MICHEL GAUQUELIN has been engaged in the study
of the relation between cosmic and biological
phenomena for over twenty years. He is at present
working in the Psychophysiological Laboratory at
Strasbourg University.

ASTROLOGY has long been a presentiment of our new
scientific world where astral influences have for the first
time been subjected to rational enquiry. The potent,
archetypal monuments of Jung's Collective
Unconscious are now appearing, in a different guise, in
the scientific journals covering physics, chemistry and
biology. As Aimé Michel says in his introduction,
'Gauquelin is a pioneer: no-one can yet say where the
thread will one day take him, but the dark labyrinth
where minds as great as Newton and Kepler once
wandered hopelessly is beginning, thanks to him, to
lead towards the light.'

'ASTROLOGY AND SCIENCE' is a first-of-its-kind
book – the most complete history of astrology available
and the best explanation of what astrology is.'

                                    Publishers' Weekly

Astrology and
Science
Michel Gauquelin

Translated from the French by
James Hughes

Mayflower

Granada Publishing Limited
Published in 1972 by Mayflower Books Ltd
3 Upper James Street, London W1R 4BP

First published in Great Britain by
Peter Davies 1970
Copyright © Edition Planète (as *l'Astrologie
devant la science*) 1966
Translation copyright © Stein and Day Inc.
1969
Made and printed in Great Britain by
C. Nicholls & Company Ltd
The Philips Park Press, Manchester
Set in Intertype Times

Contents

Preface

A MEETING AT CARTHAGE

It is easier to build up a philosophical system or follow a religion than to devote one's life to it; easier to contribute to the church collection on Sunday than to attain, through overcoming a thousand ordeals, the final stages of a state of prayer. A slack, unexamined credulity is what keeps fortune-tellers in business, and even someone who prides himself on his rationality seldom fails, when he looks through the paper, to take a half ironic, half anxious glance at the daily forecast in the astrology column. The question of whether the stars really determine his fate is conveniently obscured in the mists of his unconscious mind. It is our duty as rational men not to accept any indirect influence which charlatans and cranks might have on our behavior, but the power of myths and their persistence behind the surface clutter of equations and technology are inevitable corollaries of our intellectual laziness. As Pascal observed in trying to demonstrate the objective validity of his personal myths, nothing should be more important than to know, and as a consequence, the most dispassionate exercise of reason imposes on us the obligation to find out.

I have personally met one, and only one, man who was so convinced that the system of the universe provided by astrology was the ultimate truth that he devoted his life to it as completely as would a Trappist monk to the Catholic doctrine. I spoke only once to this strange man, on an afternoon in February 1958. He did not tell me his name and I have never seen him again. But I have often thought about him since that day. In fact I think of him whenever I wonder about the prospects of a solitary quest for truth, whenever an eloquent speaker argues for the way of solitude and points out the uncertainty of science and the insufficiency of reason.

It was at Carthage, among the ruins of the Baths of Antoninus. My guide was not about to put himself out for only one visitor, and one who was not even an American at that, and he had left me in a huge desert of collapsed arches and fallen columns. I could hear nothing but the birds, the occasional sound of cars on the Sidi Ben Said road, and the lapping of the sea. Happy in my freedom, I sat in the shade of a colossal capital of sandstone, trying to imagine what the place had been like during the splendor of Rome, or, some centuries earlier, during the terrible last assault by Scipio Africanus' men against the Carthaginian houses, which were already blazing in a voluntary holocaust.

Suddenly I noticed that I was not alone. A man was sitting near a flowering laurel not far from me and was looking at the capital. At first I only glanced at him. He was a Frenchman, I was sure. In his fifties, fair hair, a calm face, wearing a casual suit and a wedding ring. After a moment he rose, walked around the stone, touched it with his fingers, and said one word:

"Fate ..."

"I beg your pardon?"

"I said: fate. This capital is sandstone from Egypt. Yes, Egypt. Or perhaps it is from Alsace, or Vosges. Unless it comes from England. For hundreds of millions of years it slept, until it caught the fancy of a Roman architect who brought it down here. What a tremendous effort that must have taken, since it weighs quite a few tons. After which he had it sculpted. For some centuries men discussed philosophy, religion, politics and business in Latin and Greek at the foot of the enormous column which must have supported it. Now here it is on the ground. For a few more centuries tourists will wonder at its bulk, and will break off pieces to use on their desks as paperweights – look, see where a hammer has recently been used and chips are missing from it – and then it will slowly return to the earth. Or rather, to the sea, since the sea is gradually gnawing at the coast here, and a part of the site has already been drowned."

"Well," I said, "that's the fate of all stone. And wasn't this sandstone once part of the sand of the sea?"

"Certainly. But its own particular destiny is unique. This stone is weighted with thoughts, and therefore with powers."

"As for the thoughts, they are the thoughts of men and therefore no more unique than those we are exchanging now. They are the result of chance. As for the powers, I don't quite see what you mean."

My companion looked at me, it seemed for the first time.

"Do you really believe that what we are saying is purely the result of chance? All right," he added, anticipating my reply, "I don't know you, we don't know each other. We are not going to spoil the afternoon by going over the old arguments about free will and predestination. But where do the thoughts of men come from?"

For a moment I felt like answering "Yes, of course . . ." and leaving, after a polite farewell, to go on with my tour alone. But the man seemed cultivated and intelligent, and I couldn't see what he was getting at.

"Where from? Well, in cybernetics the accumulation of information resulting from a given operation can be calculated, and all mental activity, even the activity of life, adds to that information. Ever since the days of Thales, the information available on the planet Earth has been accumulated from all the thoughts of men and all the discoveries of science. That's the origin of it. At this moment as we talk, a new truth could arise from our conversation. There's nothing mysterious about that."

"That's your opinion. Do you think that by measuring the accumulation of information, and even by explaining the laws underlying it, you have explained the origin? It's as though, having solved all those school problems about filling and emptying buckets by turning on and off faucets, you claim to have discovered where the water came from."

"It seems to me," I said, "that all this has been analysed by the cyberneticists, Wiener, von Neumann, and various others."

"Don't you believe it, cybernetics is limited to calculations. And how could it be otherwise, since it is a branch of mathematics. To put it more precisely, one must admit that when a scientist discovers a new law of physics, say, he has only rediscovered that law. He doesn't invent it since it was a law of the universe before the first appearance of man, before the origin of the earth, since the universe began. The scientist is limited to the perception of the law. There is information in the minds and arguments of men, but this information existed before its discovery. If it did not, then it would be impossible to discover."

We had strayed far from the subject of the capital and its fate, and I pointed this out to him.

"No," he said, "not as far as you might think. If all our thoughts pre-existed in the universe, then this capital, and the purpose which led to its excavation, the design according to which it was carved, the speculations it induced in the minds of men, including our own, all these things are only existing for the second time in the thoughts of men – of ourselves – as a kind of addition. Everything we do and everything we are (and what we take for the essence of reality) is only a kind of vague reflection on the surface of the true reality, which eludes us and yet guides us, and gives us our deepest and only true meaning."

"The Hindus have already expressed all that, and so too has the Koran, in its way. And so, basically, have all religions."

"Certainly, but I believe that the fact that these truths were first perceived by the religions prevents us from realizing that they ought to be and are the proper subject of scientific study."

"Science? For heaven's sake, what science?"

My companion smiled and looked briefly at his watch.

"You strike me as a well-read man," he said. "I don't know if you've come across this science fiction story. The author explains how, around the year 3000, progress in radio-astronomy and other methods of penetrating space had greatly improved the range of their instruments of observation, so that men were at last in a position to define the limits of the universe. After a long series of calculations they undertook the job of putting together an image of it. First they found out that when all the calculations had been made, the universe, though enormously long in the four directions of the sky which faced each other, seemed oddly narrow in the other two directions. In short, it was very flat, like the page of a book. Toward the center, their explorations pinpointed a huge system of galaxies which were also flat and shared, to a remarkable degree, the same place in the range of the spectrum, namely, red. Some centuries later these cartographers of space made further progress, and the central galactic system began to reveal a curiously symmetrical arrangement in its general contours. When plotted on a graph it could be seen as an enormous leaf-like form; it resembled a rather blunt spearhead, or an ivy leaf, red in color.

"At the same time another team of astronomers came to the

end of their more distant calculations, and reached the outer limits of the rest of the universe. These limits were superimposed on the same graph where the central formation had already been plotted. And then at last, the ultimate word rose simultaneously in the minds of all these astronomers, the word which revealed the final secret of space-time, the word which answered all the questions which have always been raised by philosophies and religions. And this word was: 'Gin!' For the universe was nothing but a huge playing card, a trump ace of hearts which an even more colossal hand was laying down at the end of a game which had been going on for several billions of centuries.

"I see you're laughing. But did you laugh the first time you read Pascal's *Two Infinities* and came across the mite which he invited us to contemplate, do you remember? 'An infinity of universes, each one with its own firmament, planets, earth, and in that earth animals and, finally, mites.' Without cease and without end, as the expression goes. You didn't laugh because Pascal, God knows why, refrained from applying to the infinitely large that which he had imagined for the infinitely small. I deliberately said 'God knows why'; it would certainly have upset him to have imagined his God in the form of a mite. I realize that we now know enough microphysics, three hundred years after Pascal, not to believe any longer in mites packed one inside the other endlessly, like Chinese dolls. The atom is not a miniature version of the solar system, the nucleus is not a star, electrons are not planets. But the two infinities certainly do exist as he had foreseen, although they are a great deal more complicated than he could have guessed, and ultimately a great deal more interesting. Pascal's conception was of an endless series of universes, each contained inside the other but knowing nothing of it. Each followed an independent though possibly identical course, just as the images reflected in the opposing mirrors of a barber's shop repeat each other endlessly without being able to make contact. But instead of that, as we know through physics, chemistry and biology, there is a continual interaction at all levels. The particle influences us and we influence the particle. As a consequence, only the conceit which insists on man as the center of all things can prevent us from realizing that the infinitely great constantly influences us just as we influence the particle."

11

We had been walking side by side along the beach, stopping sometimes to follow the movements of a boat sailing far away in front of the white walls of Korbus. But at these last words I felt, like James Bond, something click in my brain.

"Good Lord," I said, rather disappointed. "Aren't you trying to prove to me that the most recent discoveries of science bear out the claims of astrology, that old favorite?"

"I concede that as it exists today, astrology is a collection of absurdities, like the constructions of Rube Goldberg. But imagine that in a thousand years' time a series of catastrophes had destroyed all record of the mathematics of our time, except for the immortal works of that comic-strip character. Imagine how the learned scholars, having studied them, would come to the conclusion that mathematics had never existed, except as an obvious nonsense."

"Do you mean that our newspaper astrologers are the farcical descendants of a time when astrology had its Einsteins and von Neumanns?"

My companion was silent; he seemed to be reflecting.

"Listen," he said, "you don't know me, and we will probably never see each other again. What I'm going to tell you is only a personal belief and can only have for you, shall we say, a moral significance. Think of it, if you like, as an example of the innumerable eccentricities which can be born and grow in the minds of men. So I can tell you that, having studied the principles of traditional astrology (the principles, not the methods, which are erroneous) I have found in it ... (he hesitated) ... I have found in it the key which everyone looks for before he dies. I want to tell you so that you won't get me wrong, that this key has nothing to do with horoscopes and other nonsense of that sort. Let us call it, if you like, a path or an ascent. In the rag-bag of ideas which is astrology as it is studied today, among the old conjuring books which claim an inspired source there is one, single truth. It is that of the identity of microcosm and macrocosm. But science gives us a more accurate and illuminating image of this identity."

"If I understand you correctly, astrology, such as it is today, is like a fortune teller straying among realities which await their Galileo?"

"Yes."

We were both silent: he because he seemed to be thinking

of something else, and I through politeness, for I was hardly convinced by all this. The proposition that the macrocosm is subject to the influence of this microcosm, and even that it is made up from it, was self-evident. It was true enough that I was composed of atoms, molecules and cells and that any chemical reaction in my body would affect my being and even my thought, especially if that reaction occurred in my brain, but what need was there of astrology to illuminate such a trite and obvious fact? Astrology was surely the opposite, seeking to show the macrocosm formulating and fashioning the microcosm. How could one image a universe which influenced mankind in the particular?

I recalled the words which Voltaire addressed to a nun who had claimed that her sparrow had been cured by the intervention of Providence:

"My sister, there is nothing so good as some Hail Marys, especially when a girl recites them in a district of Paris. But I do not believe that God concerns himself very much with your sparow, pretty though it is. Bear in mind, please, that he has other things to think about. He has continually to direct the courses of sixteen planets and the ring around Saturn, in the middle of which he has placed the sun, which is as big as a million of our earths. There are billions and billions of other suns, planets and comets to control. His immutable laws and his eternal confluence are the motive forces of the whole of nature. If some Hail Marys had made your sparrow live a moment longer than he ought to have lived, these Hail Marys would have violated all the laws set up for all eternity by the Great Being. You would have put the Universe out of order. You would have necessitated a new world, a new God, a new order of things."

Finally, not seeing how my companion's theory could overcome the objections of Voltaire, I decided to put them to him, in a more up-to-date form.

"I grant you," I said, "that men are always falling into the trap of taking themselves for the center of the world. Anthropomorphism is what you rightly condemn. But are you sure that you yourself have avoided making the same mistake? You say that one must be blind not to admit that the infinitely great constantly influences us, just as we influence particles. But in fact we never do influence particles, not, that is, if they

13

are considered on a particular, individual level. My hand is composed of particles, and, naturally, I can lift it. But that is a question of billions of billions of these minute entities and not of one or a few.

"Similarly, it is the attraction of the sun, certainly, which enables earth to float in space second by second, and when the earth floats there so do you and I, and all the living and dead things on it. But to go from there and say that the sun concerns itself with you and me individually, well, that's quite a step! The universe destroys us or permits us to live without knowing about us, like Voltaire's god. By believing that the stars can have a select, particular influence on your life you are imitating the nun who conceives of the Creator of the universe changing his eternal laws on behalf of her sparrow. Saturn doesn't care much about you and me! And anyway, Saturn is only a mass of various chemical components. There was a time when he was taken for a god, and that was when astrology came into being.

"Astrology continues to exist because the ignorant don't know that the god is dead. If you were right, if the stars concerned themselves with each one of us taken separately like the guardian angels in Christian theology, then Earth would concern itself with the Martians. By the Prophet, as they say around here, it would do better to concern itself with us, but you must admit it doesn't seem to give two pins for us. One of the oldest subjects of man's meditation has been the indifference of the earth to the people who live on it. Do you not accept this indifference? But if the Earth shows no more interest in us than in a block of marble, how the devil could the other stars, hidden in the depths of the sky, have any influence on us whatever?

"All these illusions are the products of minds which have been incredibly taken in by appearances. The stars are points in the sky which our ancestors took for supernatural beings because they didn't have telescopes to see the mountains of the moon, the clouds of Venus, Jupiter or Saturn. And even with the telescope, and even knowing that the earth is a very ordinary star, the imagery of our unconscious minds whispers our desires to us; our loves and dreads have not advanced with our awareness of the world. They remain infantile, emotional, and rooted in myth. Our hearts refuse to accept what our reason both demonstrates and provides evidence for: that the clouds of Venus and the ring of Saturn are inanimate physical masses, obedient to the laws of physics alone, and not vast heavenly caricatures of man, busy watching over the fate of our enterprises and the health of our sparrows. Do you remember what the king said in anger when his court was laughing at the terror produced by the appearance of a comet? 'You can talk about it without worrying,' he told them. 'You are not princes.' As if the comet made any difference! Poor, ignorant little king!"

My companion had stopped to look at me. When I finished, he slowly shrugged his shoulders.

"All that is true," he said, "but you've missed the point completely. It would be useless for me to try to make you understand in an hour something which can only come from yourself. Truths which are reached by means of explanation are small truths. The others, the only ones which count, are the result of a mental, or if you prefer, a spiritual transformation as laborious as the solution of a puzzle or the construction of a temple from a heap of stones. So I'll confine myself to telling you this. First, the old idea of the identity of the microcosm and macrocosm corresponds to the modern conception of external data existing in the universe before being taken into the consciousness of men. I don't ask you to believe but only to imagine the possibility that all your ideas, contradictory though they be, should have a fundamental existence in universal reality: an existence which is as comparable to the idea you have of it as is the intact temple to the model which the architect constructs from its ruins.

"All your dreams exist in the immense universe in a way which is real but inconceivable to your mind. And they do not exist because you dream them; on the contrary, you can only dream that which exists. As for the apparent absurdity of the macrocosm affecting the microcosm, of huge bodies like stars affecting the destiny of a man or a sparrow, I suggest that you consider whether the voluntary action of your thought on the movements of your body is not a sufficient refutation. To me, the evidence is as clear as day, and every one of my acts is illuminated by it. From it I draw a happiness and security which I would wish for you, since I find you sympathetic. Even suffering has a place there, and death fits in as a scarcely perceptible transition. And with that, sir, I bid you goodbye."

And with those words he left me, a little surprised at so abrupt a conclusion.

As I said, I have since had many an occasion to reflect on this curious conversation which took place at Carthage, a conversation of which all the ideas, if not the words, have remained imprinted on my memory. In particular, the final remark of my brief companion seemed to me for a long time enigmatic and even a deliberate evasion. Why should the voluntary movements of my body demonstrate the possibility of a particular influence of the stars for each individual?

Illumination came to me several years later with the chance fact that two books were arranged side by side on my desk: my friend Charles-Noel Martin's book, *The Thirteen Steps to the Atom* (*les Treize marches vers l'atome*), and Professor Lapicque's work, *The Neural Machine* (*la Machine nerveuse*). In a phrase of Professor Lapicque's on the *electrical* nature of the neural impulse, I suddenly imagined I heard the elegant and ironic voice of the mysterious gentleman at Carthage.

"This time," he was saying to me, "I think you have understood."

What actually happens in my organism when, for instance, I hold out my hand or when I write? Leaving aside the initial problem of my freedom to decide the movement, let us consider in detail the process which, beginning at the brain, the organ of consciousness, ends at the hand which writes these lines. What guides my hand, what animates it (and how significant the etymology of the word "animate" seems here) is a complex combination of neural impulses directed toward it by the brain. This combination of neural impulses has been known to be of an electrical nature since Galvani, Matteucci and Dubois-Reymond. But what is an electric current? The displacement of electrons. *Therefore my will both knows and can put into movement a few tiny bundles of electrons exactly as it wishes.*

The mechanism of these voluntary impulses may still be obscure, I may not know at all how the thing works, but the fact remains that among the billions of billions of electrons in my body there are some, which I can control as I please, displaced along the fibres of my conscious nervous system. I have no awareness of it, I would know nothing about it if neurophysiology had not taught me, but I spend my life doing it as M. Jourdain spends his life writing prose. And more important still, these electrons which are displaced or stabilized at my will represent the indispensable infrastructure of the whole of my conscious and unconscious life. And if the materialists are right, I am nothing other than these movements of electrons.

But what is the size of these minute particles which, under the control of my nervous system, enable me to write these lines and to think these ideas which I am expressing? Opening Charles-Noel Martin's book at pages 13 and 14, we find a table of what he has called *The Thirteen Steps,* which are thirteen gradations of the infinitely small. In this table the elemental particle is found on the thirteenth step toward the *fermi,* namely one thousandth of one billionth of a millimeter. That then is the lower limit of my voluntary action in space, the most ordinary action which controls and directs my bodily movements. And that is the lower limit only on the assumption that even lower levels will not be ultimately found.

A man 1.75 meters in height is capable of voluntarily controlling the courses of certain physical bodies 1,750,000,000,000,000 times smaller than himself. If this reciprocal influence of spatial objects separated by such extremes of size does really occur, then its possibility cannot be doubted. And if it is possible, then what will be our conclusions if we extrapolate this figure and apply it to the macrocosm?

It seems to me that this was what my companion at Carthage had meant. He believed in the possibility of an influence from the infinitely great universe controlling the destinies of men, because a man can in his own body control entitles 1,750,000,000,000,000 times smaller than himself. In order to establish the range of this extrapolation we should now ask: if we multiply the size of the human body 1,750,000,000,000,000 times do we reach the order of magnitude implicit in astronomical distances? The calculation is simple enough, the answer being about two thousand billion miles. This figure far exceeds planetary distances, since Pluto, the most remote planet, moves on an axis less than four billion miles from the sun. The relation of this figure to the solar system is 500 to 1, which means that proportionately the human body is far nearer to the stars than to the particles which compose it. By multiplying the size of an elemental particle by 10, and then again by 10, and so on till the end, 500 more such multiplications are required to attain the size of the human body than to reach the furthest planet by similarly multiplying the size of the human body. Or, if the electrons which are now being stimulated in my brain suddenly became as large as myself, and I grew in proportion, the entire solar system would appear to me as a tiny whirlpool three and half millimeters in extent.

That, then, is where the matter stands. The argument which appeals to common sense to reject the likelihood of the stars' influence on men by reason of the vast gap in size between the two may be an excellent one. But nature has made nonsense of our probabilities by constructing a whole living world – and man in particular – on an even more absurd gap in size. And it has seemed to work well enough up to the present.

But is it legitimate, as my companion thought, to apply this size-ratio to the distances between the stars? Here one can only say what it is wise to say about all extrapolations: that at first it should be developed as a game, as a means to stimulate experiment, and as a kind of stock-taking. Michel Gauquelin has devoted his life to drawing up the inventory. In this book he gives us the fullest account of his work to the present date. It must be acknowledged as the most conscientious, profound and convincing of all the refutations of journalistic and traditional astrology yet produced. At the end of a massive statistical study there remains nothing of the horoscope so beloved of our illusion-sellers. But, as generally happens in science, this cheerful and salutary demolition of eccentric fancies set up two or three thousand years ago and based on a forgotten idea has led to something else: the revelation of a new and little known field, where the influence of the stars is indeed established, but at a statistical level very different from what the authors of the black books had in mind.

The ancient astrologers no doubt had a presentiment of this new world of astral influences. Failing to find the key to it, they gave way to the prompting of all primitive thought: they constructed myths, sometimes ingenious and profound (as Jung has shown), which will always remain as a monument of our collective unconscious. But these have been overtaken by the positive investigation of a phenomenon which can still only be glimpsed. Michel Gauquelin will have been the pioneer in this arduous enquiry. No one can yet say where the thread will one day take him, but the dark labyrinth where minds as great as Newton and Kepler once wandered hopelessly is beginning, thanks to him, to lead toward the light.

AIMÉ MICHEL

Introduction

We need not launch man into interplanetary space, we need not even take him from his own country or home to subject him to the influence of the cosmos. Man is always at the center of the universe, for the universe is everywhere.

PICCARDI. *Lecture at the Palais de la Découverte, 1958.*

"It is as illusory for the scientist to decide that science has reached an end as it is for an historian to think that history will come to an end." This sentence was written by the last French winner of the Nobel Prize for Physics, Professor Louis de Broglie. It should be inscribed in golden letters on the pediment of every scientific institute, for men too often forget that science is something which lives and evolves. At every period of time the same mistake is made: the generation which is established believes the scenery of the universe is permanently fixed, and takes as unassailable what is only provisional by definition. "The known is not necessarily the real," as Jean Charon has rightly said. The "Old Guard" will not understand or admit that a new team of researchers might want to change the old scenery, or at least its color.

Hence the disillusioned judgment of another great physicist, Max Planck: "Great scientific theories do not usually conquer the world through being accepted by opponents who, gradually convinced of their truth, have finally adopted them. It is always very rare to find a Saul becoming a Paul. What happens is that the opponents of the new idea finally die off, and the following generation grows up under its influence. He who holds the allegiance of the young holds the future." [1]

And so the young must find the right road, which reminds me of a small incident which befell me personally. Not long ago (it was in 1956) I happened to be visiting the Astronomy exhibit at the Palais de la Découverte. At that time I was

1. Couderc, *la Relativité*. p. 28.

21

interested in the curious results of my studies on the influence of the stars and felt very much a beginner in many of the fields of astronomy. There was an assistant there, a pleasant and well-intentioned young man, and I asked him about the most recent discoveries relating to the planets. What had been discovered of late regarding their courses, their radiation, the part they played in the solar system? These questions left the young astronomer amazed.

"But we know everything about the planets," he answered after a long pause. "That's a field we don't study any more, no one is interested in it any longer. The new discoveries are being made in the distant galaxies. Really," he went on, with a shake of his head, "I don't see what you can hope to find that's new in the study of the planets." Then he added, suddenly rather uneasy, "You haven't asked me that question because you're involved in astrology, by any chance?"

A year later, when the first Sputnik was launched, humanity entered the space age. In the excitement shared by both America and Russia, the study of the planets again took first place as an object of scientific investigation. Now that there was hope of sending a member of the human race to another planet it was realized that hardly anything precise was known about them and that everything to do with their movements, their behavior, their atmosphere, their mass, their radiation, had to be learned again from the beginning. That is why there are now dozens of experimental satellites sent to planets which were apparently so well-known but were in fact hardly known at all.

What does the young astronomer of the Palais de la Découverte think about that today? Is he still of the opinion that there is no need to bother with the planets, and that the subject is totally out of date? Is it still of no further interest to astronomers, who are too busy with the distant galaxies? But it is true, and also a great pity, that this young scientist was doing no more than repeating what he had been taught by his masters.

The experts profess to know everything about the stars and do not like having to change their comfortable habits of thought. But when one asks if the stars have any influence on the human species, one meets an even more hostile reception. Just as it was claimed for so long that we knew everything about the planets, so it is now claimed that everything is

22

known about the relationship between man and the universe. For man is an even more prohibited subject than the sky.

The influence of the stars on man remains an apparently insoluble problem, since we are naturally a long way from knowing everything about the subject. Here two varieties of experts come into conflict without convincing each other: the astronomers and the astrologers. The former refuse *a priori* to allow that the stars might have an influence on our destinies. The latter believe it without need of proof; as far as they are concerned, twenty centuries of progress have made no difference at all. The universe as it appears to us remains *the* universe to them, unassailably and forever. And so the argument goes on, with both sides deaf to each other.

But astrology, the study of the relations between man and the heavens, does have a venerable ancestry. It was part of the earliest human inquiries into our role and our place in the universe, and it has been the inseparable companion of most of the great religions and civilizations. But all that is left of it today is an arid doctrine of prices and rates, ordered according to arbitrary rules.

In the twentieth century our ideas about the relation between man and the cosmos have ended up in one of two dead-end streets: an unyielding science and a market-place astrology. Confronted with these the public gives up, cheated of the truth. Whichever way a man's interest or sympathy may take him, he will soon run up against a wall of ignorance.

The feud between these two groups has been endless, but of late a new school of scientists has managed to break the vicious circle. For some years now these scientists have been discovering that there are certain unexpected but close connections between man and the solar system, and between man and the galaxy. So today we are in the middle of a scientific revolution. Traditional astrology still lingers on, but science should carefully reconsider some of its principles and admit that beside the superstitions of astrology there is a place for a "new and different cosmobiology."

These researchers who have lately come on the scene are scientists like any others, but their eyes see and their ears hear. No prejudice can stop them in their search for the truth. They will have to fight to get their discoveries accepted, but their ideas will one day triumph. So the problem of the stars' influence which has been considered insoluble up till now is at a turning point at the present time, heading in a new and more promising direction.

In the following pages I propose to describe the history of the relation between man and the universe. In the course of this long story there will be at first be much that is confused, there will be some strange and bewildering twists and turns with occasional shafts of light and moments of rare quality. But gradually the light at the end of the tunnel will become discernible, and finally the issues will be revealed in a new and unexpected manner: amazing issues which have never been discussed before.

The Space Age has begun, and it is therefore vitally important to construct a solidly based science of the relations which exist between men and the universe, and to find out whether astrology can add any truth to this science. If it has nothing to contribute, then we must find out what lies beyond it. Our motto must be that of all true sciences: to lose our simplicity while keeping our enthusiasm.

The Arab poet Ibn el Faridh has written that "men do not become stirred up in vain, nor do currents flow by chance. They may fall into mistake, but they are controlled by eternal truth which leads them to a certain goal."

Part One

DIALOGUE BETWEEN MAN AND THE SKY

Chapter One

THE LOVE MATCH

The old division of the universe into an objective development in Space and Time on the one hand, and a spirit which reflects this development on the other, is no longer a suitable point of departure for anyone who wishes to understand modern natural sciences. It is above all the systematic study of relations between man and nature which is the central aim of science.

HEISENBERG. *The Nature of Contemporary Physics.*

There are three great questions of humanity. Who are we? Where do we come from? Where are we going? The last would seem to be the most painful and also perhaps the most mysterious.

Philosophers will undoubtedly treat the question of our destination with much detachment, and discuss the future of humanity as a whole. They will discuss it as paleontologists treat the evolution of the species when they answer the question relating to our origins. But not everyone is a philosopher. For each of us it is our individual future which matters. "What will tomorrow bring? That is the great question," said Victor Hugo. Men had sought the answer to that question ever since they have been men, ever since they learned how to shape flints and depict their world on the walls of the caves.

"Will I have good hunting? Will I be able to escape dying of hunger?" Cro-Magnon Man must have wondered that, just as today the student awaiting the result of an exam, or the executive engaged in a new business deal might say to himself: "I would like to be older by one hour, one day, or one month."

In every age man has tried to tear aside the veil and discover what the future holds for him. The development of the idea of fate is indistinguishable from the development of human thought itself.

In the early history of humanity when nothing was certain, men noticed above all how often good and bad fortune were unequally allotted to each person. Such injustice could not be without a reason, for to the people of those days nature happened by accident. Fate was the opposite of chance.

"During my stay at Ambrizette," wrote Monteiro, "three women of the Cabinda Tribe went down to the river to draw water. They were filling their pitchers, standing near one another, when the woman in the middle was snatched by an alligator, dragged under the water, and devoured. The family of this poor woman immediately accused the other two of having put a spell on her so that she would be snatched by the alligator as she stood between them. I argued with them and tried to point out the complete absurdity of their accusation, but they answered: 'Why did the alligator just take the one in the middle, and not one of those who were at each side?' It was impossible to shake them from the notion, and the two women were forced to drink casca in an ordeal by poison. I did not discover the outcome, but it most probably happened that one or both of them died or were made slaves."

For primitive man, then, accidents do not happen. Misfortune always has an outside cause and there is always someone or something to blame for what happens to us. But in order to explain this fatal influence, one must first find the cause and identify the natural force which can lead as easily to glorious as to fatal results. So to discover the cause becomes an urgent necessity in order to propitiate it and thereby reduce its severity. Or if this is impossible, one might be able, by bringing some light to its dark aims, at least to forearm oneself against them.

Behind all the phenomena of nature they saw gods, demons, goblins and magic forces endowed with manlike wills and desires, but possessing an infinitely greater strength. What could man do to resist these forces? He had to organize his resources, and learn to recognize the mysterious afflictions which overcame him. He invented magic and appointed sorcerers, the only ones initiated to a foresight into hostile nature, and the only ones capable of reducing the harshness of its judgments. Sorcerers were the scientists of the time: those who held and withheld knowledge.

At the end of the neolithic period the strange formations of the menhirs were erected. They have a wild but impressive aspect, and mark one of the earliest manifestations of the human mind, standing as they do on the borders between history and prehistory. What is the meaning of these puzzling masses of stone and the formations in which they were arranged so many centuries ago? According to one expert, "These monuments had a religious application. We can also guess that they were associated with cults of the sun, since the formation of Kerlescan is equated with the rise of the equinox, and that of Kermario with the beginning of the summer solstice. Many others are arranged in accordance with the start of the winter or intermediate solstices, marked by the following dates: November 8, February 4, May 6, and August 8. These dates are in obvious correspondence with sowing times, the first appearance of the crops, the flowering, and the harvest. These are the only undisputed statements which have been made up to the present time on the subject of these strange monuments." [1]

At the dawn of civilization, religion, the stars, and earthly life were already connected in the mind of man. At the first appearance of writing, the Sumerian ideogram which stands for divinity is a star. From the time man first considered himself and his place in the world, he turned with awe to the marvels of the heavenly bodies, which he saw as gods and powers ordering his destiny.

In the clear sky of Mesopotamia, where the stars shine brilliantly every night, astrology was born at the same time as science and religion, the construction of towns and observatory-temples, and the rise of kings, states, government, agriculture and cattle-raising all paralleled one another. At the start astrology actually blended all these together, so that science was interwoven with religion, and the lives of kings depended upon the affairs of their nations and harvests. The

1. Fernand Niel, *Dolmens et Menhirs*, p. 43.

whole earth was answerable to and dependent on the movement of the stars, which were believed to be gods controlling the future.

In the sentence "I was born under a good star; but you were born under a bad one," none of us would have any difficulty translating the words to mean "I am lucky and you are unlucky." In all the various phenomena ascribed to fate, and in all the methods used to understand and ward off bad fortune, there was a common denominator: a belief that the prime responsibility for human destinies lay in the sky. For after all was it not always and everywhere present? "This cavern wall which suffocates us," as the pessimist Baudelaire has called it, is shaken by spectacular and unforeseeable catastrophes. How could they be warded off or understood?

Very soon, men established connections between their daily lives and what they saw in the sky. Agriculture followed the seasons, and the seasons followed the sun. Springtime and harvest depended on it, and everything seemed to run in time with the rhythmic movements of the sky. The men of those days lived in a world which they accepted at face value, and the most striking phenomena came from the sky: thunder, lightning, seasonable or unseasonable rains, refreshing or destructive winds. Men put their gods in the sky, for they felt confusedly that their lives depended on it. They were sure that those glittering points of light which stared down at them from one end of the horizon to the other did not shine there without any meaning. So, behind the planets which hung in the sky or crawled like flies over the turning surface of the globe, the first Chaldeans imagined that powerful deities were concealed. They tried to understand the meaning of these divine lights and to follow their courses in order to read the judgments of fate. A new code would enable them to unravel the secrets of the future, and for a long time this remained as a naive crosscheck on our knowledge of the future. This was astrology.

If by some miracle a modern scientist were to meet a Chaldean, there would be an almost complete lack of understanding between them on both sides, for modern reasoning is no longer the same as it was at the dawn of civilization. When men were closely bound to nature and yet had practically no knowledge of its laws, all natural phenomena seemed to be alive and endowed with wills of their own. A river could, if it wished, change course and flow upstream. The moon could, if it wished, disappear piece by piece and be reborn anew from nothing.

Investigation by psychologists into the mentality of children enables us to get a glimpse at what might have been in the minds of the first watchers of the sky. Piaget has recorded this conversation with Hubert (age 10):

"Can the moon do what it likes?" asked Piaget.

"Yes," the child answered. "When we walk it follows us."

"Does it follow you, or doesn't it move?"

"It follows me. It stops when I stop."

"And if I walk as well, which of us will it follow?"

"Me."

"Which?"

"You."

"You think it follows everyone?"

"Yes."

"It can follow everyone at the same time?"

"Yes."[1]

So for Hubert, as for all children of his age, an optical illusion so familiar to adults as no longer to be noticed is enough to give the moon a will, and therefore a mind of its own. The moon follows us, therefore it must watch us.

Here is another child's point of view, again recorded by Piaget:

One winter morning, when the sun shone into the room, Jean-Pierre turned to his mother and said, "That's nice, the sun has come in to heat the radiator."

The tendency of the child, then, is to regard the objects in the sky as though they were large children, good or naughty, and possessing curiosity and wills which are more or less good. Let us go back four thousand years to the Chaldeans at a time of lunar eclipse. The priests announced that "The god Sin is being attacked by seven demons, he is in agony in the sky, he is growing dim." Hence it was vitally necessary to ward off the end of the world which might follow from the eclipse. Marguerite Rutten has explained the procedure: "It was decreed according to ritual that as soon as the eclipse began, the priest had to light a torch on the altar and chant dirges for

1. Piaget, *la Représentation du monde chez l'enfant.* p. 215.

the fields, the rivers, and the great divinities. In addition, for the duration of the eclipse the inhabitants had to remove their turbans and cover their heads with their clothing. In order to prevent the catastrophe from reaching the town they had to shout until the eclipse came to an end, and as soon as the moon reappeared the priest extinguished the torch on the altar."

This is a far cry from the cheerful "eclipse parties" which people nowadays hold on the Butte Montmartre! Like the young child of today, the Chaldeans inhabited a world of dreams, or rather of waking nightmares, since the signs in the sky tended to carry an ominous meaning for them. It was a nightmare in which they tried desperately to ward off the deadly fates which threatened them through the agony of their captors, the star-gods.

Primitive man was afraid of the forces which surrounded him, and especially of the frightening, unexpected occurrences in the sky. Wishing to rid himself of this fear he made use of a mechanism which has become very familiar since its explanation by Freud: he unconsciously projected his dreads onto the objects which had inspired them; by so doing he endowed the stars with familiar powers similar to those all around him and even to his own.

Thus the men of that time located their fantasies in the sky. To the Chaldeans, who lied in a warm country, the scorpion with its terrible bite was a dangerous creature. The stars also induced a fear in them, and they therefore projected the image of the scorpion onto the sky.

Thus began the creation of a strange and fantastic mythology, a mixture of real and imaginary animals which all the ancient peoples superimposed upon the sky. Hence the plumed serpent of the Mexicans parallels the fish-goat of the Chaldeans; and the Egyptians' sow, which can gobble up the sun, parallels the poisonous scorpion of the Babylonians. A major stage in the history of human thought is marked by the apparently spontaneous creation of this miscellany of animals in different parts of the world. It provides a striking proof of the reality of Jung's archetypes. Man possesses not only identical methods of reasoning and understanding, but also a totality of images which carry similar meanings in all the continents. The sky is the same for all, and so is the response to it. That is why astrology has been universal and that is also why ideas showing a surprising basic similarity have brought forth a swarm of monsters on the earth, monsters whose nature is both human and cosmic.

But man did not stop at projecting symbols of his fear onto the sky. He also identified himself with the stars he observed, thus displaying a convenient defense mechanism: the stars then became objects capable of assuming men's own misfortunes, sickness, and fear. Thus a prayer of the ancient Estonians is addressed in all candor to the moon, asking it to take on the pain and weariness of men: "Hail, new moon. I must become young and you must become old. My eyes must become bright and yours dull. I must become as light as a bird and you as heavy as iron."

Gaston Bachelard has perfectly expressed this tendency of men to project their cares unconsciously into the sky, and the role which dreams and poetry have to play here: "On this great drawing board of the night diagrams have been scrawled in mathematical reverie. But they are false, all these constellations are beautifully false. For stars which are in fact completely separate are joined in a single figure. Imaginary lines are drawn between the points of reality, where isolated stars gleam like diamonds. The dream, like a great master of abstract painting, has used a bare minimum of points to portray all the animals of the zodiac. *Homo faber,* that idle wheelwright, sets a chariot without wheels in the sky; the laborer, dreaming of his harvests, pictures a simple ear of corn. The zodiac is the Rorschach Test of all humanity."

If a man projects himself onto the sky, he is himself the sky, identifying himself with the constellation he is looking at. So a person who is born under Aries, the sign of the Ram, will himself be a ram, with an impulsive, butting character, and a voice which may be sharp and with a trace of a bleat. Under Taurus he will be obstinate and unsubtle; and under Leo his character will be royal, as befits the king of the animals.

The fact that whole countries have shared the same collective imagination might be thought surprising, but this is not only because the minds of their peoples have been formed in the same mold. It is also because, as they were faced with the same problems, so the struggle took on a social aspect. When a number of people have joined forces the unknown becomes less intimidating. This also has been noted by Bachelard:

"That ram, young shepherd, which you are caressing as you dream, it is there above you, turning slowly in the immense night. Will you find it again tomorrow? Point it out to your companion, and then let the two of you work together in depicting it, recognizing it, and speaking to it intimately. Thus you will prove to yourselves that you have the same vision, the same desire and, in the lonely darkness of the night, you will see the same phantoms fade away. How life grows greater when dreams become shared!"

Thus a whole nation's people created identical beliefs for themselves and no longer fell into disorder, since everyone was joined in the struggle with their fate. Tower-observatories were built, which the priests ascended, and after centuries of patient observation they finally learned the secret of the stars' movements, the secret on which their fates appeared to depend. Astronomy was born, but it was astrology which made its birth possible.

If the notion still persists today that the secret of our fate resides in the movement of the stars, it is because it corresponds to something deep and lasting in the minds of men, something akin to the need to eat, or fight, or make love. It is a naive and subjective way of understanding the world through oneself. The brain of man is hardly any different now from what it was five thousand years ago. That is why we find the same fantasies in the twentieth century as in other times, though the fantasies may be concealed beneath an easily removed veneer.

Astrology, it must be firmly stated, has continued to survive in many areas of ordinary life. The most rational of men will admit that his field of activity is invaded by notions which come directly from it, which he may not even notice himself. Even time is divided in a way which preserves many astrological formulas so obvious that they pass unnoticed.

A year is the time it takes for the earth to go around the sun. A month is the interval between two moons. We owe the four weeks to the four quarters of the moon. There are twelve months, as there are twelve signs of the zodiac. The astrologers' ideograms of the planets and the signs of the zodiac are still employed by astronomers (an amusing thought when one thinks how little they like even the mention of astrology). In France each day of the week is dominated by a planet: Sunday by the sun, Monday by the moon, Tuesday (mardi) by Mars, Wednesday (mercredi) by Mercury, Thursday (jeudi) by Jupiter, Friday (vendredi) by Venus, Saturday by Saturn. There are twice twelve hours in a day, as there are twelve astrological houses.

Even the important festivals in the calendar have an astrological basis. Christmas is celebrated in the winter solstice when the days, which till that point have been shortening, begin to grow longer. Easter is celebrated at the spring equinox, when nature wakes from its winter sleep and the flowers bloom.

We describe qualities of character in terms borrowed from astrology. A daydreaming person is said to be "mooning around." Someone of erratic character might be thought "lunatic" because, like the image of the moon, his mood is subject to fluctuations. An energetic step is called "martial," and a hearty laugh is "jovial." Verlaine describing his bitterness said, "I am saturnine." All these analogies derive from the most orthodox astrology.

It is therefore true that the charisma of astrology still has importance even with the most rational men, and often enough we might feel in our heart of hearts a twinge that the cosmos might just be purposeful for good or ill and it might just have something to do with our futures. But actually our fate has nothing to do with all this fantasy of the skies, as we shall see from an examination of its history.

Chapter Two

DIVORCE

When the world was thought to be exactly as it appeared to the eye, men believed that there was a harmony between celestial and earthly phenomena. A similarity in the universe created a matching similarity among men. The circle of the heavens was fixed and immutable, for the stars returned to the same places in the same forms. Therefore, "there was nothing new under the sun."

An hypothesis of man's fate depends to a considerable extent on what one imagines to be the fate of the universe. Now, as we know, the ancients were often misled in their conception of the world and mistaken in their explanations of the movement of the sky. Understandably they were equally mistaken in the matter of man's fate.

For the Assyrians and Babylonians, the earth was the center of the universe, which was like a kind of oyster. The sky had the shape of an upturned bowl, from which hung the divinities of light, the stars and planets. Then, in the sixteenth century of our era, an obscure canon called Copernicus dared to claim that the earth was not the center of the universe, but, on the contrary, it turned around the sun: although men seemed to see the sun rise and set, this was an illusion which had induced an erroneous belief that it was controlled by the earth and in orbit around it. His theory was considered scandalous, the Church condemned it and later Galileo was compelled to deny it.

But gradually it had to be acknowledged, there was no doubt about it: the earth was not the center of the universe. And as a result the question arose that if the sky had not been made especially to surround the earth, were men any longer at the mercy of a heavenly dispensation?

However, faith in astrology continued strong. If the moon had no influence on terrestrial matters, how could tides be explained? Then Newton propounded his law of universal gravity, a principle of far-reaching explanatory value. Gravity, the force which is everywhere and operates on everything at once, including the most remote places in the world, and something in common with the idea of "harmonies," as the Ancients had conceived it. But Newton's law was scientific, and it was this, as the science historian Thorndike has said, which "definitely replaced astrological law." Newton could be satisfied with his work, for, according to one story, he had enrolled at Cambridge to see "what truth there was in the pronouncements of astrology."

At all events, the law of gravity was sublimely indifferent to all the things of the world. It appeared to trouble itself little with the lives of men, and men of science began to take pride in proclaiming that the heavens were quite detached from the sphere of human activity.

After Galileo's magnifying glass, the telescope enabled science to replace the old and worm-eaten furniture of the sky with more impressive and gigantic structures, though no less strange.

For instance, it had been believed that the sun was symmetrical, a perfect and unchanging sphere in the heavens. But it was nothing of the sort. The golden disc was periodically covered with spots, as the young German Jesuit Scheiner discovered in 1613. This gave rise to a new scandal. "My son," said his superior, "I have read my Aristotle several times right through, and I can assure you that he has never mentioned any spot on the sun. The reason, you can be sure, is some fault either in your glass or your eyes." Today it is not only recognized that these spots exist, but it is also known that the sun is capable of even more surprising activities. On occasion it suddenly emits, for reasons still only slightly understood, huge torchlike flares of radiation which may extend for thousands of miles. It turns on its own axis and sends out into space, and particularly into the earth's atmosphere, all kinds of particles and waves. Altogether, it acts in a way which would have seemed unbearable to the peripatetic philosophers of Aristotle's time, who wanted to make his star the symbol of the perfect circle.

And in spite of all efforts to glorify it, the sun is of only minimal importance in the sky. When earth was demoted from its central place, the sun was awarded the crown, but soon it was necessary to recognize that our senses had once again been deceived. The "king of the stars" was in fact only a lowly pawn on the immense chess-board of the universe. The Milky Way, "the great ocean of milk" as the Hindus call it, captured the attention of the astronomers. Then one of them could pronounce it as our own universe, a galaxy of thousands of millions of stars. The sun is only one star among the others, drawn along in the huge wheel of the galaxy. The sun was like a minor chieftain ruling over the planets, of which our earth was one, a humble empire which it took along on its course among the constellations.

But as telescopes became more and more powerful the universe increased further. The galaxy itself, the empire which included the sun and the earth, was in its turn found to be only the outskirts of a greater universe. The sky was seen to be filled with thousands of other galaxies like ours, floating at unimaginable distances from us. At last, the universe was revealed as an expansion of millions of galaxies flying away from one another though already separated by infinitely vast distances.

Astronomers competed with each other in proclaiming that this universe was beyond any scale of man's. How could it be imagined that our tiny and insignificant persons could affect in any way whatever these vast and staggeringly distant entities? We were scraps of flesh and blood stuck to our little globe by an effect of the earth's weight, gravity, the single cosmic law which included us all in its universal and indifferent influence.

And so astronomers lost interest in human matters as they contemplated the immensities in the skies. A century after Galileo had first turned his glass upward to observe Jupiter's satellites, a Dutch scientist, Leeuwenhoek, employed an equally magical instrument to observe the earth: the microscope had gained its credentials. Leeuwenhoek, with the help of a vision suddenly increased a hundred times, discovered a strange, incredible world which no one had seen before. He realized that what had appeared to be a clear, empty drop of water was in fact crawling with minute and variegated creatures. He realized that life on earth was quite different from what had been thought. There too the ancients had been taken in by appearances.

What these investigators gradually discovered through the medium of their microscopes was so absorbing and so new that they no longer concerned themselves with anything outside their immediate environment or the earth and its atmosphere. In this constricted but fascinating territory they learned to understand the vast distances within the infinitely small. They discovered that the world was made up of molecules, and that these molecules were composed of even smaller particles, the atoms. As their various instruments became more efficient their restless curiosity drove them to discover that even the atom was not the ultimate constituent of the universe. Certain particles could be identified even within the interior of the atom, around whose nucleus electrons constantly circled. The chair on which I sit and the table I am leaning on to write are only constructions of an incredible number of these spinning particles.

I too consist of these minute particles, but, like all living things, whether animal or vegetable, my body has a larger base unit than the atom or the molecule, namely, the cell. In the last century the German, Schwann, showed that the cell was the structural base of all living things from the amoeba to man and its remarkable properties became familiar to observers. Also in the nineteenth century a quiet but brilliantly gifted monk, Gregor Mendel, discovered the first laws of heredity during his researches among certain varieties of the pea. And after him a new breed of scientist came into being, the geneticists. Their answer to the question of our fate was heredity. For within the cells they had found long, threadlike structures which were responsible for the transmission of hereditary traits. They called them chromosomes, and remarked that they were made up of smaller units, genes, which were set out in great numbers along the length of each chromosome. At the moment of conception, these chromosomes were redistributed in a manner almost like a lottery.

In this way nature plays heads and tails with our physical and mental qualities, and decides at the moment of conception what we will become later. How? By means of a code which has recently become a little more intelligible, thanks to the work of two American scientists, Watson and Crick, who were both awarded the Nobel Prize in chemistry. They have explained that the genetic code is formed like the perforated card of a computer program, and our fate is written on the program. All the information stamped on the code will eventually become reality. Our youth, age, and maturity are printed there at the moment of conception, thanks to an extraordinary and very complicated substance called desoxyribonucleic acid (DNA for short), which has a different structure for each one of us.

But if we can decipher our genetic codes, can we therefore also decipher the future? It is not only our physical strengths and weaknesses which are printed there, but also character predispositions and intelligence. It is all there, even to the moment when the complex machine of our body will become disordered and break down for ever.

A good proof of this opinion may be found in the example of twins. If our fate is written in advance in our cells, two individuals who have drawn an identical number in the lottery of heredity ought surely to have identical lives. Dr. Kallmann of the Psychiatric Institute of New York has been studying this question; over thirty years he examined 27,000 pairs of identical twins, and his conclusion was that "every being has inside him a clock set at the moment of his birth which predetermines particularly illnesses and accidents."

A simple example of Dr. Kallmann's provides food for thought: twins who were deserted at birth by their parents and raised by their adoptive families in two different countries nevertheless both chose a military career and at their retirement had both reached the same rank of colonel!

But here perhaps there is an idea which will make the astronomers scowl behind their telescopes, and the astrologers prick up their Chaldean ears: the twins were born under the same relative position of the stars. Could that be the reason why they had the same fate? No, for here there is an important difference. It is not because they are born under the same star but because they have the same hereditary luggage that twins often share the same destiny. This can be shown by comparing the performance of non-identical twins who are born from different eggs. Now, although these are born on the same day, like identical twins, they show considerable differences of character and of subsequent destiny, unlike the usual case of identical twins.

Is it correct then to say that the effect of heredity extends to all our life? According to the great poet Maeterlinck: "It could be said that what happens to men is that which they want to happen to them. We should not forget that nothing befalls us which is not, like us, in nature. And the most unexpected freaks of fortune often take the actual form of our thoughts."

That might explain a certain innate awkwardness in men who always fail in whatever they undertake, or the insolent good luck of the fortunate people who succeed in everything. Would not a man's manner of reacting in his life go far to explain such lives? That was certainly the opinion of a young Viennese psychiatrist at the end of the last century named Sigmund Freud. He took as his field of study, not the human body, but the human mind, and he examined it with a special sort of microscope. By psychoanalysis he discovered that what had been considered obvious and rational motives for our actions often had an unconscious, irrational origin. Once again, man was not what he had assumed himself to be. Psychology and psychoanalysis have enabled us to penetrate an unknown world, and have provided us with a guide to understand the complications of human lives. Like genetics, it assumes that our fate is within us. Psychology has taken for its own the famous remark of Schiller: "The stars of your destiny are in your heart."

In the face of such exciting discoveries, biologists and psychologists were fully occupied with what happened on Earth and thought about nothing else. They had too much to do for the rest of the universe to have any interest for them. A permanent divorce, based on a striking temperamental incompatibility, was established between the microscope and the telescope. The gap between astronomers and biologists grew wider and wider, between those who wanted to know what the universe was made of and those who wanted to know what man was made of.

By the twentieth century the gap between the world of galaxies and the world of living cells had become a yawning gulf. Between the two there flowed the more or less stagnant and muddy stream of astrological notions. The sky of the astronomers was not concerned with men's future, and man as revealed by the biologists had no need of the sky to know his destiny. Despite its ancient place in the heavens beyond his control, his fate had become earthly and internal. Man's future was to be found in his genes and in his deepest thoughts; he carried it within him.

Chapter Three

THE RECONCILIATION

Man had explored the universe and now believed that the skies had no meaning for him. He knew that his future depended on his genes and his own mind. Half the scientists had turned their backs on the other half. But should not science strive for universality, for the resolution of apparent contraries, and a generalization of its laws? Was it not better for scientists to be alert to this fact than to keep their eyes glued to their instruments and take no intrest in the world around them?

"Biologists, look at the structure of the universe, perhaps it will help to enrich your own science. Astronomers and physicists, spare a glance for living things. The temperamental incompatibility, the divorce between your instruments, has reached the point of rupture. As you accumulate data from your experiments, do you not see that the established rules fail to explain all the facts?"

There were appeals of this kind from isolated researchers, but science as a whole remained deaf to them. Then, on April 12, 1961, the amazing news was learned that there was a man in space; his tiny satellite was orbiting the earth. All the contradictions had failed to jerk the scientists from their rut, but Yuri Gagarin succeeded. If man had begun to travel in space, was it not time to consider the importance of the effects which space could have on man? So at last the great question was once again raised.

The great French biologist, Laborit, has written: "Is there anything more saddening yet more exciting than to be a man in the middle of a hidden universe incomprehensible in its finality, a universe which reaches us through the narrow openings of our senses, and yet fashions and blends us; a universe which existed before us and will continue on when we are no more; a universe in continual flux like ourselves; we, who attain a sense of stability and interruption through artificial means; we, who mold a finite world with the apprehension of the infinite?

"In our discouragement we look down at the constricted horizon of the earth. We imagine our world wandering and spinning in space, and try to gain comfort from the olive tree close at hand, its leaves trembling in the evening air, or from the roar of the city, its pain and labor, or from the presence of those men who, confined in the same cosmic vessel as ourselves, do not seem upset at the fact. We feel comforted by the swarming life all around us. . . .

"And then hope slowly returns to the biologist who guesses at a link, or rather a prevailing continuity, between the anaerobic bacteria which he treads underfoot, the last red glow of the setting sun, the white leaves of the olive tree, his wrist watch which tells him the family is waiting for him to come home to dinner, and the oil tanker which returns to port."[1]

So he conceives the biologist "who guesses at a link" between the universe and man. But besides the biologist there are also physicist-astronomers, one of the most famous of whom, Fred Hoyle, has defended the idea that we are primarily the "stuff of the universe." The materials which form living tissue, from lichen to man, may have a different architecture, but they are made from the same substance as the whole of the universe. A hydrogen atom on the star of Sirius is no different from one which exists on earth and circulates in our bodies.

Scientists who have studied the origin of life on earth have come to the conclusion, with the Russian biochemist Oparin, that life appeared first on the surface of the sea. It was caused by the reaction produced in the atmosphere then through the luminous and ultra-violet energy proceeding from the sun. Unknown to his superiors, a young American researcher of twenty-five, Stanley L. Miller, went back literally three billion years – in his laboratory. He succeeded in confirming conclusively the correctness of Oparin's hypothesis: the sun is indeed the creator of life upon earth.

In 1946 the Nobel Prize was awarded to Hermann J. Muller for discovering how mutations are produced; he altered the genetic base of sex cells by bombarding them with X-rays. A radical alteration of our biological destiny could follow

1. Laborit, *Du Soleil à l'homme*. pp. 9–11.

directly from prolonged exposure to such rays. We know that the cosmic rays which reach us constantly have a penetration as strong as Muller's X-rays. What effect might they not have had on the evolution of life?

Even more extraordinary is the very recent experiment with "radio-controlled" cells. John H. Heller and A. Teixeira-Pinto, the American scientists, also changed the arrangement of chromosomes. This time weak radio waves were used which had been considered incapable of having the slightest effect on living matter as well organized as this.

X-rays are one end and radio waves the other end of the entire range of recorded radiation. These rays reach us in unimaginable quantity from the sun, the planets and the galaxy. It is a matter of urgency, particularly at a time when man has left the protective barrier of the atmosphere and launched himself into space, to know whether the rays which reach us in this way have the same effects as those used by scientists in the laboratories. If the cosmos played as essential part in the first appearance of life on earth, why should it not also play a part in the evolution and destiny of living creatures?

So, thanks to Gagarin, increasing numbers of astronomers, physicists and biologists are willing to reconcile their sciences. They are becoming eager to meet and collaborate to build a new science which will examine the relation between man and the universe.

Biologists are aware that the earth is not a central, self-contained unit, and astronomers are aware that the skies can affect our lives. But does there remain a common denominator which might help us to connect the evolution of the universe with the life of man?

There exists one really fundamental characteristic of the universe: it is subject to rhythms. The Ancients had already stressed the rhythms of nature, without always perceiving the precise consequences. They are found as much in the infinitely great as in the infinitely small, as much in organic as in inorganic matter. The wave which carries a photon of sunlight is recurrent, just as the sun itself is recurrent in its eleven-year cycle. Mendeleiev has left his name to posterity by demonstrating that the elements of nature can be classified according to a law of recurrence. Astronomers teach us that stars have an immensely long life cycle, and that their age can be predicted according to their color, from which it can be seen whether their demise is near or far away.

In nature there is nothing which does not follow a pattern of vibrations. There are minute vibrations on the scale of the atom, as in Planck's well-known quanta, for instance. Elsewhere there are immense vibrations which affect the entire universe. May not the present expansion of the universe be followed in the future by a period of retraction? Rhythm and recurrence exist everywhere.

Living matter is no exception to this rule. Rhythmic cycles are found everywhere: in the carrot, the amoeba, the giant tortoise, as much as in man. Some of these rhythms are familiar to us, such as the respiratory rhythm or the rhythm of the heart. Discharges of neural impulses also occur rhythmically: the brain sends out regular and recurrent waves, and all our biological processes are subject to cycles of varying length.

To go further into the matter, these rhythms seem to operate like internal clocks whose mechanisms control the whole of life. From the most elementary reactions of the cells to the most complicated reactions of the whole organism, everything operates by rhythmic vibrations. As the biologist Thorpe has concluded, the presence of biological clocks is probably universal in nature as it exists on earth.

Where do these bodily rhythms come from? Are they chance effects or are they connected to an environmental necessity? What should be said about the 24-hour rhythm which controls our sleeping and waking hours? All the authorities are agreed that this rhythm fits in with a biological restructuring, as recurrent in man as in the animals. In a very real sense, we are not the same person at ten in the morning as at ten in the evening; our tension is different, our cells do not divide at the same rate, our kidneys do not discard the same elements, our brain does not function at the same rhythm. An American expert, Aschoff, has come to the same conclusion in this matter as the Russian, Bykov; the rhythm of our internal clocks depends on another rhythm which cannot seemingly be put out of order, the alternation of day and night.

If man were taken from this dependence, when, for instance, he is launched into space, would his organism not lose this well-ordered synchronization of his bodily functions? Would his internal clocks not start to run irregularly, each at its own pace, with possibly disastrous results? This question has become crucial for all the successors of Gagarin who will be sent into space where there is no day or night. How will they withstand over a long period the absence of the 24-hour "time-keeper," which controls their biological processes like a metronome? Will their internal clocks gradually fall out of time with each other? These questions, vital for interplanetary flights of the future, have led to a considerable expansion of research to find out how our internal clocks are controlled, and to what extent the "time-keepers" which we find in our ordinary environment are necessary to us.

Careful calculation has shown that not only the alternation of night and day but also the seasons, the years, and many other cosmic cycles are also "time-keepers," providing us with certain rhythms. Authorities like Brown, Bennet and Webb have demonstrated that there are cycles in living creatures which are geared to the course of the moon, others to the rotation of the sun on its own axis, and so on. It seems well established that living things may make use of an internal clock independent of all known cycles. But this biological clock can conform to many different recurrences imposed by the environment, of which the most important is the length of the day.

It will certainly be necessary to train the internal clocks of astronauts who will have to tolerate, in their flights into space, the absence of the rhythms of day and night. But, as Professor Piccardi has said: "We need not take a man from his own country or home to subject him to the effects of the cosmos, for the universe is everywhere." The earth is a cosmic vessel, as Laborit has put it. Drawn by the sun in the galaxy, we are all somewhat in the position of Gagarin, but our situation seems more comfortable than his because we are more used to it.

If the rhythms of a man are artificially disorganized by making him submit to unusual experimental conditions, it has been confirmed that his internal clocks become disordered. But what would happen if our cosmic "time-keepers" were themselves disordered and changed? We now know that the heavens are not fixed, so the question is a natural one. Is not the functioning of our body altered, upset and disordered when the cosmos which surrounds us is changed? The sun, for example, the agent of all life on earth, is subject to certain sudden shifts of mood. These shifts violently agitate the needles of compasses, disturb the atmosphere, and form *aurorae boreales*. Surely men who live at the heart of these disturbances must also feel their consequences? We should find out and know whether our own internal clock is upset when the cosmos is disturbed.

By asking whether earthly, and particularly human, phenomena are influenced by cosmic effects we are once again raising the question which had once been tackled by astrology: do the stars have any influence on men?

But there should be no mistake about it. The intention of the scientists who are taking on this problem is not at all to bring astrology back into good repute. Besides, the astrologers did not ask whether such an influence existed; they stated categorically and *a priori* that it did exist. The scientist's task, on the contrary, is to clear all the mystery from the question of astral influences. It is no longer a matter of handing on the tradition of vague and occult relations between "what is above and what is below," but to formulate new laws with clarity, and then to establish them by modern methods. It is no longer a matter of seeking what are the good or bad "purposes" emanating from the stars, but to understand their physical nature, which is indifferent to our own fate. The sky of the astrologers belongs to the Ancients, and it is limited to the stars of the solar system; that of the new scientists is, on the contrary, the infinite universe where new discoveries are constantly being made. There is no longer any attempt, as in astrology, to forecast an event in everyday life, but to put in order quantified data and see whether the various cycles of the cosmic clock and the various cycles of the living clock coincide at any point.

For a new aim new methods are required. The modern scientist will no longer be satisfied, like the astrologer, to discuss at random this or that case which happens to come into his range of vision. He will collate a great quantity of data, fully aware of their origin, and will carry out an exhaustive study before stating that surprising influence is verified by the facts. At this stage the laws of statistics and particularly the celebrated laws of chance have enabled him to bring an entirely new response to the question of whether the stars have any influence on men. Without statistics one would have to rely upon impressions which are generally fallacious; without its laws there could be no definitive answers. The Chaldeans, and then the Greeks, were too impatient in finding an answer to the question of influences which come to us from the sky. But today if one wants to go to the trouble of looking for the truth, it is not impossible to find.

In the course of this book we will be able to establish the difference between error and reality, between the world of astrology and modern research, between astrological forecasting and scientific prediction. But there can be no doubt that the results of the latter will often be as fantastic as were the fantasies of the former. It is common knowledge that reality often surpasses fiction. The world is always stranger than we imagine.

Few people have yet heard of these new scientists who are seeking to understand the relations between the sky and earth. But though their names are not mentioned in school or even at college, they will certainly figure in the reference books of the next century. Our aim is to make them known now. We shall follow each step of their thought as it developed and see how they have managed to explain facts which are sometimes evident, but which were formerly written off as the effects of chance and without significance.

But what if they did have significance and were not accidental occurrences? In any case, what precisely is chance? Sganarelle, the false doctor, used to say: "If your daughter is dumb it is because she has lost her powers of speech." This is a non-explanation, an evasion; just as often it is not an explanation to ascribe something to chance, but a sleight of hand which conceals our ignorance of the real causes. If we had a knowledge of the whole of nature would chance still have a place? Astrological explanations of our fate have been replaced by the acceptance of coincidences stripped of all magical content. This marks a considerable advance in man's thought, but sooner or later new explanations will have to be advanced to take the place of these "coincidences."

The history of science shows that the better a subject is understood the less room there is for chance. Increasingly often, concealed causes are found for the "coincidences" of nature.

Science has a duty to eliminate the effects of chance and to replace it with known and predetermined laws; only science can release us from our ignorance.

This ignorance was good enough for many traditional scientists, and still is good enough for them when confronted by apparently absurd natural phenomena. But every day there are courageous pioneers engaged on "pushing back the frontiers of accident," as Professor Chauvin has expressed it. A number of small facts which were considered insignificant but did not "fit in with" the known laws have been shown to have considerable importance.

Thus the fascinating research of Professor Piccardi has been based upon a question which seems almost ridiculous: why can the insides of boilers be cleaned more easily on some days than on others? We shall see how the German scientist Bortels tracked down the "accident" which sometimes prevented water from freezing when the temperature was six degrees below zero; how the Japanese biologist Takata spent all his life obstinately finding out why in spite of all the established laws, the human blood in his test tubes was violently disturbed one day when mixed with certain chemical reagents which had had no effect on it before; how even the time of birth is not as "accidental" as had been thought, and is perhaps not completely independent of certain cosmic "time-keepers."

Won't this make astronomers in their observatories furious, and delight astrologers in their offices for astral consultations? When hypotheses as strange as these are advanced, shouldn't one first of all be sceptical rather than admiring? Are we being told that the future now lies in cosmic rhythms? Is there a distinction between what we referred to as "time-keepers" and what astrologers bluntly called astral influences?

There is a distinction; astronomers may rest easy and astrologers should not rejoice too soon. These new pioneers claim that the future in the sky is still obscure, the future, that is, for ourselves as individuals with our own little problems. What the scientists are discovering, fascinating though it may be, would never satisfy an astrologer's client, for it would not answer such questions as whether he will make a happy marriage or live to be a hundred.

The astrologers promise a horoscope for everyone, individual horoscopes with individual forecasts. A true scientist could never promise that. "We are unable to say whether that spot which is at the moment appearing on the sun will affect a particular individual," he would say, "because our predictions are not designed for individuals. They are developed according to total statistical laws. The world is linked to the stars through the laws of probability, not through any benign or malign purposes involving any particular individual."

"One death is an accident; a hundred deaths is a tragedy; ten thousand deaths is a statistic." This epigram of the great mathematician Henri Poincaré points up the conflict between statistical laws and individual lives, and shows that the second is dependent on the first, but actually determined by it only within certain limits. For human destiny, as Voltaire said, is as hard to weigh as the eggs of a fly in a spider's web.

There have been mathematicians who have tracked down chance and brought it to defeat in its own territory. They have discovered that the world, or at least a large part of it, is governed by the laws of probability. In a sense, nature would seem to be playing a continual game of dice. This major discovery has given high hope to scientists but would never satisfy the student of astrology.

Each weekend we can state with statistical certainty that the following Monday a given number of deaths will occur on the highways. But for someone who is actually on the road this certainty has no significance. What he wants to know is whether he himself will have an accident, whether it is his fate to be killed next Sunday if he takes out the car.

The statisticians, after calculations involving numbers of cars, accidents, and miles covered, will be able to tell him that his chances of ending his career Sunday at the bottom of a cliff, if he takes out the car, are 0.003%, and may advise him to go by train or air instead. But the motorist will not take such an answer seriously, because he can say, with some appearance of reason, that at the end of his journey he will be either alive or dead, but not nine hundred and ninety-seven thousandths alive.

The statisticians will shrug their shoulders impotently and, if the driver is still uneasy about the outcome of his journey, he will go off and consult either a clairvoyant or an astrologer, according to his taste. For we can be sure that the astrologer will answer the question of whether he will return safely from his journey or not, precisely and in detail.

The astrologer and the scientist are divided by mutually antagonistic attitudes of mind. Emil Borel has said: "Statistics do not enable us to predict a specific phenomenon, but merely to express a total result relative to a sufficiently large quantity of analogous phenomena." This is in a sense an admission of impotence toward the particular. Hence the findings of the laws of probability are not interesting to those people who want to know what is to happen to them individually. Their individual fate will not necessarily be in accordance with the general rule.

Insurance companies know how to tie up statistics and the individual, and they do it with style. The fact that they make money is a good indication of the accuracy of their calculations, and proves the reality of probability ase related to humans. In a sense they represent a victory for the large majority over the isolated individual.

If you are sixty an insurance agent may call on you and advise you to take out a life insurance policy, explaining that his statistical tables still predict a life-expectancy of around ten years.

Does this mean that you will live to seventy, and at that precise moment will abruptly pass on? Will all your future plans be based on this prediction?

Obviously not, since this possibility is far from being a certainty in your case. It does not take into account the age of your arteries, or the banana skin on which you could slip tomorrow, or a number of other factors which will be decisive in your case. The agent who wants you to take out a policy has no idea whether you will one day celebrate your hundredth birthday, nor does he care. He knows that as a group his clients of sixty live, on the average, a further ten years, and that is all he needs to calculate his profit. Whereas in your case what matters is to know for sure whether or not you will reach seventy, or eighty, or a hundred. In short, you are interested in your future in terms not of probability but of certainty.

It does not matter that the chances of winning the top prize are minimal when one buys a lottery ticket. The important thing to the buyer is the knowledge that he has that chance, and the words of the astrologer will foster his delusion.

The astrologer claims to be able to reveal a man's individual future, whereas scientists like Piccardi, Bortels and Takata would never make such a claim. Therefore there will for a long time to come be a parallel coexistence (less peaceful than inevitable) between the pioneer scientists investigating the influence of the stars on earth and the adherents of ancient astrology. The latter will maintain its parasitical existence for a long time, for astrology is the dark side of the human imagination, whereas the others are defenders of its bright side.

It is to be hoped that the superstitions will gradually disappear, but the date will certainly not be tomorrow for they cater to a human need which scientists cannot satisfy, at least for the present. Therefore, in this book astrology will have a place alongside recent discoveries on the influence of the stars. "It is no waste of time to find out how others have wasted their own," Bouché-Leclercq, the historian of astrology, has said. But in our opinion it is far more interesting to understand the world as it really is. Numerous fresh discoveries on the influence of the stars, incredible though they seem, will show us that the cosmos, though indifferent to us as individuals, nevertheless provides a measure of our lives, and this measure is the whole universe.

For if the new pioneers cannot state with precision the date of someone's marriage or the winning number of a lottery ticket, they do offer something better to anyone capable of transcending the petty aspect of his own individual future: a magnificent panorama, a new destination for the human species enlarged to the scale of the cosmos. What these investigators are offering is something so deeply interesting, so fantastic, and also so true, that it is certainly worth all the self-regarding fantasies which astrology sends floating around our minds.

Part Two

FIVE THOUSAND YEARS OF MODERN ASTROLOGY

Chapter Four

THE STRUCTURE OF ASTROLOGY

What do you think of astrology? In my opinion it is a very great, very beautiful lady who comes from a time so distant that she cannot fail to hold me under her spell. I can see no finery or elegance in the purely physical world to match hers. Moreover, she seems to me to have in her possession one of the highest mysteries of the world. A pity that today, at least for the uncouth, a whore has been enthroned in her place.

ANDRE BRETON

Astrology is as old as man, and has existed since man has been capable of thought. His earliest thoughts concerned magic, and the earliest magic involved the sky, as the mysterious formations of the prehistoric menhirs testify. And when, four thousand years ago, the astrologer-priests climbed to the top of their towers to foresee the future of their country and their king, astrology was already a very old concept.

Today the year 2000 is knocking at the door. All around us the world has changed, but astrology is still there, exactly the same but stronger than ever. It represents a significant problem which cannot be ignored. It is an object of study for the economists, and all their conclusions concerning it are in agreement.

"If its place in society is to be assessed by the number of printed words devoted to it, then it is certainly more important than that allotted by our society to astronomy and math-

According to the astrologists, each sign of the zodiac governs a part of the human body.
Astrological man. Wood engraving, Paris, 1491. – Photo Garnier

ematics," Jean Porte, an official in INSEE, has written. "Its budget exceeds both that of scientific research and that of the steel industry," another economist has reported. "There are 30,000 astrologers or affiliated members in France, and they all earn a good living," according to a third, "and their clients come from all levels of the population. The position is the same abroad." Today astrology is a flourishing industry, and its popularity is assured.

"What do you associate with the words 'The influence of the stars'?"

"I think of astrology and the signs of the zodiac."

"Do you believe in astrology?"

"Yes and no . . . there might be something in it."

"Do you know what your sign is?"

"Of course. I was born in August, so I am a Leo."

"How did you find that out?"

"By reading the horoscope in the newspaper for fun. You must admit they sometimes get it right . . ."

The above is an interview with a man in the street chosen at random during a public opinion poll. One final statistic: according to the most reliable estimates, thirty out of a hundred people believe in astrology and thirty think there is 'something in it' and know their signs and those of their acquaintances. There are therefore only forty out of a hundred people who do not believe in it at all, and even among these there are some who are not always quite sure.

In the light of the incontestable accuracy of the figures, the question arises whether this robust survival from the past is attributable entirely to human stupidity. Or perhaps the popular intuition is right and the scientists are wrong to reject astrology out of hand without going into the matter?

At all events, it deserves an objective analysis. What are the rules of the astrological game, the record of its progress? When was it born? What are its real origin, its history, its successes and failures? Is what survives today worth anything scientifically. Is it worth a great deal or nothing whatsoever?

In any case, what exactly *is* astrology? Definitions of it are easy enough to find:

"Astrology is the art of predicting the future through observation of the stars." (Larousse)

'It is the longest illness ever to have afflicted reason."
(Bailly)

"It is a very great lady who has come from the beginning of
time." (Breton)

"Astrology is quite simply the art of predicting the future."
(Robert Amadou)

"The longest lasting and the most universal religion in the
whole epoch of humanity." (Berthelot)

Astrology is a science, a royal art, the opposite of a science.
It has a superior quality, for the few only. It is a folly, the outcome of an infantile process of thought. On the one hand it
may be called monstrous pride to believe that human destinies
could possibly be connected to the motions of the planets and,
on the other, a lesson in humility through the discovery that
we are totally dependent on those motions.

Whence all these contradictions? At least they demonstrate
that astrology is not as simple as all that. The following pages
are therefore devoted to a survey of the game of astrology,
from which we shall see how relevant it is to the present day.

A BRIEF SUMMARY OF
MODERN ASTROLOGY

We shall follow the practice of modern astrologers and refer
to the subject which they teach as "modern astrology." But
we should remember that although this may on occasion borrow the terminology of nuclear physics, behavioral psychology or modern psychoanalysis to defend or explain itself, it
actually relies, in arriving at its daily forecasts, entirely on the
inexhaustible source of the ancient *Tetrabiblos* of Ptolemy
(second century A.D.). Whatever its form, modern astrology is
still Greek astrology built on a Chaldean hypothesis.

An account of its growth will be given later on, and we need
not go into it at this point. It should suffice to provide a brief
"astrology for beginners" of the kind a student might read for
a comparatively unimportant exam.

The material will therefore be presented in table form, together with the way it is used. We will in general make use of
the formulae of a contemporary astrologer who is very well
known without being original in his teachings. In this way we
shall avoid charges of ignorance as regards the present-day

splendors of this doctrine, or of basing our observations on the cheerful hoaxes of men like Francesco Walder who, though renowned for his weekly horoscopes in a woman's magazine, is also capable of explaining the difference in character between two parrots by reference to their dates of birth. It should be emphasized, however, that this side of astrology is also part of modern astrology, whatever some people might claim.

THE SOLAR SYSTEM

Although astrologers no longer concern themselves with it, the reader may find it useful to know how their theories relate to the sky. The world of astrology is the solar system, consisting of the sun and the planets orbiting around it. To this should be added the moon, Earth's satellite.

We should have an idea of the relative distances between the different members of the solar system. They are, in order of distance from the sun: Mercury, Venus, Earth with the moon orbiting around it, Mars, Jupiter, Saturn, Uranus, Neptune, and Pluto.

If we imagine the solar system reduced in size one billion times, the sun would be in the middle, a sphere $4\frac{1}{2}$ feet in diameter. Sixty yards away would be Mercury, a small disk 5 millimeters in diameter. Venus would be next, a disk 12 millimeters in diameter and 108 yards away, and 150 yards away Earth would be a disk of identical size. At 225 yards there would be a smaller disk, Mars. Then would come the large planet of Jupiter, which on this scale would be 5 inches in diameter and 780 yards away; then Saturn, 4 inches and 1400 yards. Finally, at the end of the solar system after Uranus and Neptune, the planet Pluto, $\frac{1}{2}$ inch in diameter and $3\frac{1}{2}$ miles from the sun. These distances, which are considerable in relation to those on Earth, are very small compared with those of the stars: in fact the nearest star is seven thousand times further away from the sun than Pluto.

THE ECLIPTIC AND THE ZODIAC

The astonomers compare the sky around us to a giant sphere, with Earth, reduced to the negligible size of a point, at the center. The ecliptic is the full circumference of this sphere, which the sun covers in one year, at the rate of about one degree each day.

Of course, this motion is only an apparent one. In fact it is Earth which orbits round the sun in the same period of time. But astrologers are only interested in apparent motions and, in any case, at the time when astrology was born no others were known.

In this heavenly sphere the planets and the moon follow the same route as the sun. They all move inside a zone which does not extend further than 8 degrees either side of the ecliptic. This circular belt of 16 degrees is called the zodiac, and has been divided into 360 degrees by the astronomers. The astrologers split up this 360 degrees into groups of 30 degrees each. These are the celebrated signs of the zodiac which are so important in astrology: Aries, Taurus, Gemini, Cancer, Leo, Virgo, Libra, Scorpio, Sagittarius, Capricorn, Aquarius, Pisces. The sun enters Aries, the first sign, on the 21st of March, the Spring equinox. It enters the second sign, Taurus, on the 21st of April. Hence a familiar definition: if you were born between the 21st of March and the 20th of April you are an Aries.

The further away from Earth they are, the more slowly the planets appear to move along the signs of the zodiac. Thus the moon takes twenty-seven days to go through the twelve signs, whereas Pluto takes 250 years to do it.

Moreover, as seen from the Earth, the planets appear to undergo "changes of speed," and sometimes even seem to go backward. But this again is a question of appearances. In fact, the planet progresses uniformly in its orbit. "It is the year-long journey of Earth which puts these twists into the planets' perspective against the background of the distant constellations," explains Couderc. "And the speed of Earth is regulated with the speed of the planet to decide its apparent progress" — which is what interests the astrologers.

THE SIGNS OF THE ZODIAC

The signs of the zodiac are the cornerstone of astrology. If he knows the sign he was born under, a person can learn much about himself from it. We therefore take this opportunity to set down for the reader the various signs and their meanings.

(The text in quotation marks has been taken from the work of Andra Barbault: *Défense et illustration de l'astrologie* [*A Defense and an illustration of Astrology*].)

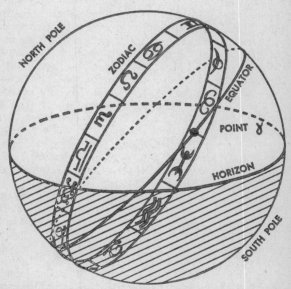

The ecliptic is a great circle of the celestial sphere traced by the course of the sun in a year. The lane of the ecliptic is inclined from 23° to 27° from that of the celestial equator. It is therefore not perpendicular to the line of the poles around which the earth rotates in its daily movements. The point where the ecliptic cuts the celestial equator is called point gamma. The sun passes point gamma on March 21, the vernal equinox. The zodiac is a belt of the ecliptic 8° wide. The planets follow this path. The zodiac is divided into twelve signs of 30° each.

If you were born between March 21st and April 20th:

ARIES

"Under the rule of Mars: spontaneity, warmth, aggressiveness, elation, enthusiasm, strength, passion, courage, a spirit of initiative and enterprise, a zest for conquest, novelty and adventure. Full of vivacity but lacking in self-control or perseverance. Impulsive, rash, and inclined to outbursts of temperament. An original and exploratory mind. Politically an advocate of force, an extremist."

If you were born between April 21st and May 20th:

TAURUS

"Under the rule of Venus: stable, well-balanced, calmly confident, strongly sensual, with a powerful appetite for life, simplicity, serenity, a slow tempo. But occasional rages and violent reactions. Faithfulness, steadfastness, industry, obstinacy, stubbornness, grudge-bearing, patience. A practical and realistic mind, common sense. Firm, faithful and jealous in his feelings. Politically, peace-loving, protective toward the interests of his class."

If you were born between May 21st and June 21st:

GEMINI

"Under the rule of Mercury: versatile character, flexible, light, youthful, clever, subtle, skillful, ingenious, gifted with know-how and very adaptable. But often unstable, anxious and complicated. A smart type, shrewd, cunning, having special skills, venturesome, sparkling, witty, excitable, nervous. A lively, quick mind. In love matters likes to flirt or play games, or forms an intellectual bond. Politically, a theoretician or propagandist."

If you were born between June 22nd and July 22nd:

CANCER

"Under the rule of Moon: a slow-moving character, sensitive, emotional, impressionable, easily swayed, delicate, dreaming, maternal. Shy, pensive, self-effacing, retiring, childish, melancholic, attached to memories, the past and his family. In love tender, family-oriented, a 'mother hen.' Politically unrealistic because over-imaginative."

If you were born between July 23rd and August 22nd:

LEO

"Under the rule of the sun: a strong character, forceful, strong-willed, conscientious, idealistic, radiant, striking, abundant, powerful, virile, commanding, full of authority, having an ambition which achieves its aims, egotism, pride. A lucid, clear, logical mind. In love matters, big-hearted but not free from selfishness. Politically, gets to the top posts."

If you were born between August 23rd and September 22nd:

VIRGO

"Under the rule of Mercury: simple nature, modest, retiring, sober, reserved, prudent, patient, with an eye to the future, precise, well-ordered, regular, clean, scrupulous, also eccentric. Practical, methodical, and with administrative ability. An observant, analytic, critical intelligence. In love matters, undemonstrative, serious, inclined to celibacy or a marriage based on good sense. In politics, practical, reasonable, a supporter of order and organization."

If you were born between September 23rd and October 22nd:

LIBRA

"Under the rule of Venus: balanced and moderate, with a sense of proportion, harmony, appreciation of shades of meaning. In character, uncommitted, conciliatory, peaceful, indecisive. Qualities of friendliness, courtesy, sociability, mildness, kindness. A mind with a gift for comparisons, standards and harmony. In love, refined, well-disposed, understanding. Politically, moderate, between the two extremes, fair, conciliatory, enduring."

If you were born between October 23rd and November 21st:

SCORPIO

"Under the rule of Mars and Pluto: an instinctive nature, violent, passionate, undisciplined, rebellious, imperious, hard, aggressive, sometimes full of hatred, but also anguished, obsessive, morbid. An instinctive mind, a 'nose' for the good, curiosity. In love, obsessed by sex, suffering outbursts of passion. Politically, favors violence, is extremist, aggressive, fiercely militant, combative."

If you were born between November 22nd and December 20th:

SAGITTARIUS

"Under the rule of Jupiter: thoughtful nature, reasonable, tendency to good works, conciliatory, trustful, loyal, generous. Persuasive, perceptive intelligence, more philosophical than practical. In love, a calm, honest and straightforward sentiment: if thwarted, free and far-ranging affections. Politically on the side of the underdog, can be tolerant and conciliatory, or rebellious and in conflict."

If you were born between December 21st and January 19th

CAPRICORN

"Under the rule of Saturn: uncommunicative nature, enclosed, reserved, sober, disciplined, calm, reflective, patient, cold, detached, ambitious, with distant objectives. A rational mind, objective and rigorous. A geometric, abstract spirit. In love, calm and detached but faithful; a celibate. In politics, ambitious."

If you were born between January 20th and February 18th:

AQUARIUS

"Under the rule of Uranus: a light and airy nature, vibrant, ethereal, sensitive, emotional, and idealistic. Lacking in spirit, but self-sacrificing and able to devote himself to a higher cause. A free-ranging, up-to-the-minute mind, interested in progress, reform, new ideas. In love, independent, whimsical, friendly. In politics often a progressive and in favor of reforms."

If you were born between February 19th and March 20th:

PISCES

"Under the rule of Neptune: a nature which seethes and bubbles with concealed passions; fluid and unstable impressions, indefinable sensations and emotions. Inclined to fantasy, evasiveness, hyper-sensibility, impressionability, indecisiveness, uncertainty; compassion, devotion, self-sacrifice. A poetic mind, intuitive, sensory and penetrating. In love matters, sensual of mystical, self-sacrificing and dedicated. In politics, produces visionaries, leaders of popular movements, or adventurers."

THE DIURNAL MOTION AND
THE TWELVE HOUSES

Earth turns on its polar axis every twenty-four hours, and this is called the *diurnal motion*. Because of this rotation of the earth, all the stars appear to travel across the heavenly sphere in the course of a day. For instance, if the sun takes 365 days to cover the zodiac, it takes 24 hours to cover the whole sky from one sun-rise to the next.

The astrologers, in taking into account the alternation of day and night, decided to treat the span of a day like that of a year in miniature. And just as they divided the zodiac into twelve signs, so they divided the diurnal motion of the stars into twelve parts, which they called the Houses. Each planet in the solar system crosses the twelve Houses in 24 hours, or rather, appears to do so. The Houses are numbered I to XII, in a reverse direction from the diurnal motion of the planets, beginning at the Ascendant (the point of the zodiac which is rising at the time of the birth under consideration).

Astrologers attribute a special importance to the Ascendant: in a scheme of birth, the sign in which the Ascendant appears is as important for the interpretation as that in which

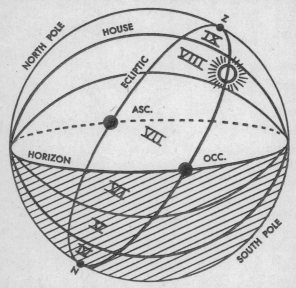

For any given time and place, the astrologers divided the celestial sphere, like an orange, into twelve sections known as the twelve Houses. The stars which most interested them were close to the ecliptic and it was there that the boundaries of the twelve Houses were most significant.

The most important boundary areas, called the "cusps" of the Houses, are the points where the ecliptic meets the horizon at the Ascendant (Asc.) and Occident (Occ.), and with the meridian at the sun's zenith (Z) and nadir (N). The Ascendant, where the ecliptic begins to rise above the horizon, is the point from which the Houses are numbered in decreasing order. In this order, the daily movement of the celestial sphere makes a complete rotation of the zodiacal belt through all twelve houses in a period of twenty-four hours.

the sun appears; these two signs mingle their influences. If, for instance, you were born on the 15th of April, the sun is in Aries, but if your Ascendant is in Cancer, then in your case the warm and impulsive character of Aries will be tempered by the dreamy, "stay-at-home" nature of Cancer. That will make you, according to the rest of your scheme, either a domestic tyrant or an affectionate head of the family. The calculation of the Ascendant is a complicated business, and we refer the reader to a specialized work for further details.

THE SYMBOLISM OF THE HOUSES

The meaning attributed to the twelve Houses of astrology:

First House: The personality of the subject.

Second House: Money, fortune, goods, possessions.

Third House: The subject's social world, brothers and sisters, relations, neighbors, education, communications, travel.

Fourth House: Parents, hearth and home.

Fifth House: Pleasures, amusements, games, love, creativity, children.

Sixth House: Known as "the Hospital of the zodiac." Chores and obligations; work, health. Small animals.

Seventh House: Marriage and partnership. Lifelong opponents, declared enemies.

Eighth House: Death, inheritance from others' deaths.

Ninth House: Religion, philosophy, long journeys. Large animals.

Tenth House: Profession, career, vocation, awards and honors.

Eleventh House: Friendships, and other kinds of help and support.

Twelfth House: Called "the Hell of the zodiac." Ordeals; secret enemies; snares and ambushes, illnesses, and various misfortunes.

A planet is described as "strong or dominant" if it is in an "angular House," that is, the 1st, 4th, 7th, or 10th House; "moderately strong" when it is in the 2nd, 5th, 8th, or 11th House; and "weak" if it is in a "cadent House," that is, the 3rd, 6th, 9th, or 12th.

THE SYMBOLISM OF THE PLANETS

In astrology, the symbolism of the planets is as detailed as that of the signs of the zodiac. We should note that for the astrologers all the members of the solar system are treated as planets, even the sun and moon. Here is what each planet will yield to you if they are "strong" in your horoscope (for instance, if they occupy one of the following "angular Houses": 1, 4, 7, or 10).

The Moon governs childhood, digestion and menstruation. It bestows a sensitive nature, emotional, impressionable, easily influenced, dreaming, whimsical, poetic, idle, weak. *Dispositions*: an affinity with food, clothing, children, animals, water, and small objects. *Events*: offspring, home, family life, journeys.

Mercury governs adolescence, the nervous system, and the respiratory system. It bestows an adaptable nature flexible, skillful, clever, ingenious, subtle, delicate, changeable, variable, unstable, versatile, malicious, and sly. *Dispositions*: representatives, middle-men, dealers, translators, mechanics, small businessmen, intellectuals. *Events*: study, journeys, business, material interests.

Venus governs the first stage of adult life, the evacuatory and genito-urinary systems. Bestows a lively nature, gay, graceful, courteous, gentle, sensitive, elegant, attractive, loving, frivolous. *Dispositions*: an affinity with the recreational aspect of earthly life, with art and esthetics. *Events*: the pleasant things of life, gratification, love affairs, worldly success, happiness, luck.

The Sun governs young adulthood (20 to 30 years), the metabolism, the circulatory system, eyesight, heart, and brain. It bestows a proud nature, magnanimous, aristocratic, powerful, generous, open, sometimes arrogant. *Dispositions*: an affinity with culture, objects of value, parades; high posts. *Events*: a social role, office, honors, fame, a lofty position.

Mars governs the beginning of maturity (40's), the muscular system, compulsive behavior. Bestows an energetic nature, robust, courageous, manly, aggressive, active, frank, impulsive, tyrannical. *Dispositions*: an affinity with iron, fire, hard, sharp, pointed and dangerous objects. *Events*: strong feelings and conflicts, enmities, traps, waste, loss of goods, lawsuits, operations, accidents.

Jupiter governs maturity (50's), the liver, blood stream, stresses the important needs of life, greediness, carelessness. *Dispositions*: an affinity with men, animals, and plant life, wood, parades and shows, churches, banking and restaurants. *Events*: life's happy events; well-being, comfort, success, wealth, status.

Saturn governs old age, the skeleton and the skin. Bestows an introverted nature, reserved, cautious, patient, reflective, calm, deep, well-balanced, serious, faithful, melancholic. Tendency to be pessimistic, self-centered, solitary. *Dispositions*: an affinity with the soil, minerals, insects, laboratories, libraries, monasteries, places of retreat, mountains. *Events*: responsibilities, celibacy, disappointments, failures and sacrifices; losses, bad luck, unhappiness, rejection, mourning, illnesses, death.

Uranus governs tension, swellings, intake and output. Bestows a character which concentrates systematically on the means to the attainment of a position of importance and privilege; assertion of character, independence, originality, eccentricity, cynicism, excessiveness. *Social life*: belonging to an elitist organization of people with special skills, progress, innovations, engineering, industry; commercial associations, capitalism, imperialism, fascism, dictatorship.

Neptune governs an inability to differentiate confusion, and a tendency to exaggeration. Bestows a highly sensitive and highly emotional character, impressionable, with many facets, diffuse, uncertain, imprecise; given to good works, dedication, masochism, fantasy, evasion, utopianism, idealism. A sensitive, intuitive, ultraperceptive mind. *Social life*:

involved in popular movements, anarchy, demagogy, scandal, chaos, revolution; syndicalism, democracy, socialism, communism.

Pluto governs the shadows and the invisible. It expresses the demonic side of life and draws on deep aggressive instincts, Freud's death-wish. It is concerned with great ordeals and disasters, deaths, agonies, sacrifices. It has some affinity with unorthodox fields: the art of the medium, clairvoyance, occultism, symbolism, psychoanalysis, speliology ... and subjects like sexuality, espionage, secret societies, Nazism, the atomic bomb.

NOTE: Uranus, Neptune and Pluto were discovered respectively in the 18th, 19th, and 20th centuries, and obviously have no place in ancient astrology. But, as has been shown, astrologers have found no difficulty in conferring attributes on these planets which are no less detailed than those of traditional planets. A modern planet requires a modern significance: for instance, Uranus=fascism, Neptune=communism, and Pluto =the Nazis or the atomic bomb. It is remarkable that the astrological observations concerning Pluto are so precise when one realizes that this planet was discovered less than 40 years ago, and that the astronomers have still not calculated all its physical characteristics!

THE SYMBOLISM OF THE ASPECT OF THE PLANETS

The "aspects" are the angles formed between the stars, as seen from Earth, and considered two by two in the zodiac. Their angular distance is calculated on the ecliptic. Astrologers attach a particular importance to certain of these angles, above all those of 0 degrees, 60 degrees, 90 degrees, 120 degrees, and 180 degrees. The following meaning is attributed to them:

Conjunction: (when there is no gap between the planets, and they are side by side in the zodiac): the influences of the two planets are mingled; hence a favorable interpretation with good planets, (Venus, Jupiter), and an unfavorable one with bad planets (Mars, Saturn).

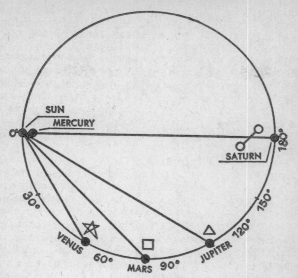

The Aspects

The circle in the diagram represents the ecliptic. The sun is shown on the same degree of the ecliptic as Mercury, that is to say, in conjunction with Mercury. Venus is 60° from the sun, in sextile. Mars, at 90° from the sun, is in quarter. Jupiter, at 120° from the sun, is in trine. Saturn, at 180° from the sun, is in opposition. These are the principal aspects used in astrology.

The sextile (an angle of 60 degrees between the stars) and *the trine* (angle of 120 degrees between the stars) are both beneficent aspects. *The Quarter* (angle of 90 degrees between the stars) and *opposition* angle of 180 degrees between the stars are both harmful aspects.

Since really accurate aspects are very rare, astrologers permit, in a scheme of birth, a latitude of a dozen degrees for the aspect to be still valid. This is what is meant by an *orb*. For instance, an angle of 117 degrees instead of 120 degrees is still a perfectly acceptable *trine*.

THE ASTROLOGICAL SCHEME

Let us imagine that at the exact moment of birth a photograph of the astrological sky had been taken. The planets would each have a place in one of the signs of the zodiac, the Houses would be set out beginning from the Ascendant, and the planets would be at particular angles between them. This would be the birth chart, also called, wrongly, the horoscope.

The task of the astrologer, when he has calculated and arranged all the astronomical elements of this chart, is to decipher it and to make clear all the signs of fate which are contained in it.

In an astrological scheme, everything is contained in the signs, the aspects, the planets, and the Houses. Astrologers deny that one has the right to judge the destiny of a "native" on the basis of one factor alone; this would be an unimaginable heresy. Thus the planets "take on the character" of the sign they are passing through, and add their own symbol to it.

For instance, Venus in Taurus (a sensual, amorous sign) will give good results, for Venus usually governs this sign. But if Mars (the planet of war) is in Cancer (abode of the dreaming moon), it will produce a bad forecast. Likewise when the moon crosses the sign of Scorpio (a sign of Mars), for this sign, as has been shown, is of an aggressive character, and does not fit well with the calm and imaginative aspect of the moon. Their encounter produces lamentable results, and woe to the poor human who has "the moon in Scorpio."

Here are some details of this unfortunate situation described by André Benbault:

> *Moon in Scorpio.* This one of the basic elements of the female "vamp," possessing a destructive attitude (the Praying Mantis type: Duchesse de Montpensier) and of the masochistic woman who seeks self-destruction in love (Marie Vetsera, the heroine of the Mayerling drama), or merely of the erotic woman. (A. de Noailles). The man is more or less attracted to one of these female types, or may only feel fear of women (Louis XVI). Or he may be prey to more or less obsessive fantasies (Berlioz, have a morbid imagination, or be at the mercy of an aggressive

drive releasing violent passions which may be acted out (Goering) or sublimated (Racine, Mauriac).[1]

Destroyers, sublimated or fearful or aggressive, or prey to fantasies . . . what a choice and what a variety!

But the planets do not only occupy a sign. They also and at the same time dwell in a House. Thus, if Venus in Taurus is also in the fifth House, she will bestow numerous and happy offspring; in the sixth House she will bring agreeable employment, or delightful little animals; in the seventh House, a beautiful woman or a charming husband, etc. All these declinations are favorable.

Nor should the aspects which the planets receive and send out be forgotten. These too affect the symbolism of the whole. Venus in a bad aspect, in the fifth House, will perhaps provide numerous offspring, but they will cause many worries by their wasteful habits. If Venus is in the sixth House and receives an unfriendly eye from the other planets, the little animals will be unbelievably disagreeable, the work will be somewhat disreputable, perhaps involving gambling or (in the rare case where the "illusion" of Neptune is included) even brothels. . . .

Evidently, the total picture is very complicated, and it requires particular care to formulate, from the birth under consideration, a forecast which is both complete and takes into account all the elements of the problem (and also finally turns out to be accurate!). The great art of astrology is to keep track of all the combinations of aspects, signs, planets, and Houses.

Let us take an interesting historical case (and one which, occurring in the past, will have the advantage of not being proved wrong after the event), and see how an astrologer would interpret it. For instance, why, according to Barbault, was Henri III emotionally the least well adjusted of all the French kings?

> Saturn is in VII and in double square with a moon-Venus opposition (the latter in exile), and this opposition is also in minor dissonance with the sun. Section VII is therefore "touched" at the same time as the three symbols. This delicate and intelligent prince had an extremely sensitive character which had been damaged by an excess

1. *Traité pratique d'astrologie*, p. 145.

of mother love. At eighteen, when he was acclaimed as a hero and had made some reputation as a Don Juan, despite his honors, pleasures, and the adulation of the court, he suffered from the sadness and motiveless regret of a discontented man. There was one great love in his life, Marie de Clèves, and he was loved in return, but she married the Prince of Condé. That was the downfall of Henri, who sought oblivion in the strangest excesses: his homosexual tendencies came to the fore, he was seen dressed as a woman, painted like a whore, dressed in all kinds of finery, and kissing boys.... However, he had not renounced his love: in his exile in Poland he dreamt of marrying Marie, but on his return to France she died (Saturn in VII is master of VIII and is the aspect of Venus in the VIIIth sign). Then his great grief broke like a storm, and he suffered collapse, despair, disgust. Emerging abruptly from his apathy he decreed, in his despair, commemorative ceremonies, dressed his court in mourning, and even wore a costume embroidered from head to toe with small death's heads.... At twenty-three he married Louise de Vaudemont-Lorraine who would always love him; but this love was to be unrequited and the union sterile. In his twenty-fifth year, with the authority of Catherine, the barrier which separated him from homosexuality and the partial domination of his "darlings" was to collapse....[1]

It is not our intention here to produce a treatise on astrology. We will only remind the reader that astrologers, besides the predictions which are worked out from the birth charts, also claim the ability to foresee good and bad times, from the astral motions which they observe subsequently. They are therefore interested in the *transits* of the planets, that is, their passage over a place of particular importance in the chart, and in the yearly horoscopes which they call the *revolutions of the sun*. At each anniversary a new horoscope can be calculated, and will provide a forecast for the coming year.

In this way the death of a person and his manner of death can be predicted, by observing an exceptionally malefic convergence in a year which is astrologically ill-omened.

Let us see, for instance, why Napoleon's career ended trag-

1. *Ibid.* p. 301.

ically on May 5, 1821, the day of his death in Saint Helena. An astrologer can easily explain it to us:

The moon was transiting his planet, situated in Section VIII, which is Venus 7 degrees from Cancer; and this moon was in a manner transporting and relaying unto Venus the opposition which Uranus and Neptune were sending against the planet at 3 degrees from Capricorn in Section VIII."[1]
The Emperor really had no chance of getting out of it!

That, then, is modern astrology. But where did this astrology come from? How did it develop? What is it worth? It is essential to learn about its history before going further, toward the true mysteries and the true discoveries.

1. *Ibid.* p. 315.

Chapter Five

THE NIGHT OF ASTROLOGY

Once there was a very ancient people who lived over three thousand years before Christ, in a place today called Mesopotamia. These were the Sumerians and, like all other primitive peoples, they worshipped the forces of nature. They were a nation of fishermen, hunters and farmers, and they therefore imagined that these forces contained gods of fertility and fecundity.

Their gods were originally from the earth, but they were conscious of the continual presence, overhead, of a cloudless sky and soon began to notice the strange relation which existed betwen the movement of the sun and that of the seasons, the times of sowing and harvest, and the relation between the moon, which lit the caravans crossing the desert, and the mildness of the night. In this way the cult of the god Sin, embodied by the moon, grew up, and the cult of the god Samash, embodied by the sun. Sin, the moon-god, was a man of ripe age with a beard of lapis lazuli. He crossed the sky in a boat which was the crescent moon. Samash, the sun-god, was his son. He was lord of the year, which he covered in 365 days.

After the Sumerians came another people, the Chaldeans. They too believed that the whole world was arranged according to a magical design. The whole of nature contained a meaning which was often dangerous and disquieting. They therefore had to counter-attack against a hostile destiny. Their imaginative powers created an amazing number of procedures for discovering the future and warding off the evil fates. The Chaldeans searched for omens in dreams, in the aspect of the liver at animal sacrifices, and in abnormal births. They were even the inventors of physiognomy, finding animal likenesses in the features of human faces, from which they deduced indications of character.

In this mass of magical operations, there was one which had a start on the others and soon surpassed them all: that of "the signs of the sky." The Chaldeans were a pastoral people, and they thought they had evidence for their belief that the movements of the sky participated in the fate of plants, animals, and men on earth. Perhaps a study of these celestial movements would enable their fates to be predicted; and prediction would lead to foreknowledge of what would happen, storms, rain, winds, wars, victories, and defeats; in a word, perhaps they would be able to discover the future and its perils and to preserve themselves from them.

As a result, watch towers were built in Chaldea, more than three thousand years ago: the *ziggurats,* some of which, such as those at Ur, Uruk and Babylon, reached a height of 300 feet. These towers were formed from a succession of terraces, sometimes painted in the seven colors of the stars of the solar system. At the top of these towers, far from the dust of the towns, priest-astrologers kept a constant vigil, relieving each other day and night.

For century after century they patiently observed, taking advantage of the clearness of the Mesopotamian sky. Thanks to their untiring observation they accurately recorded the principal movements of the sun, the moon, and the planets. But there was a radical difference between these patient watchers and modern astronomers. The former believed that the sky was swarming with life close at hand and the stars were lamps hung from its cupola like an upturned bowl. When he was at the top of his tower the priest-astronomer believed that by stretching out his hand he could almost touch the celestial vault. This presumptuous notion comes up again in the legend of the tower of Babel (the ancient name for Babylon). Excellent and exact observations, but a magical sky ... astronomy and astrology were born simultaneously, under the sky of Chaldea.

The Chaldeans divided the sky into three parts which they called "the celestial ways." There was the "way of Anu" which followed the heavenly equator; "the way of Enlil," which followed the tropic of Cancer and "the way of Ea," which followed the tropic of Capricorn. Very soon, the priests had noticed that the sun and the moon, that is, the gods Samash and Sin, followed a similar route in the sky, which they called "the way in relation to Anu." The Chaldeans were specially interested in the constellations which these two great gods "happened" to cross on their journey. To identify this route with precision, they established the site, among the constellations, of thirty-six of the brightest stars, which they called "the counsellor gods." The "counsellors" surveyed all that happened both in the sky and among men. Then from these "counsellors" the Chaldeans named twelve "chiefs" of the constellations which the sun and moon regularly passed through. Each of these twelve "chiefs" held sway over a part of the sky called "Berou." So this first map of the sky contained the outline of what later became the zodiac with its twelve signs. The strange names of the "berous" have largely come down to us, the venerable ancestors of the signs which we know so well and which we see used as much by astrologers as astronomers.

What names did these strange counsellors and celestial chiefs have? They were given the names of monsters, and for this reason: the Chaldeans had created an entire mythology, fantastic and bizarre, which can be found in one of mankind's first great poems, the celebrated "Creation" of Babylon. The clay tablets, covered with cuneiform script, have come down to us and been deciphered, and in it is the notion that monstrous animals came to life at the time when "there was nothing but darkness and water." The poem describes men with "the hindquarters of a horse and the forequarters of a man, having the form of hippo-centaurs," "bulls with men's heads," "four-bodied dogs with fishes' tails." In another part, the birth of these monsters is described as follows: "The mother of the abyss dressed the terrifying dragons in horror ... She created the hydra, the huge lion, the foaming wolf, the scorpion-man, the raging tempests, the fish-man, the capricorn (a goat with the tail of a fish) ... In all she created eleven monsters." Another ancient Babylonian legend tells how the hero Gilgamesh had to fight against eleven monsters and their leader. This could well be the twelve constellations with their astrological interpretation. Gradually, Chaldean mythology placed these strange creatures in the heavenly vault. Thus the constellations were named one by one, and by the Assyrian epoch some of the present names of the signs of the zodiac are there: Taurus (which was then at the Spring equinox), Leo, Capricorn, and Scorpio.

In the course of watching "the path of Anu," the Chaldeans established a surprising fact: that there were other "lamp-divinities" besides the sun and the moon which also moved along this heavenly road. Their behavior seemed strange in the middle of the multitudes of stars holding a constant position in the sky. The Chaldeans had discovered the five planets. They called them the *bibbus*, which meant "wild goats," as opposed to the tame and placid herds of fixed stars. The *bibbus* were regarded as "interpreters," because their course, which was carefully studied with many observations, announced future events. Each *bibbu* was the abode of a god, and its course in the sky declared the benevolent or malevolent intentions of the god who lived in it.

The beautiful evening star, the planet Venus, was the dwelling place of the goddess Ishtar, a most important deity since she reigned over fertility and fecundity. The planet Jupiter was the dwelling place of the god Marduk; it was both the planet of the king and the king-planet, just as Marduk was king of the gods. For the majestic course of Jupiter strays least from the ecliptic, center of the "path of Anu." The god who lived there was not a calm one: Marduk had the power to unleash storms and cataclysms. The planet Mars was "the red planet," the home of Nergal, the violent and malevolent god of war. Saturn, a remote, pale and quivering planet, was the kingdom of the god Ninurta. Ninurta was like a second Marduk, but colder and more thoughtful; he was aged and dwindling, and further withdrawn from the earth. But his remoteness was not to be trusted too far, for he too could prove himself an irresistible god, unleashing storms or life-giving breezes according to his whim. Mercury was said to be the dwelling place of the god Nabu and was given many epithets by the Chaldeans because of the great difficulty they had in observing this star. (Mercury is very close to the sun, and it is difficult to see it through the fiery rays of the star of day.) They called it the sparkler and the burner, but also the stubborn one, the enemy, the wicked one, the leopard, the fox, since it understood so well how to trick its watchers.

Naturally, the attributes of the planets were not chosen at random. The existing gods and their mythology were distributed among the stars, as Bouché-Leclercq says, "according to imagined connections between the glitter, color, status, behavior, and the customs of the wandering stars who were the kings of the heavenly hosts, with the divinities which had already been created by the same imagination." A remarkable alliance between the human imagination and the world of appearances.

The astronomer-priests did not have a wide clientele; in fact, to begin with, they had only one client, but a noteworthy one: the king. Through divination of the stars the king, and later certain leaders, tried to gain advance knowledge of the political events involving their country and their own personal lot. In this matter Chaldean astrology was more exclusive than astrology today, since it was not for everyone. In addition, the Chaldean astronomer-priests based their forecasts on the rise, fall and color of the stars, but were not particularly concerned with birth dates. Forecasts based on birthdays appear very rarely almost at the end of the Chaldean epoch; and, even then, only the king of the country had the right to one.

The official astrologers were required to send their observations to the sovereign at regular intervals. These royal astrological letters are the most lively account we have of Chaldean astrology. The king was a difficult, demanding and urgent client. Sometimes the questions he asked were difficult to solve. Here is one letter which betrays the embarrassment of the chief astrologer:

> The twenty-seventh day of his month – which was that stated – concerning that star of Jupiter about which I have formerly written to the king, my lord, as follows:
>
> In the path of Anu was it seen, but it was low and in the twilight, it was not clear. . . . On rising, it appeared distinctly under the Chariot, which stands in the way of Enlil.
>
> For the Chariot, its definition is complete, but for the definition of Jupiter *Mul-Babar*, which is in the way of Anu, on the subject of which I have written formerly to the king, my lord, it is not completely defined. May the king my lord take good heed. . . .[1]

That is the letter of a cautious astrologer, and one who recommends caution to his king. It may be wondered whether the latter was satisfied with this manner of evading precise answers. But sometimes the astrologer was more positive, and

1. Extract taken from the work of M. Rutten, *la Science des Chaldéens*, P.U.F. 1960.

deliberately risked even a gloomy prediction. Witness a certain Zakir, addressing himself to King Sennacherib (letter 1214):

"In the month of Tammuz, in the night of the tenth day, the constellation of Scorpio approaches the moon. This is its meaning: when at the rising of the moon Scorpio stands at its right horn, during the year there will be a swarm of locusts. They shall devour the harvest. . . ." Obviously Zakir did not lack courage, nor was he afraid to upset the farmers of the district.

Our knowledge of the forecasts which the Chaldeans could make is also drawn from the discovery of collections of documents. These documents were made up of prescriptions based on earlier observations, and could be automatically used when the same conditions again appeared in the sky. The chief of these collections is called the *Enuma Anu Enlil*. It is largely devoted to the eclipses, shape, and quarters of the moon, and the halo which sometimes surrounds it; but there are also other forecasts, a number of which are entirely meteorological and form the section known as *Adad* (the god of mountain peaks). Here is an example:

"If it thunders in the month of Shebat, there will be a plague of locusts." Or again: "If the moon has a halo, the month will be wet or cloudy." It can be seen that at that time astrology was concerned with the prediction of atmospheric disturbances.

Other predictions take external politics as their subject: "If the moon is visible on the fifteenth day, the omen is favorable to Akkad, unfavorable to the Subartu." Or it could be about the king's own fate: "If the sun stands in the place of the moon, the king of the country will be secure on his throne." Or again: "If Mars draws near Gemini, a king will die and there will be a feud."

Sometimes the forecasts even dared to fix the cost of living: "If Jupiter seems to enter into the moon, prices will be low in the country."

The Chaldeans drew their forecasts particularly from the appearance and disappearance of the stars at the line of the horizon. The forecasts which could be made from these astronomic observations were catalogued with a precision remarkable for the time. F. Thureau-Dangin has translated from the tablets of Uruk belonging to the Musée du Louvre in the following example. These are of particular interest since they are rare examples where the forecasts are related to the date of birth. But it is clear that, when "if a child" is written, the child referred to is that of a king.

If a child is born at the moon's rising, his life will be cheerful, happy, perfect and long.

If a child is born when Venus rises, his life will be calm and pleasurable; wherever he goes he will be loved; his days shall be long.

Sometimes the forecast was more subtle astronomically, involving the observation of two stars at the same time:

If a child is born when Jupiter is rising and Mars is setting, he will have happiness, and will see the downfall of his enemy. [But on the other hand] if a child is born when Mars is rising and Jupiter is setting, later on the hand of his enemy will take him captive.

According to Chaldean logic, the difference between these last two forecasts is easily explained: since the child is the son of the king, he is himself a future king; Jupiter is his planet. As it rises it dominates Mars, the harmful planet, which disappears below the horizon. Hence "he will conquer his enemy." Hence, also, in the opposite case, he will be conquered by him.

The whole of antiquity and the Middle Ages have reflected the exceptional value of the Chaldean science. Its exceptional quality lies in the precision with which it manages to describe the phenomena of the skies.

A simple example: Kidinnu, master of the school of Sippar, calculated the synodic lunar month with astonishing accuracy to the nearest 0.6 of a second, as being 29 days 12 hours 44 minutes 3.3 seconds, whereas it is in fact 29 days 12 hours 44 minutes 2.7 seconds!

In addition, it should not be forgotten that our calendar and all the sub-division of time which we use today have been directly inherited from the Babylonians. It was they who actually divided the solar year into twelve months corresponding to the twelve revolutions of the moon around Earth. Ours is therefore still a calendar based on sun and moon. Finally, the Chaldeans divided the day into twelve hours or *berus*, which are double hours according to our way of measuring time. These hours were divided into 60 minutes and these into seconds. As M. Rutten has pointed out, "We may have divided the day into 24 hours, but our watches have kept a dial of twelve." In that respect our watches are Chaldean!

Admittedly, the astronomer-priests did not seek to go beyond the world of magical appearances to understand the mechanism which underlay the motions of the sky. The Greeks were the first to try to achieve that task. However, it was the Chaldeans, and they alone, who established the precise tables from which the more abstract imagination of the Greeks could operate. And the latter never remotely succeeded in collecting so many material records.

Our admiration for the Chaldeans should be without reserve when we realize that the precision of their measurements was arrived at with instruments as primitive as the clepsydra and the gnomon to measure time and the height of the stars above the horizon.

Through this spirit of patient inquiry they had a universal influence, which allowed them to reveal to the four corners of the world their knowledge of the motions of the sky and their astrological ideas: in Egypt, Greece, India, China, and later, by means of the Arabs, in Europe up to the twentieth century, and no doubt beyond.

But to understand the history of astrology since the time of the Chaldeans, we have to follow two very different routes.

The first leads to the East. It is also a roundabout way, because it takes us to the four corners of the world: Egypt, China, India, and the astrology which is "outside time," namely, that of the Mexicans. All along this winding road astrology maintained its original quality of stimulating speculation both about the nature of the world, and about religion and philosophy. Here the individual is of little importance; he is lost in a universe which is almost as alive and purposeful as ourselves.

The second route is a straight line which leads to the West, reaching the Renaissance and then our own time by way of Greece and Rome. This road is traveled by an astrology which becomes increasingly isolated; in the course of centuries it has become more or less completely cut off from the science and religion which it once owned outright. Hence it may be said that it has become a kind of ghost of its former self. This astrology has become the province of the "horoscopes for everybody." If we meet mainly priests on the first road, on the second there are mainly charlatans.

Chapter Six

A MARRIAGE OF RELIGION AND SCIENCE

Astrology is not just the trash that we know today, which was fathered by the Greek imagination. Our popular astrology is cut off from its eastern origins, and the astrological advice which can be read on the back of tickets issued by weighing-machines is only a dismal caricature of it. However, on further reflection, all astrological consultation, even the most serious, is today only a caricature of what it once was. Up to a certain point it can even be claimed that it is no longer astrology.

In a general sense, astrology parallels man's attempts to understand both the way the world works and human destiny. For many centuries it has been a universal idea of the world, *the* universal idea of the world; a kind of prehistoric monster with science as its head and religion as its hind-quarters. This astrology is found along the paths which lead back to the old civilizations.

EGYPT

In Egypt the high priest of Heliopolis (the City of the Sun) was from the beginning of history honored with the title of "astrologer-in-chief." This post was held by, among others, Potiphera, the father-in-law of Joseph in the book of Genesis.

Even in the most distant ages, the Egyptians took an interest in the sky and its omens, but their mental attitude differed sharply from that of the Chaldeans and so did their astrology. Since they were a people who depended entirely on the Nile for their livelihood, they made it into a fertility god. But it occurred to them that the sky might have called forth the beneficent flood of the river, for each year it happened when Sirius, a very bright star, was ascending at the same time as the sun. They concluded that it was the combination of Sirius' beneficent action with that of the sun (a combination which only happened once a year) which made the Nile overflow its banks. Then everything in the arid soil of Egypt came to life again. Hence the beginning of the new year in Egypt coincided with the rise of Sirius in conjunction with the sun.

In their preoccupation with the star of Sirius, the Egyptians took no particular interest in the constellations of the zodiac from which the Chaldeans took nearly all their omens. They were satisfied with a vaguer astrology, based on the sun, the moon, eclipses, and noticeable meteorological phenomena.

However, for a long time they were credited with the invention of detailed astrological zodiacs. This belief was founded on the discovery of zodiacs like that of *Denderah,* which was imagined to be of the greatest antiquity. But it is now known that the Egyptian zodiac dates only from the Roman epoch.

Under the last of the Pharaohs the religion of the Nile gave way to Chaldean astrology as revised and amended by the Greeks. This became popular throughout the ancient world and yielded an unexpected harvest. The great sage of the time, the celebrated Ptolemy, wrote his *Tetrabiblos* at Alexandria, a book which became the astrologers' bible in the ancient world. At that time Egypt was one of the great centers for students of divination of the stars. During the later periods of Egyptian history the influence of the stars took on such importance that scholars have been able to reconstruct the life of Egypt in the Greco-Roman age by means of the facts referred to in the astrological consultations of the time.

CHINA

In China, more than two thousand years B.C., the worship of the heavens was strictly associated with agriculture, and then became an actual law of society. For the thinkers of the time, historical cycles were confused with the motions of the sky, and astrology, as a fundamental part of the established order, became the imperial cult of the heavens. The emperor was called "the son of Heaven."

In China a close relation was established between the four seasons and the four points of the compass, from which came a very old custom which "the son of Heaven" underwent, and which now seems strangely uncomfortable to us. The Chinese emperors of the prehistoric period before the Chou dynasty (second millennium B.C.) spent each season of the year in that part of their square palace which corresponded to the relevant point of the compass: the east in Spring, the south in Summer, the west in Autumn and the north in Winter. Thus the emperor identified himself with the season and the sky. But it should be acknowledged that, for the poor carnal body of "the son of heaven," this desire to identify with the weather and the seasons must have entailed the discomfort of stifling in Summer and freezing in Winter.

His body and his life were the standard of measurement of the whole universe. The emperor was so perfectly in harmony with the stars that astrological predictions were vested in him.

However, this great power could be a two-edged weapon, for if he did not play his part of controller of the heavens to perfection, these could rebel against him and be thrown out of order through his fault. René Berthelot has provided a dramatic example: "The collapse of the First dynasty, the Hia, in the eighteenth century B.C., may have been precipitated by the failure of their advisers to make correct astronomic forecasts, and by the appearance in the sky of irregular and unforeseen phenomena. An eclipse of the sun occurred which had not been announced by the princes Hi and Huo, whose ancestors had been entrusted by Yao with the task of governing the seasons. It was believed that the mistakes arising from their faulty observations of the sky had destroyed the harmony between celestial phenomena and the sequence of events on Earth. Since this disorder in the sky indicated that it had turned against the Hia dynasty, it became necessary to find a new emperor to restore order and re-establish an accord between the sky and the Earth. Thus the mistaken calculations of an astronomer had serious political consequences."

Nearer our own time, in the second century B.C., the Emperor Wu had a spiral tower which may have been derived from the Chaldean ziggurats. In addition, he had a terrace made so that he could look at the moon, and at the foot of the tower a lake one thousand feet square was dug. When he went up to the terrace to see the reflection of the moon as it appeared in the lake, his court was ordered to take to boats and make merry in the moonlight.

On other occasions when Wu stood on the terrace which communicated with Heaven, he commanded young girls and virgin youths to dance in couples so as to influence the divine powers, while torches made a shower of stars around them. The rhythm of this dance imitated the circular motions of the world of planets. These delightful celebrations are described by the great Chinese historian, Sseu-ma tsien, a contemporary of Wu.

In China, astrology was identified not only with the Emperor but also with religion, and to a considerably greater extent. This was the case in Taoism, for instance. Kwan-Tse, the famous Taoist author, wrote: "The *Tao*, which is made manifest in the heavens by the sun, is made manifest also in the hearts of men ... It is the living force which brings existence to being. Here below, it brings forth the five varieties of cereal, and up above it ordains the movement of the stars."

Thus the *Tao* is like the astrological lore of the first Sumerians, namely, the living force of the whole universe is also that of man. As a result of this, respiration was considered of major importance in China, India and Polynesia, since the air was supposedly full of "the seeds of life."

For his part, Confucius has declared the purpose of the Emperor as follows: "One who governs the people by means of his virtue is like the pole star which keeps still in its place, while the other stars circle it." And another Chinese moral philosopher proclaimed that one should "universally love every being and every thing, since Sun and Earth are but a single entity."

But the actual practice of astrology in China was always at a primitive level. For instance, the *Fen-Chui* almanac (meaning "wind and water", which was intended for the use of farmers, is a very naive mixture of astrology and alchemy. It provided methods of keeping track of the sun's and the moon's courses in the 28 constellations (the Chinese did not use a solar zodiac of twelve signs but a lunar zodiac of 28 signs, because the moon takes 28 days to cover the zodiac), their supposed influence on the five parts of the human body, and on the five primary colors in nature.

There were also applications of a theory linking the macrocosm (the whole universe) to the microcosm (the human body). The Taoist magicians of the first centuries of the Christian era believed that in every part of the human body there lived deities who were also gods of the sky, the earth, the constellations, mountains and rivers. By means of meditation it was possible to see the cosmic deities living inside the body, and also to acquire from them psycho-physiological prescriptions and moral precepts relating to health and welfare, through which the organism could be cleared of evil spirits and influences; it would be purified by breathing, the absence of coarse foods, and exposure to sun baths and moonlight which would pervade it with celestial influences. Thus purified and unburdened, it would ascend to the sky, where man would partake, body and soul, of immortal life.

INDIA

In India, vague and disorganized traces of an astrology dating back to the earliest times deeply pervade the various philosophies and religions.[1] It is hinted at in rituals which are

kept with the same fervor today as formerly. For instance, the crowds of pilgrims at Benares are unknowingly referring back to the origins of this astrology when they make the pre-dawn descent down the steps which run for miles alongside the river. At the hour when the night is about to end, the faithful, turning toward the East, await the moment when the rising of the sun will enable them to purify themselves of their sins by leaping into the sacred waters of the river.

Similarly, at Allahabad, where the greatest pilgrimages in India (and the greatest known to the world) take place from time to time, the pilgrims go to bathe in the confluence of the Jumna with the Ganges toward January, and particularly in the years when a certain conjunction of stars occurs. This indicates a connection between this water cult and astrology.

Astrological conceptions, though very indistinctly formulated, are found in all the religious writings of India. In the *Vedas,* dates of sacrifices are appointed at the new year and the full moon; and the stars are the guardians of the *rita* which is both the cosmic and the social order: "around the sky runs

1. But there is also a modern astrology in existence in India today which is related to the type afflicting the West, and was presumably imported in the nineteenth century by the British Raj. There is currently a famous representative of this astrology, Raman, who teaches it at the University of Mysore as though he were an accredited and official academic.

the sleepless wheel of the *rita*, the wheel of twelve parts: the year."

In the *Upanishads,* Brahma is given the title of "ordainer and inspirer of the universe." The celebrated dance of Siva, which is so often represented in statuary, symbolizes the rhythmic movement of the universe, with which the god associates man through his dance. And it should not be forgotten that the twisted cross is an Indian religious symbol, the *swastika* representing the circular course of the sun around the cross of the four points of the compass. This symbol, then, is related to the most archaic cosmic conceptions of humanity.

In conclusion, it should be noted that the concept of *karma* is in some ways more astrological than astrology. At birth, according to this view, a destiny heavier than the circle of the stars weighs on us. Good and bad actions carried out in earlier existences have an effect on future life according to a cycle reminiscent of the cycles of astronomy.

MEXICO

The first archeologists who discovered the old abandoned cities of the Mayas were respectfully amazed at the size of monuments apparently devoted to the study, through magic, of space and time. Here is an example described by Berthelot:

"Copan was a city which endured for four centuries and which, between the years 400 and 600 A.D., must have been in existence at the high point of the Maya civilization. It was a city of astronomer-priests who had an observatory and established a calendar. The temple was an exact rectangle, and was built at the top of a wide staircase on the summit of a pyramid of terraces, like those of Babylon. The large public building of Copan is oriented in the same way as a Chaldean temple or a Chinese palace, facing the four points of the compass."

The gods of the Mexicans, like those of Chaldea, reigned over both meteorological phenomena and animal life, and they had their dwelling places in the stars.

Three great gods were worshiped by the Aztecs:

Huitzilpochtli (the humming-bird magician) was the god of war and hunting, but also of the sun at its zenith, the overwhelming midday sun.

Tezcatlipoca (the smoking mirror) was also omnipotent and omnipresent. His name came from the mirror in which he was reputed to see reflected all the events of the world.

Quetzalcoatl (the plumed serpent) was lord of the planet Venus. The legend told how once the plumed serpent Quetzalcoatl was sacrificed on a pyre, and afterward a brilliant star, Venus, was seen to rise from the flames.

This Venus-serpent with feathers is of the same essence as the fabled creatures of the Chaldeans. The Mayas attached particular importance to this planet, minutely studying its different motions, whereas they seemed uninterested in the other planets. They were specially impressed by its disappearances: when, at recurrent intervals, it drew near the sun and passed into the fire of its rays, they believed that this was the death of the planet-god; when it drew away from the sun again and reappeared before the eyes of its worshipers, they believed that their plumed serpent had been brought back from the dead at the same time as the most brilliant of the planets.

These phenomena were forecast in advance with astonishing accuracy, but the carefully calculated dates marked the execution of terrifying rituals, which Jacques Soustelle has described in *Aztec Daily Life*:

"In their heart of hearts the Aztecs could not have had much confidence in the future. Their universe was vulnerable and at the mercy of catastrophes. Every fifty-two years the peoples of the empire were filled with fear, when the sun set on the last day of the 'century,' and there was doubt as to whether it would ever reappear.

"All fires, both in the cities and the country, were put out, and anxious crowds hurried to the foot and onto the slopes of Mount Ulxachtecatl, while on the summit the priests watched the constellation of the Pleiades. At the moment when it reached the meridian, the astronomer-priest made a sign. The captive was stretched out on the stone, a flint knife pierced his chest with a muffled sound, and a fiery torch was turned quickly around on the gaping wound. Then, miraculously, the flame spurted up, gaining life, so to speak, from that mutilated chest, and, in the midst of cries of joy, messengers lit their torches and left to carry the sacred fire to the four corners of the central valley. In this way the world had once again escaped destruction."

Among the Mayas, the astrologer-priests also concerned themselves with specific predictions of events or persons. They predicted the fate of a child according to his birthday, depending on whether that day was designated favorable or ill-omened in the sacred calendar. Every day's name was represented by a sign, and the sign of the day of his birth dominated the man till his death. It even determined his death and therefore his tenure of life. Naturally, they tried to cheat their fate a little; if a child were born under an inauspicious sign, a few days would be allowed to pass, until a more favorable sign, before naming it.

The calendar could also be consulted by those wishing to know an auspicious time to start an undertaking. And when a marriage was arranged, the astrologer-priests would conjoin the birthdays of the young man and the girl to decide if it would be happy.

Unlike classical astrology, this calendar was drawn up in advance, and the motions of the stars were not taken into account. However, the resemblances between Mayan and classical astrology remain considerable, and some archeologists and historians have come to wonder whether this astrology, like the Mexican civilization itself, was an entirely original creation of these peoples.

But the archaeological exploration of Central America is still comparatively recent, and contemporary discoveries, which are often sensational, have led some authors to believe that the ancient peoples of America knew considerably more about astronomy than has been commonly supposed. The discovery of a Venusian calendar at Tiahuanaco, near Lake Titicaca, might be supposed to indicate, according to the theory of the Russian academician Kotelnikov and of Professor Shklovsky, that the ancient Incas were looking into a problem which is still not clear to contemporary astronomers: the rotation of Venus on its own axis. If they had solved this problem it would have been no small feat, but at present this is no more than a daring hypothesis. However, there can be no doubt that, in the years to come, the study of the Central American civilizations will come up with some surprises concerning both the knowledge of astronomy and beliefs on astrology of these peoples.

There are some strange analogies which have made some people suspect a very remote Chinese influence, which itself was influenced by an even earlier Chaldean astrology, and approached Mexico by way of the Pacific islands, where here and there strange traces of a distant past still linger on.

Egypt, China, India, Mexico, these are only some important stages which have marked our random exploration of the numerous historical dialogues between men on earth and the skies. But it is high time we broke off our meandering journey through the old cosmic beliefs and returned to the road leading to school, and particularly the astrology class. For as yet we have not learned a word of our own classics or the way in which the Greeks turned Chaldean astrology into the doctine of "a horoscope for everybody," that excellent piece of imitation jewelry whose artificial glitter is with us today.

Chapter Seven

THE FOUR BIBLES OF ASTROLOGY

In the first century of the Christian era, one of the most famous sages of his time, the Greek Claudius Ptolemaeus, born in Egypt, undertook to summarize the information which his age had collected on the universe. In a first volume, *The Almages,* he set down what was known about the motions of the sun, the moon, and the planets, and he put forward an explanatory system which did not yield its place till Copernicus, in the sixteenth century, postulated that the earth was not the center of the universe.

His second work was in a sense an astrological version of the first. Ptolemy called this wonderful but tenuous intellectual construction the *Tetrabiblos,* namely, the four books. Today these four books are still the "bible" of the astrologers.

Greek astrology has in fact come down through the centuries almost intact, and may be found in identical form in this age of interplanetary voyages. Why has it had this extraordinary career? It it more effective than the other astrological doctrines which originated in Chaldea, and which have prospered little all over the world? No, its success may be attributed in part to the Greek genius for constructing beautiful edifices of abstract thought. It has also benefited from the general acclaim with which everything from Greek antiquity has been received by Western Europe. But, above all, it has proved ideally adapted to public taste in developing the fascinating idea that astrology can be within the reach of the humblest mortal, and can reveal to him his own personal future.

Berosus, a priest of the temple of Marduk in Babylon, was a Chaldean, born in 330 B.C. By virtue of his profession he was both astronomer and astrologer. Aound 280 he undertook the task of writing three large volumes in Greek called the *Babyloniaca,* in which he recounted the history of his country, Chaldea, devoting a large part of it to astrology.

The Greek world was immediately infatuated with this book. For the first time they could read in their own language all the knowledge accumulated over the centuries by the astronomer-priests. In the face of this success, Berosus set himself up at Cos, a small but very wealthy Greek colony, and initiated a course of astrology. He also instructed the medical students of the school of Hippocrates which was located there.

Naturally, the Greeks of this time already had some knowledge of astronomy, but they lacked precise records and detailed doctrines. On the other hand, thanks to her great philosophers, Greece was intellectually prepared to accept the teaching of Berosus. The predominant authority was the classics, so that the concepts of astrology commanded allegiance almost at the outset.

The most famous Greek philosophers had not waited till Berosus before expressing intuitively the same idea as his. Pythagoras sixth century B.C. applied his brilliant intuitions concerning number to the movement of the stars. He regarded the seven planets as a heavenly lyre, and allotted to each of them one of the seven notes of the musical scale, according to its respective distance from earth.

Plato (429–347 B.C.) had developed a theory of planet-gods in the *Timaeus*. And the whole of Platonism was ready for conversion to astrology. Plato's heaven was filled with models of everything which existed on Earth, models themselves copied from divine ideas. The whole thing was a vast wheel whose axis, a spindle of steel, rested on the knees of Necessity; thence fell to Earth souls which had already been sifted, sorted, and stamped by the motions of orbs turning inside with a sonorous rumbling, and these souls vibrated in concourse with their eternal harmony. These are the "vibrations" and "harmonies" which will recur in astrology at every corner of the road.

Aristotle (382–322 B.C.) carried such weight that he contributed "more than any other factor to the founding of popular astrology, to its general acceptance, and to its maintenance up to modern times," says Couderc in his work on astrology. "Our world, according to Aristotle, was necessarily connected to the movements of the upper world. And all the power in our world was controlled by these movements."

But if the Greek intelligentsia accepted Chaldean astrological doctrine right away and with enthusiasm, it could not disown from one day to the next its own ancient and prolific mythology. It was therefore necessary to naturalize the symbolism attributed to the zodiac and planets by the Chaldeans as far as possible by bestowing on them names taken from the Greek pantheon. But it was not always easy to make them fit the symbolism dreamed up by the Chaldeans.

The planets were Hellenized by finding equivalents between the Greek and Chaldean gods. It was easy to find substitutes for Ishtar, the goddess of love and fertility, and Nergal, god of war. Aphrodite and Ares were the obvious choices. The planet of the king, Marduk, was also naturally attributed to Zeus, himself the king of the gods. But it will be remembered that the Babylonian Marduk was hardly a kindly figure, releasing storms and cataclysms at his whim. The planet which had become Zeus must needs be accorded a greater serenity and a greater benevolence toward humans. Ninurta, the cold one, became Kronos. The planet was apparently small and far from Earth, and had been regarded by the Chaldeans as a dethroned and cooling sun, somewhat in the same way as Kronos had been dethroned in Greek mythology. But there too the character of the planet-god had to be perceptibly altered: Ninurta unleashed storms or fertile breezes; Kronos was a wise old man, morose and a little malevolent. As for the planet Nabu, it was attributed to the wily Hermes. But the Greeks did not keep the unfavorable attribution of the Chaldeans; instead of being a god "of fire and mischief," the planet was only "artful,"as befitted the deity of words and tradesmen.

Finally, a role had to be given to the sun and the moon in the astrological concert. It will be remembered that the Chaldeans had seen the moon as a masculine deity, Sin, and Samash, the sun, was his son. The Greeks, who had been watching the stars for a long time themselves, had their own point of view: the moon became feminine, and they reversed the order of generations: Helios, the sun, was the father of Selene, the moon.

Gradually, under the pressure of the Greek pantheon, the sun, the moon, and the five planets took on a whole range of meanings and influences which were endlessly embroidered. Each of these stars controlled a certain part of the destiny of men. Nothing was left out, neither intelligence, nor character, nor, above all, good and bad luck. Ares and Kronos (Mars and Saturn) became the "great malefics," whereas Zeus and Aphrodite (Jupiter and Venus) became the "great benefics." All these characteristics have remained exactly the same through the centuries, and have been brought up to date by only a slight rephrasing of the language. They can be found in our brief summary of modern astrology, written by the pen of a contemporary astrologer (see pp. 58–70).

As for the gallery of monsters represented by the Path of Anu of the Chaldeans, the Greeks not only modified it to suit themselves but also gave it its name for posterity: the zodiac, which means "the road of life." They improved it as well, giving it the standardized, definitive form which we know. The Chaldeans had left some blank spaces along the Path of Anu. These were filled by the Greeks, who gave a precise name to each of the signs of the zodiac and an equal space of thirty degrees. They were also the ones who established the width of the zodiacal belt at eight degrees either side of the ecliptic.

In describing the signs of the zodiac, they also sought creatures from their own mythology which might correspond to those of the Chaldean Way of Anu. The sign of Scorpio is an example. In the Babylonian legend, the hero of Gilgamesh, in the course of his epic journey, is attacked by the scorpion-man who guarded the sun. For the Greeks, the scorpion was sent by Gaia, Earth, to slay the skilful but overly gallant and vain hunter, Orion. The mythic scene was still enacted in the sky, where the two actors found themselves transported, for as soon as Scorpio arose the star of Orion sank below the horizon.

The example of Scorpio provides an illustration of how, by analogy, psychological meanings were gradually attributed to the signs of the zodiac. Thus the scorpion, a creature which brings death with its venomous sting, was supposed to have an aggressive, destructive influence. It was he who demolished and destroyed, but was also capable of rebuilding on the ruins he had caused. At any rate, those who were born under this sign were never at rest.

Thus, gradually, the fabled animals of the Chaldeans were dressed in more or less suitable Greek clothes. Soon the celestial menagerie could put up a "full house" sign. A definitive list of its incumbents is summarized in this mnemonic verse from the Middle Ages:

Sunt Aries, Taurus, Gemini, Cancer, Leo, Virgo, Libraque,
Scorpius, Architenens, Caper, Amphora, Pisces.

(These are the Ram, the Bull, the Twins, the Crab, the Lion, the Virgin, the Scales, the Scorpion, the Archer, the Goat, the Watercarrier, the Fish.)

Each sign had, like Scorpio, a particular character, and it transmitted this character to the humans born under its influence. Our brief summary of astrology outlines the subtleties of each sign, which have not changed since the most distant times.

In Chaldea, where the government had been theocratic, only the king and the country had a right to forecasts of the future. The designs of the planet-gods did not concern the ordinary mortal. Besides, forecasts based on the date of birth were drawn up only in exceptional cases. What mattered was the appearance of the sky at the moment when important events seemed likely to befall the king and the country. In the place of this astrology of the State, the Greeks quickly substituted something more democratic, thanks to two concepts which appeared simultaneously: first, the date of birth made it possible to forecast the future of the newborn child through an examination of the stars at that moment, and secondly, everyone, even the most humble servitor, had the right to a "personalized" horoscope.

How did this idea of a horoscope based on the date of birth come into being? The success of the astrologers in Greece encouraged an increasing number of people to review their economic position with the object of asking them which day would be auspicious for their enterprises. There were no longer enough "signs of the heavens" to provide information for everyone. It apparently soon occurred to the astrologers that the dates of birth of their clients were presumably the most important events of their lives. An examination of the sky at that precise moment should enable them to know, once and for all, the pattern of their future lives. It then became sufficient to study the sky on one occasion only in order to answer all the questions asked by the client.

"Astrologers were led to concentrate all the influences capable of being calculated on to this moment of birth," writes Bouché-Leclercq. "Thus, by dint of philosophy, use of the theory of the microcosm, and subtle distinctions between what is the case for practical purposes and what is the case in fact, they built up something which could be called a basic doctrine, not of astrology in general, but the astrological method known as *genethlialogy*."

In fact, this only amounted to one of many methods, but since it assumed the stars' involvement in the personal destiny of everyone, this lucky discovery thrived. And today our highly individualistic society ensures that the doctrine of genethlialogy and horoscopes for everybody should continue to command a fascinated clientele.

The assumption that everyone had the right to know his individual fate by consulting his date of birth caused the Greeks to make their astrological doctrine both more extensive and more complicated. The basic idea was simple: at birth, a child was influenced by "the star which was also born," that is, which rose at the same time. This star became the "master of his fate." At the beginning all the stars – sun, moon, planets, and distant stars – answered his purpose. But gradually the astrologers wearied of consulting the whole sky and concentrated their attention on the zodiac, which was its most familiar zone, and one in which all the co-ordinates had been gathered together in detailed tables. This was the circle which they chose to examine for the planet or fixed star which rose at the exact moment of birth to foretell the child's destiny. Every day a large number of children were born, all of whom had to be given a different future; so the planets and the fixed stars of the zodiac were no longer enough. The astrologers then concentrated on the hour of birth itself, and from that day the term "horoscope" was coined, a word which means literally "that which looks at the hour." The horoscope is the precise degree of the zodiac rising at the moment of a child's birth. Whether or not it contained a planet or star, it was believed to play a decisive part in the future life of every newborn child.

Now it was absolutely necessary for the Greek astrologers to diversify their predictions to such an extent that no two children ever had the same horoscope, and therefore the same fate. As a result, they lost touch completely with reality because, of course, this "degree of the horoscope" seldom actually corresponded to any rise of a planet or star.

It will be seen that horoscopes do not have at all the meaning which readers of the astrology columns in newspapers attribute to them. The horoscope as formulated by the Greeks is still used by serious astrologers, but it is not a vague daily forecast applicable to everyone at the same time. According to the definition of astronomy, it is "the degree of the ecliptic which rises above the Eastern horizon at the exact moment of birth." Modern astrologers prefer to use its Latin name, *ascendant,* when referring to it, and the word horoscope is generally used to refer to the state of the whole sky at the moment of birth. Thus the horoscope became an abstraction, a self-contained entity, without an actual astronomic presence to justify it. However, from this time onward it has been just this abstraction in the sky which has carried fundamental weight in deciding a man's fate, for it fixed the sky, as though in a photograph, in a determined pattern which was different for everyone. It was now possible at that prophetic moment to interpret the aspect of the sky in the entirety of all its components: planets, aspects, signs of the zodiac, and Houses. In the spinning mechanism of the sky, the wheel of destiny was suddenly halted. The planets were like balls which had rolled into certain compartments and had to be interpreted in the light of the compartments they occupied. Now we can get a glimpse of the admirable complexity of the system.

Since the horoscope was calculated at the precise moment of a child's birth, the sun, moon and planets would all be at different heights in the sky. One of these stars might be near the horizon, another at the top of its course, and a third beneath the horizon and out of sight. Therefore each had its place in the sky.

In order to give greater meaning to the place which each planet occupied in the sky, the apparent movement of the sun around the earth every 24 hours was regarded as a miniature version of its yearly movement, a sort of year which passed 365 times more quickly. By means of this peculiar reasoning, an analogy could be drawn between the yearly and the daily courses of the sun. The astrologers therefore divided the "day" into twelve parts, in the manner of the twelve signs of the zodiac. Each day the sun passed through these twelve

Houses of the sky, 365 times faster than it passed through the signs of the zodiac. The planets also went through the whole of the zodiac, like the sun, and so they too crossed the twelve astrological Houses in 24 hours, but each at a different time.

This analogy could not remain unexploited, and so the Greeks gave a detailed meaning to each of the Houses, as they had done for the signs of the zodiac. This innovation was typically Greek, and it was adopted by the whole of the Ancient World. It can be read without any alteration in the astrology handbooks of today. The different meanings of the twelve Houses are outlined in our brief summary of astrology.

Behind the meanings given to the Houses there are often bizarre, symbolic and unexpected reasons. For instance, astrologers especially pity the fate of the "first place" above the horizon, which they have numbered XII, and also its opposite, number VI, which has first place below the horizon. This is how an astrologer of the Roman epoch, Manilius, explains their unfavorable influence:

> The first place in front of the horoscope is the "gate of toil," a sad place, full of discouragement before the start of the climb. The opposite place, which has just plunged into night, is also gloomy, and with better cause; it is a "second gate of toil." Why is the place which goes up behind the horoscope called, with good reason "the horrible dwelling-place of Typhon" like its counterpart? It is because these places are gloomy and anguished, like Typhon blasted and buried beneath Etna. He is suspended above the setting and fears to fall into nothingness, and he who climbs behind the horoscope fears to slip on the slope.

In the sky, the stars did not operate singly, but often in concert. The Chaldean formula, for instance, will be remembered: "If a child is born when Jupiter rises and Mars sets ..." The stars were thought of as alive and animate, and could therefore be in sympathy or disagreement according to their respective positions in the sky, and these feelings affected humans. The matter was not worked out in detail by the Chaldeans. They only took note of planets which were face to face, that is, in opposition, and in that case the forecast was rather favorable: opposed planets did not look at each other from the side, but full in the face, and therefore supposedly acted together.

But the Greeks like numerical precision, and therefore made use of other angles formed by the planets. From this, the theory of "aspects" was born: some angles were considered to have a bad influence, whereas others were supposed to have a beneficent one. The aspects of the planets are vaguely based on Pythagorean theories, but they amount to a kind of celestial artillery where good and bad rays intersect.

When considering the 360 degrees of the zodiac, the Greeks attached particular importance to the sort of angles which could be found in simple geometrical figures like the triangle, the square, and the hexagon. These were interpreted according to a poetic symbolism. For instance, why was an angle of 60 degrees considered beneficent? The answer was to be found in the beauty of the hexagonal cells of bees, for a "sextile" makes up one of the sides of the celestial hexagon linked to the 360 degrees of the zodiac.

The task of explaining all the details worked out by the Greeks in their astrological doctrine would be an endless one; but that is not our aim. These details naturally had plenty of variations, and often contradicted each other, but their reasoning, which was both logical and mathematical, had a precision which aroused admiration. Thus the Greeks gradually covered over the livelier, more primitive, animistic theories of the Chaldeans with cold reason. But behind this logical screen the planet-gods who lived in man and for man still survived.

These planet-gods had their moods. For instance, when they seemed to move forward in the sky more slowly, it was thought that they must be annoyed and therefore their influence would be malefic. They had friendships and enmities among themselves, just as humans did. The moon, for instance, got on badly with Mars, for dreams and warfare do not go well together. In their course through the signs of the zodiac the planets (literally "the wanderers") passed through constellations whose accord with them varied. Just as a traveler who passes through several countries likes one and dislikes another, so the planet-gods "rejoiced" in certain signs of the zodiac (the expression is an astrological one) and felt "in exile" in others. Thus the sun "rejoiced" when he passed through the sign of Leo because the sign "resembled" him and because it was a Summer sign. He was "exalted" when he entered Aries because the Spring was starting. He was "in exile" in Libra because Autumn came at that point. And he was "in his fall" in Aquarius because it was Winter. It is interesting how often astrology betrays the fact that it is a creature of the Northern hemisphere. If they had come from Australia these interpretations would be reversed!

But if it is easy enough to understand why the sun's mood changes as it changes its sign, the planets' shifts of temper are often less comprehensible to the novice. Thus Venus is "in exile" when it crosses Aries, and when it crosses the next sign, Taurus, it abruptly "rejoices." Why? The mystery seems impenetrable. At any rate, these shifts of temper are considered of great importance in the interpretation of a scheme.

It was not only the case that the date of birth contained good or bad omens for the whole life of the individual, but also it was possible to diagnose, from the birth chart, the moment in a man's life when the stars would act to set in train the earlier predictions. The principal landmarks of a man's life, which made it possible to specify particular events in it, were the anniversary chart. Each year, at the hour and day when the sun returned to the place it had occupied at his birth, a man's anniversary chart could be calculated. If it was good, the year would be good. If it was bad, the year would be ill-omened. But the forecast of a scheme of birth could show an opposite tendency to that of an anniversary chart and therefore both were taken into account at the same time. (This practice is still carried on by astrologers of the present day.) In this the Greeks were again referring back to a very old idea, namely, that the seed of a plant contained in itself, at the moment it was put into the ground, the exact time when it would flower, ripen, and wither. The Greeks grafted their pseudo-logical mathematics onto this idea, and the horoscope of birth became a sort of game, which a man had to play all his life. At some times he won, and at others he found himself in dangerous surroundings where he was penalized.

The rules of this game were based on the passage of the stars as the years rolled by in those parts of the horoscope of birth which were considered especially "sensitive" – places, that is, which important stars had occupied at the moment of birth. Naturally, these places contained nothing in particular, but they had been sensitized once and for all at birth, and each passage of a planet in one of these places reactivated its sensitivity.

Let us imagine, for instance, that you were born with the sun at ten degrees of Aries, and that the malefic Saturn chances to pass over this point; then everything begins to go wrong in your life. But if Venus or Jupiter make a "transit" there, all your worries disappear. Thus it may be seen how the scheme of birth could be extended into the future. By these means not only the date of a marriage and certain kinds of success could be specified, but also accidents and even the death of the subject. The latter would occur if there were an exceptionally malefic convergence of death-dealing transits in a year which was itself especially inauspicious. An example illustrating this formula will be found in our summary (p. 70).

Once Greek astrology had used all its subtlety and artistry to construct a scheme, it still had to be interpreted. We have seen the arsenal of infinite possibilities which it had at its disposal. The planets, sun, and moon all assumed a different character according to their place in the zodiac and in the Houses according to the angles between them. Astrologers had to know how to weigh up the pros and cons of the benefic and malefic influences which were concentrated on the child at this moment of birth. The consultation was concerned with those areas of a man's life which have always been of particular interest: health, wealth, success, love . . .

It was a hard task. They could find assistance through reference to books of precedents and prescriptions, but an important part of the interpretation had to be of a personal nature. As the most famous of them all, Ptolemy, began his *Centrilop*, "Every judgment arrived at by an astrologer must be the result of his intuition and his science." The modern astrologer is in the same position. The symbolic keyboard on which he plays is always more or less the same, and the same eternal themes are requested by his clientele. Nothing has changed. Astrology was born fully armed from the Greek imagination, like Minerva from the brain of Jupiter, and it threw itself into the conquest of the Western world. It still lives on, and in the next chapter we shall describe its story.

Chapter Eight

TWENTY CENTURIES OF HOROSCOPES

ROME

The Roman world, brought up on the Greek civilization, had docilely taken its major gods from the Greek pantheon. There was no difficulty about translating Greek into Roman astrology. Zeus became Jupiter; Aphrodite, Venus; Ares, Mars; Kronos became Saturn; and Hermes became Mercury. These are the familiar Roman names of the planets which we still use today.

In practice, however, astrology had a difficult time in getting started in Rome. Unlike Greece, Rome had an ancient tradition of fortune telling which was closely intertwined with its religion. For centuries decisions of state had been at least partly determined by the flight of birds, the observation of thunder and lightning, and the entrails of sacrificial victims. The augurers themselves formed a significant part of the priestly class and were often members of the aristocracy.

At first, the nobility were sceptical, and regarded this new kind of divination with some contempt. It flourished among the common people, but that was of little importance, since it was practiced by simple charlatans who were for the most part quite ignorant of both astrology and astronomy. They were called *Chaldei,* in memory of the wisdom of the ancient Babylonians, but this was rather to insult their memory. The main activity of these Roman chaldei, it appears, was to forecast the winner in chariot races, whence the name "circus astrologers" which they were derisively called by the historians of the time.

The continual disorders in the social framework, the revolutions and wars and also the expanding population of Rome, all prepared the way for an acceptance of the influence of astrology; but it still did not come without trouble. In Rome the soothsayers were a professional body which was willing to defend its ancient privileges stubbornly. Feeling that their clientele was slipping away through the competition of the astrologers, they counter attacked vigorously. In 139 B.C. a decree of Cornelius Hispallus drove from Rome and Italy "the chaldeans, who exploit the people under the false pretext of consulting the stars." But by virtue of a mechanism familiar enough to all ages, this persecution made the astrologers seem more interesting, and their condemnation chiefly brought them publicity. The decree was defied to the point of consulting the astrologers by letter.

A comet which appeared just at the time of the death of Julius Caesar was the object of a power struggle between the two great rivals, the soothsayers and the astrologers. The former tried to interpret this phenomenon in the manner of lightning and thunder, but they were soon left behind by the astral interpretations of the astrologers. Finally, a man of encyclopedic knowledge, the Stoic Posidonius, decided the whole of the Roman intelligentsia in favor of the astrologers.

It was this man who built or put the finishing touches to the fortress of astrology. Now that it was guaranteed by a sage as renowned as this instructor of the Roman aristocracy, the people of the nobility who had till now been suspicious of or indifferent to the subject were forced by fashion to declare themselves adherents of astrology. As soon as it became fashionable, the curiosity of the dilletanti produced a crowd of practicing astrologers who wished to have nothing in common with the "Chaldeans" of the public streets. These new people were experts in manipulating numbers and geometrical forms, and reclaimed from their leader the title of "mathematicians," which had fallen into disuse since the disappearance of the Pythagorean schools. Until that point astrology had been nourished on philosophical argument and the unquestioning faith of the common people; now it occupied a place between these two extremes, a place where it could settle down and grow prosperous. This was in a rich, literate society which had reached, without exceeding, a degree of scepticism which dismissed the old beliefs and left the field clear for new ones. Greece provided the astrologers, and Romans, long accustomed to their role as disciples, admired, consulted and paid them.

The great men of Rome were not the last to consult the

astrologers. At the beginning of his career Octavius had had as teacher the mathematician Theogenes. When he became the Emperor Augustus, he made Theogenes his confidant and collaborator, and, according to Suetonius, "soon had so much confidence in astrology that he made public his genethliac scheme, and struck silver coinage with the sign of Capricorn — the sign he had been born under."

The Emperor Tiberius also believed, but with some reservations. More than once he had astrologers thrown from the rock where he built his palace when their predictions seemed suspect or unflattering to him. A certain Thrasyllus, however, became his confidant and astrologer. Thrasyllus was assigned to draw up horoscopes of the most prominent people and to denounce those whose fate seemed to mark them for the Empire. Tiberius then had them executed without mercy, to avoid any eventual rival. This seemed a good idea to Domitian also, who used astrology in the same way.

It is also said that Septimius Severus, when he was still Prefect at Lugdunum (ancient Lyons,) was already consumed with ambition and spent much of his time studying the horoscopes for girls to marry. When he learned that there was one in Syria whose birth chart predicted that she would marry a king, he asked for and married her. She was the future Empress, Julia Domna.

Great men must be imitated, and soon the whole of the Roman intelligentsia swore by astrology, whether in art or literature. Bouché-Leclercq has described this snobbery vividly.

"Under Augustus, astrology was decidedly fashionable. Everyone prided himself in having some smattering of it, and writers heaped on allusions which they knew would be understood by the nobility. Never had the stars held such a place in literature. . . . The portraits of the great diviners, Melampus, Tiresias, Chalcas, Helenus, were all touched up to include 'the science of the stars,' without which they would have seemed unworthy of the reputations. . . . Virgil, a somewhat clumsy practitioner of flattery, offered Augustus the suggestion that he should replace Libra, the Scales (for his justice and fairness were as great as the sign of the zodiac's) . . . Lucan willingly put Nero in the place of the sun . . . Horace assumed a kind of affectation to show that he had some inkling of astrology . . . he mentions that Mycaenas and he had to consult some

103

astrologers who found their birth charts 'extraordinarily in harmony.' Propertius was not content, like Horace, to make passing allusions to the mysteries of the new science. He introduced an astrologer into his work.... As a Stoic, Seneca believed in astrology. His tragedies are riddled with tirades where the heavens are taken to task.... Descriptions of the stars, and real or imagined celestial phenomena, tended to become a mania among the literary."

Women were not exempt from this mania, far from it. In his *Satires,* Juvenal ridiculed frivolous women in high society who fell for the great Chaldean art without being able to understand the smallest rudiment of it.

Naturally, astrology was still to encounter certain difficulties during the history of Rome. It was attacked by Cicero, for instance, in the name of reason and logic (of which more in the next chapter). There was still an attempt to bring down the utter charlatans who really went beyond the limits, like a certain Crinas of Marseille "who prescribed special diets for his clients based on the motions of the stars according to a mathematical formula, and who at his recent death left ten million sesterces (Pliny, XXIX, paragraph 9)." Later on, the astrologers were also to have trouble with the early Christians, who condemned the fatalism of astrological teaching.

But the jurists had no longer any recourse against it when the very famous and learned Ptolemy brought out his *Tetrabiblos,* thus giving astrology its credentials. From the fourth century A.D. it was all over Rome. A certain belief in astrology became part of the general way of life, and thereafter only extreme forms of it were regarded as superstition.

During the decline of Rome, and especially after the distracted reign of Heliogabalus, not just the prominent, but all people were afflicted with an outbreak of occult sciences which resembled a debauch. This certainly made a contribution toward the political and moral disorganization of the Roman Empire.

THE ARABS

After the disappearance of the Roman world, submerged beneath the barbarian invasions, astrology also disappeared in the turmoil. But if it was almost entirely eclipsed in Europe until the Middle Ages, the Arabs, who had become the sole trustees of the ancient literature, provided it with a new field of operation.

The most famous names in Arabian science took an interest in astrology, which they connected as much with medicine as with astronomy and mathematics. Avicenna, the renowned Arabian doctor (980–1037), always combined his practice of medicine with astrological prescriptions. Albumasar, the famous astonomer, wrote a treatise summarizing the Egyptian and Greek traditions in *The Flowers of Astrology*. Another great Arabian astronomer, Albategnius, drew up his *Treatise Concerning the Advantages of Astrology* at the same period, and established a system of division of the terrestrial sphere. Among the Arabians, the whole of physical science was a kind of vast astrology.

But although they produced a large literature, the Arabians lacked the inventive genius and the originality of the Greeks. After the twelfth century, they too let astrology slip into the magical world of all-purpose prescriptions. The chief merit of the Arabians lay in having passed on the writings of the Ancients. But was it really a service to the modern world to have brought it the *Tetrabiblos* together with the *Almagest?*

However, it should not be forgotten that in the Arabian world astrology was soon united with and counterbalanced by Islam. This monotheistic religion did not easily reconcile itself with an essentially polytheistic astrology, but, in spite of everything, the two systems did manage to get along fairly well; the fatalism of *Mektub* ("it is written") bears witness to a state of mind which was by its nature akin to astrology.

THE MIDDLE AGES

In Europe, astrology began to show its head again in the eleventh and twelfth centuries. But it was not an essential problem to the people of that time. Their faith was so strong that it sheltered them from any curiosity about their existence. For them, their lives began and ended in God.

On the occasions when astrological pronouncements saw the light of day, despite the Church's hostility, it was only to announce terrors and the end of the world; in 1179 the civilized world was thrown into panic by the writings, originally published in the German countries, of a mysterious John of Toledo. These predicted that all the planets would come together in Libra in the year 1186; such a conjunction in a sign of violent winds implied a general catastrophe; 1186 would be a year of calamities, and in September there would be earthquakes and violent storms.... The news spread like wild-fire: in Germany, caves were dug; the Archbishop of Canterbury decreed times of fasting; in Byzanthium, the windows of the imperial palace were walled up; in Persia and Mesopotamia caves were gotten ready. The month of September passed without a cataclysm.

Maybe so, but the obscure John of Toledo had come very near a prediction which might have altered the course of history: there may have been no violent winds in Europe that year, but this was the time when the terrible invasion of Genghis Khan took place. Instead of digging caverns, preparing caves and fasting, they should have mobilized armies and built fortifications.

THE RENAISSANCE

In Italy during the Renaissance, astrologers worked in broad daylight; they were scientists and almost officials. Besides astronomers, universities had special professors who taught astrology, although it was forbidden by the Fathers of the Church. Pope Sixtus IV maintained, like the *condottieri,* "planetaries" who established a favorable time for journeys, wars, or merely entertainments.

Similarly, when Milan's Chief of State, Ludovico Moro, decided to marry, he did so after consultation with the chief astrologer, Messer Ambrogio da Rosato. The marriage was arranged for January 17, 1491, the day of the god Mars, and therefore favorable to the birth of a boy, which was of course what Moro particularly wanted.

At this time, all the sages and scientists in Europe were more or less interested in astrology. Paracelsus (1493–1541), the great doctor and inventor of Hermetic medicine, developed a theory of medicine in which alchemy and astrology played a preponderant role. All the great astronomers practiced astrology. Indeed they were obliged to do so, for it was stipulated by order of the king that the astronomer's task was not only to observe the motions of the stars, but also to draw up astrological almanacs containing predictions. It should be added that the astronomers of the time accepted this obligation without any objection, for they were equally convinced of the reality of astral influences.

The great astronomer Johann Muller, known as Regiomontanus, was connected to the court of the king of Hungary, and provides an example of this. He anticipated Copernicus' discoveries, but he was also the inventor of a new way of dividing the sky into astrological Houses which is still in use today. Copernicus himself did not draw up horoscopes, but he had no difficulty in accepting the aid of a notorious astrologer, Rheticus, in completing and bringing out the first edition of his famous book, *De revolutionibus orbium celestium* (1540), which explained that the earth turned round the sun. Tycho Brahe combined a solicitude for precision and perfect objectivity in astronomy with classical astrological beliefs. As for Kepler, astrology was at least as dear to him as the laws of the stars' motions which have made him immortal.

Emperors, kings, and princes throughout Europe once more maintained, as at the high point of Roman history, their personal astrologers. After a thousand years of silence, astrology had made a shattering comeback into the Western world.

Astrology was a constant companion of the kings of France, at least until Louis XIV. It may be said without exaggeration that all the members of the House of Capet were more or less smitten with astrology. The House of Valois were hardly less convinced of the truth of the revelations taken from the aspect of the stars.

Charles V, for instance, provided his general Du Guesclin with a personal astrologer to guide him in the dispositions of his strategy. A portrait of Louis XI would be incomplete if his taste for the stars were omitted: "In his case, the influence of the astrologers equaled that of Tristan l'Hermite and Olivier de Daim."

Of all the characters in the history of France, none was more influenced by astrology and magic than Catherine de Medici, the wife of Henri II. She had tradition on her side, for the whole family of the Medicis had for a long time used — and misused — the advice of astrologers. Her long reign was marked by the presence of three famous astrologers whom she relied on successively for advice. The first was Luc Gauric, a Neapolitan of humble origin. Then came Nostradamus, the most celebrated astrologer in the world (and the greatest charlatan as well). He really achieved glory after the publication of his prophecies in which he claimed to have foreseen the death of Henri II, "on a field of battle and in single combat." When Nostradamus went, the second part of Catherine de Medici's reign was dominated by the sinister figure of the Florentine, Cosimo Ruggieri, astrologer, magician, and caster of spells. He believed neither in God nor in the devil, nor, very probably, in astrology either. The queen built a columnar observatory for him near Saint-Eustache, which was afterward demolished.

Henri IV had a character very different from Catherine de Medici's. But although he was highly skeptical about astral divination, he nevertheless ordered Doctor Roch Le Baillif to draw up the horoscope of the dauphin and rewarded him with the title of First Doctor to the King.

The birth of the child who was to be Louis XIV on September 5, 1638 at Saint-Germain-en-Laye has been described by Voltaire. At the very moment of the dauphin's birth at 11 minutes after 11 in the morning an astrologer who had been standing in the antichamber of the queen hurried out to produce the birth chart of the child. This astrologer was an important person, Jean-Baptiste Morin de Villefranche, who was responsible for the first serious studies into the question of longitudes, and who held the Chair of Mathematics at the Collège de France.

However, under Louis XIV astrology suffered a serious setback. In 1666, Colbert founded the Academy of Sciences and expressly forbade the astronomers there to study astrology. Whether through conviction or through fear of losing their posts, the latter complied in the prohibition. Astrology lost its privileged position as a discipline, at least officially, never to be seen again at the Sorbonne or the Collège de France. However, another field still lay open.

The invention of printing enabled astrology to reach the depths of the country. There it took a popular and practical form which it had not possessed for the literate of the towns. Its influence was spread in the form of almanacs; the first were printed in the fifteenth century, and they are still found today. It may be said that almanacs were still found on the bedside table of the peasant until the arrival of radio and television.

These almanacs were designed for simple people and in a sense they recalled the preoccupations which had brought astrology to life three thousand years before. They contained advice and forecasts about subjects like sowing times and the kind of weather the year would bring. Some almanacs specialized in health topics. They indicated propitious times to bathe, shave, purge oneself, or let one's blood. And they also explained the astrological origins of diseases.

The almanacs were expensive and they were certainly not within the range of every pocket, but they used to be loaned and their contents were spread by word of mouth.

They reveal an odd mixture of Greek astrology and Christianity, expressed in a naive, rustic style, since they were produced by people who knew little for people who knew nothing. There was even a book of hours, slipped in betwen prayers and illuminated prints, and a list of the parts of the body influenced by the planets, written in rhyming verse:

> "The Sun watches over the stomach,
> Saturn the lungs,
> Venus the kidneys,
> Jupiter the liver,
> Moon the head . . ." and so on.

A drawing illustrates this anatomy lesson: between the legs of a figure there crouches a fool, complete with cap and bells; this was the emblem of the brain brought under the influence of the moon.

THE TWENTIETH CENTURY

With the dawn of the twentieth century, astrology seemed no more than a flickering flame, whose guttering light was no longer fed by anything except the naive and unpretentious forecasts of the almanacs. But then something rather curious happened. Two books appeared within a year: a remarkable historical study called *Greek Astrology* written by a member of the institut, Bouché-Leclercq, and a *Manual of Spherical and Judiciary Astrology*, by a man called Formalhaut, which

"That which is on high is like that which is below." The stars correspond with the parts of the body.

was a great success. So astrology was once more revived by these two books at a time when the Institut had demoted it to the level of historical fantasy.

This revival was particularly evident in France after the end of World War I as a result of the efforts of an enterprising astrologer Paul Choisnard. With his adherents, he brought a whole swarm of cranks and charlatans in his wake. The period between the two wars saw a new invasion of the world press and literature by astrologers. The first exponents of the "astrological forecast" in mass circulation papers appeared around

1930. Some books of "astrology for everybody" were incredibly foolish and shameless yet had a really wide sale. Thousands of Fakirs, Wise Men, and "Professors" set themselves up in fairground booths or luxurious offices from Hollywood to Paris. It once again became smart to know about astrology, and the same mania which had tainted the Latin poets did not spare some modern authors. William Butler Yeats, André Breton, and the Surrealists joined that group which contained Virgil and Horace. Although still outcasts, "serious" astrologers imitated official scientific institutions. They formed "faculties," they held "conventions," and tried to make use of modern discoveries in physics and psychology to breathe new life into the moribund body of astrology. Unfortunately, these endeavors concealed an extensive lack of learning and in the end were nothing but everlasting variations on themes first proposed by Greek astrology. Behind the new jargon borrowed from modern science, it was still Ptolemy and the *Tetrabiblos* manipulating the well-worn strings.

In 1936 Hitler addressed the International Congress of Astrology in these terms: "I heartily thank those participating in the third congress of International Astrology, and wish them every success in their work."

The rise and fall of Hitler have a certain place in astrology; for did not Hitler plunge the world into war on a particular date, based on his faith in his astrologers? A president of Columbia University, Nicholas Murray Butler, claimed that Hitler was frequently in consultation with five astrologers, and that in 1939 these advisers told him that the month of September would be the high point of his career. Whatever he should consider a good thing to do to add to his reputation, that thing should be done before that time.

The claim of the President of Columbia University does not seem to have been confirmed by other historians. However, it is certain that, in accordance with the Nazi taste for the esoteric, Germany bestowed official recognition on "scientific astrology," and had appointed a certain Karl Freidrich Schule to be provisional head of the new Union of the profession of Astrologers.

All that we have in the way of records is the personal diary of General Jodl, Chief of Staff of the Wehrmacht, and this is full of astrological allusions. It contains a formal command issued to the German Ambassador in Norway to meet the Norwegian authorities at a certain day and hour in order to break off diplomatic relations at such a time, an equally formal order to an admiral to attack *at a certain precise time*, making it clear that the whys and wherefores of this precision were not his concern to know.

Did Hitler, like the Roman emperors and Renaissance notables, have his own private astologer? Several names have been put forward. It is said, for instance, that in the Munich *putsch* of 1923 he consulted someone called von Sebottendorf. Later he supposedly made use of the services of a woman, Elizabeth Ebertin. But the name most often mentioned is that of Karl Ernst Krafft, who was born at Basle in 1900, and was the most famous astrologer of his time in 1939.

Krafft, according to Professor Hans Bender, drew up Hitler's horoscope, in which it is specifically stated that the Fuhrer's climax would come in 1941–42, and that he would have to win the war by 1942 at the latest, or else catastrophe would occur in 1945. It is assumed that Krafft's private journal, which is still in his mother's possession, would tell of his dealings with Hitler.

But it was chiefly Rudolf Hess, Hitler's heir-apparent and complete confidant, who protected the astrologers. When Hess fled to England, Hitler in his fury turned against Hess's protégés, and several well-known astrologers were put in concentration camps. Even Krafft did not escape this fate, dying at Buchenwald on January 8, 1945.

The taste of Hitler and his men for astrological forecasts may be explained in terms of the occult, mystical atmosphere which pervaded their minds. In *The Morning of the Magicians* Pauwels and Bergier devote a long passage to some more or less frantic doctrines about the cosmos which were popular in the dictator's circle. The doctrine of Horbiger may be taken as an example: History proceeds in cycles, both on earth and in the cosmos; for the laws of the sky are the same as the laws of Earth, and the whole universe takes part in the same motion, and is a living organism in which everything reverberates with everything else. Men's fortunes are linked to the fortunes of the stars: that which happens in the heavens happens on earth, and vice versa. Horbiger would have felt at home in Babylon! This theory is very close to "ancestral astrology," and Hitler found in it a confirmation of his historic role. While it is difficult to determine whether his beliefs in the cosmos and the planets helped him in his political rise it is certain that they played a part in his thought and action.

Chapter Nine

ASTROLOGY ON TRIAL

During its Chaldean period astrology was regarded as something self-evident, self-explanatory, and beyond argument. But when it reached Greece it met its first enemies. In order to overcome the opposition its adherents now tried to go a little further than the simple rules which they had learned; they looked behind these laws for the reason why the stars could influence the future lives of men.

Many astrologers think that their art is sufficient in itself and needs no demonstration. Whether they are of the present or the past they see in the science of the stars a symphony of universal intercourse. This is a wonderful conception of the world, a cathedral which need no building, for it is already built and has only to be wondered at and understood for one to live harmoniously within it. For disciples of this school divination is divine revelation, a kind of extension added to human intelligence.

We have seen how men have tried from the beginning of history to understand and to pierce the veil of the future and to have something which they could admire and appeal to, something they could hold on to in misfortune. They have imagined the whole universe as a living organism with its own life. They claim that it is a *macrocosm,* and that man is an identical but miniaturized version, a *microcosm.* Everything which happens on a universal scale also happens within man, and the knowledge of the motions of one enables us to know the future of the other, since their inner workings are the same.

This idea is significantly superior to the popular astrology which we know. It is a mystic philosophy, a way of comprehending life, and a different world from that of science. In a word, universal symbolism is a religion, and as such it occurs in China, India, Pre-Columbian America, and in all ancient civilizations. This code of astrological faith is succinctly summarized as follows in the hermetic book *The Emerald Table*, said to have been written by the god Hermes Trismegistus himself.

> It is true, without falsehood, certain and very real,
> That that which is on high is as that which is below,
> And that which is below is as that which is on high,
> In order that the miracle of Unity may be perpetual.

This is very impressive; but how can this vast, vague conception of a microcosm analogically related to a macrocosm be put into concrete form? How can it explain the detailed and highly specific prescriptions of Greek astrology? This Olympus of pre-established harmonies is soon lost again in the attempt, and honored astrologers of the past, like contemporary ones, are either at a loss to do so or founder in a morass of half-baked analogies. Here are some eloquent examples taken from the *Centrilocus* of the much-venerated Ptolemy (in the *Centrilocus* Ptolemy made a digest of his *Tetrabiblos*. He collected the essence of his astrological thought into a hundred aphorisms).

> 27th aphorism: "Venus confers beauty and perfection to that part of the body indicated by the sign of the zodiac where she is situated." (By referring to the zodiac-man on page 110 the reader may easily imagine what is conferred by the planet along the twelve signs.)
>
> 52nd aphorism: "Planets ruling the birth of tall people are in a position of elevation at the time of their horoscope ... those ruling short people are in declining Houses."
>
> 53rd aphorism: "Planets ruling the birth of thin people have no latitude; those of strong or fat people have a latitude."
>
> 56th aphorism: "When the moon is in the first quarter, its humors will swell the body until the end of the second quarter; but when the moon passes into the two other quarters, the humors will grow less and the body diminish."

Many "symbolic connections" of the same type can be found in the writings of modern astrologers. This example came to light in the pages of an entirely serious astrological review:

> If a plaster cast is taken of the child's head at the moment of birth, and if, at the same time, an etheric cast is made of the heavenly vault as it was above the place of birth, the two forms will correspond exactly.

Evidently, the loftiness of fine symbolic doctrines soon collapses into a comforting pop-astrology when our own small persons are involved.

Symbolic astrology seeks to express a communion between man and the whole universe. Great writers and moral thinkers of every country have been inspired by it. At the start of Christianity, Christian writers regarded this astrology-religion as a kind of rival which used methods which were basically and fundamentally wrong, for it posited a number of gods or forces of nature whose rigid and blind fatalism allowed no freedom of will to man, instead of a single and all-powerful god. The first Church Fathers therefore saw astrology as a demonic monster which had to be fought. Its harmful nature, amorality, and determinism threatened to turn the believers from the way of righteousness. Its determinism was particularly dangerous: since God was sole master of the future, it was impossible that the stars should be a cause of men's destinies. This idea is already found in the writings of Saint Ephrem from the fourth century: "If God is just, he can not have set up geneathlic stars, whereby men would necessarily become sinners" (*Carm, Nisib*, LXXII, 16).

However, some Church Fathers condemned the immoral aspect of astrology without disputing its effects on men. In *The City of God*, Saint Augustine uses a thorny and somewhat contradictory argument to finally reject astrology because it is opposed to the idea of Divine Providence; but at the end of the argument he adds that while astrologers have "so often found answers which are wonderfully true, it is not because of their imagined art, but through the inspiration of demons." (*Civis Dei*, V, 7.)

If Christianity rapidly took over from the polytheism of astrology in the Western world, it did not entirely break free from it but stole some elements of the astral philosophy. How could it have been otherwise, since astrology and Christianity were born in places geographically so close to each other?

With a rival as insidious as a popular religion of the stars it was no wonder that Christianity should absorb it and turn some of its chief elements to its own account. This is what the Christian Church consistently did in order to accommodate rival pagan superstitions. The two fundamental dates round which the year of Christian celebrations is built are those of the birth and rebirth, or resurrection, of the Messiah: Christmas and Easter. After a long period of indecision, the Christians chose dates which had marked the beginning of the year for the gods of the sun, that is, they put the birth of the Messiah at the time of the Winter solstice, when the days begin to lengthen, and his resurrection at the Spring equinox, when the days begin to be longer than the nights. As for the instrument used in the torment of Jesus (a T-shaped device used for the punishment of slaves), the Christian Church, after some indecision, decided to represent it as two lines intersecting each other at right angles, which was the traditional symbol of the four points of the compass and of the sun's course in the cults of sun and life. And, as in these cults, Christians of the first centuries established the custom of turning toward the East for prayer, that is, toward the rising sun.

Many other details reveal how astrological ideas infiltrated early Christianity: the darkening of the sky which indicated the death of Christ; his resurrection on a Sunday, the day of the Sun; and, especially, the fact that his birth was announced by the star of the Magus Kings.

At the beginning these Magi were not kings. They were only Chaldean astrologers. Saint Jerome acknowledges without difficulty that they were genuine astrologers, but the legend turned these Arab magicians into kings.

In the ensuing quarrel between the church fathers and astrology, the star of the Magus Kings was a considerable embarrassment to the Christians, for its presence in scripture was true astrology, holding the high jurisdiction for which it had been designed. For at the birth of Christ this star proclaimed royalty. Even a royal horoscope for Jesus Christ meant a destiny for the man-god and also appeared to be a guarantee of authenticity for astrology provided by God himself.

Christians got around the contradiction by claiming that

the star did not belong to the repertory of the astrologers but was merely a witness, a sign of the coming God, and in no sense a cause. But this problem of the star of the Magus Kings shows that a subject of astrological concern had penetrated the heart of Christianity. Ultimately, the belief in a heavenly life after death, the idea that souls go from the earth to the sky and that God's operation extends from heaven to earth, represents the same basic idea ("Our Father which art in heaven ... thy will be done on earth as it is in heaven ...").

The Church, however, even during the Middle Ages and the Renaissance, did not persecute astrologers systematically. In fact there was hardly a war between Christianity and astrology. Some astrologers were burnt as sorcerers, but this was rare. The reason for this lay mainly in the important and ingenious teaching of the great Latin theoretician Plotinus, who lived in the third century. This neo-Platonist philosopher taught a theory reconciling Christianity and astrology.

What most disturbed adherents of Christianity, as we have seen, was the idea that the stars could control men's fates. But if the will of God could be set above their influence, would not the conflict between the two beliefs be eliminated? This was the basic postulate of Plotinus: celestial bodies should be denied any claim to being the efficient cause of human events. The stars did not produce these events, they were only the signs which announced them.

In that case, how did the stars work? In the same way as birds of omen: "Just as birds, whether they fly or come to a halt, tell us by their feathers and cries of events in the future of which they know nothing, in the same way it is possible to say that Jupiter is health-giving and Mars terrible, for happy events are signified by the one, and by the other unhappy events.

"They are, therefore," adds Plotinus, "like writings constantly being inscribed in the heavens, or rather, inscribed there once and for all." But how does this pre-established harmony between celestial motions and the earth below enable astrologers to produce accurate forecasts? Plotinus puts forward this explanation by way of example: "Just as with a living being, by virtue of the single principle on which his nature depends, it is possible to assess one part by another; an examination of his eyes or some other part of his body allows us to estimate his ways." In the universe, therefore, the stars have no actual, physical influence. "The active cause is the soul, the inspiration of the great animating spirit" (Enneades, IV, 4).

This world soul was only a step away from God himself, and the Church Fathers gladly made the transition with ease. Thus some of them, like Saint Thomas Aquinas, could announce with a clear conscience that they were convinced followers of astrology.

Thanks to the ingenious doctrine of Plotinus, astrology and Christianity ended by making a sort of marriage of convenience, or at least a relatively peaceful coexistence. Later, some priests and even a number of Popes during the Renaissance were to countenance astrologers, on condition that they acknowledged that the stars they consulted were only signs of God's will, and not direct causes of human destiny. At the present time, the Church condemns the use of horoscopes, but does not reject the possibility of an astral influence on men.

But some disturbing questions remained to be answered. How did astrologers claim to define the nature of astral influences? How did they know that a certain planet was beneficent, another malefic, or more or less, as the case might be? How could they justify the ridiculous notions associated with the figures of the zodiac, which were purely imaginary forms; or the influence of planets on signs and vice versa, when we have long known that the planets are a vast distance away from the constellations, and only seem to be fixed there through a trick of perspective?

There have been astrologers who have decided to take up an apparently scientific point of view in order to find proofs of even the craziest propositions. These men had no time for vague analogies and universal symbolic harmonies. The influence of the stars had to be explained in terms of physical forces and mechanisms and by no means through the intervention of a world spirit. Unfortunately, they did not know how to distinguish between analogy and scientific laws, between chance coincidences and data from painstaking observations repeated and confirmed a thousand times. Their "physical astrology" therefore turned out to be a pseudo-science and a caricature of the genuine article.

The first "physicist astrologers" made their appearance in

119

Greece. They passed serenely through antiquity, the Middle Ages, the Renaissance; and at the present time these "physicists" are still familiar figures. But their more intelligent arguments have actually had quite an effect on science.

The motions of the sun and moon have, by any evidence, a real physical influence on terrestrial phenomena: the seasons, the growth of vegetation, and the temperature necessary for life on earth are dependent on the sun; and the tides of the sea are dependent on the moon. Eratosthenes in the third century B.C. almost perfectly described the effect of the moon on tides. "The moon draws the sea after her with a powerful suction," wrote Pliny as well. This is a favorite and convincing argument of the "physicist astrologers." Why should this star, which glimmers so faintly and yet can move the sea, not also be capable of influencing the moods of men and animals?

But overextended, the argument became absurd; it was also noticed that the tides were higher at the solstices, and this effect was attributed to the passage of the sun through the "cardinal" signs, Aries and Libra. This was the "physical" proof of the effects of the signs of the zodiac! In addition, it was known that the height of the tides depended on the width of the angle between sun and moon, and that the least extensive tides always occurred during the moon's first and last quarters. This was the "physical" proof of the influence of planetary aspects. According to these people, the influence of each planet was also connected with physical considerations. Thus Ptolemy claimed that Jupiter was beneficent because its climate was temperate, being situated at an equal distance between the fires of Mars and the snows of Saturn. An explanation was also put forward for the effects of the Houses on planets: Ptolemy stated that a planet which had just risen had a weak but bad influence "because its rays fall on Earth at an oblique angle, and are diluted by the moistness of the horizon's mists."

Why was the moment of birth so important? Answer: because the child resembled soft wax on which the seal was stamped. At the moment of birth the influence of the stars was like that of an archer who, by an instantaneous act, produced all the consequences of the arrow's impact when it reached the target.

These astral influences reached us through "emanations" sent out by the celestial bodies. If it is difficult to understand how purely imaginary forms like those of the constellations could send out these "emanations," one might recall the belief that dogs became rabid during the Dog-days (July 22–August 23: the period when Sirius, the Dog-star, rises and sets with the sun). Obviously the Dog of Sirius influenced its terrestrial counterparts.

Today, explanations based on "emanations" seem ridiculous, but those who believe in astrology feel the theory of emanations provides a better explanation of remote-controlled effects than the force of gravitational attraction for more modern thinkers, since only the effects and not the cause of this attraction are understood. However, when contemporary astrologers want to justify their beliefs with "physical" arguments, they prefer to borrow the marvelous apparatus of modern science, and shamelessly jumble up an equally mysterious collection of X-rays, electromagnetism, conditioned reflexes, and psychoanalysis with a batch of quotations from Ptolemy. One astrologer wrote a mathematical work, *Astrology Corroborated by Science*, where he coolly invents an invisible ray of cosmic origin: "the odic wave." This remarkable wave explains the whys and wherefores of astrology in all its details … for the very good reason that it was created for that purpose! Another, even more recently, has discovered why the twelve signs of the zodiac have a physical reality: "I have learned," he states, "that radioactive fallout from high altitude explosions of hydrogen bombs does not cover the surface of the earth evenly, but is arranged in *twelve lines* pointed toward the poles in a manner resembling the parts of an orange. Is that not conclusive?"

If these interpretations of the stars' influence left the Church Fathers completely indifferent, they have in all ages enraged scientists hostile to astrology. Scientists have joined in denouncing these explanations as the most transparent charlatanry.

But, since supporters of "physical" theories have wanted above all to seem rational and objective, they and their doctrines are most effectively attacked with arguments taken from experience, common sense and reason. This type of criticism of the astrologers is not lacking; here are some important objections.

It very often happens that two individuals are born at the same time. According to astrology, they would have to have the same destiny. As Carneades pointed out two centuries before Christ, this is certainly not the general rule. Cicero too has raised the question: "Were all those who perished at the battle of Cannae born under the same star?" (*De Divinatione*, II, 47).

And how do they explain the different destinies of twins born virtually at the same time, and therefore beneath the same sky? How is it possible for one, for instance, to die at an early age, while the other has a long life? The astrologers' defense is that twins are never born at *exactly* the same time, and that a small difference in the degree of the horoscope can completely alter the wheel of his fate. Arguing with astrologers on this issue has been useless for centuries; for instance, Sextus Empiricus criticized the idea of the horoscope and showed that it was impossible to note exactly the moment of birth; obviously if very great accuracy were really necessary, all the forecasts of the astrologers would be wrong from the start. Later, Pope (St.) Gregory put forward a similar argument: "Some children take a long time to emerge from their mother's womb; in these cases, would not the head and feet be born under different signs?" The astrologers had a remarkable answer to this, and one which demonstrated how well equipped they were for arguments of this sort: "This in fact proves," they said, "that a powerful intellect may often be found in someone whose legs are weak." As one weary astronomer said, "arguing with astrologers is like punching a feather pillow; you flatten one part of it and another fills out."

Critics of astrology still had other arguments left. They asked, for instance, how the future could be predicted according to a man's date of birth, when his life actually began at his conception. A horoscope drawn at conception should be the only important one in forecasting his destiny.

Actually, this objection did cause some embarrassment to ancient astrologers. Most replied that the moment of conception should indeed be important; and, in making more detailed astrological analyses, they did try to obtain this information. Forecasts based on schemes both of birth and of conception became the last refinement in the subject, and it is said that the Emperor Augustus had this rare privilege.

Unfortunately any hope of gaining accurate information in this matter had to be given up, for it was nearly always impossible to establish the moment of "impregnation," even to the nearest hour. The birth chart was re-emphasized and justified as far as it could be. In general, Ptolemy's pronouncement on the matter predominated: "Conception is regarded as the natural beginning of life. But the moment of birth, though subordinate to the other, is endowed with a greater energy, since this energy is brought to bear on a complete human being and not a seed, and is added to a similar influence already brought to bear on the embryo" (*Tetrabiblos*, III, 1). Ptolemy therefore supported the bold and unprovable hypothesis that a child is born when the configuration of the sky is the same as at its conception. He then shrewdly extricated himself from this last difficulty by assuming the time of conception to be a first reading, though harder to establish than the second, of a similar configuration of the sky.

Enemies of astrology had still not come to an end of their objections. "If," said Cicero, "the state of the sky and the positions of the stars have so great an influence on all living things at their birth, it follows necessarily that this influence bears not only on humans, but also on animals. Can anything more absurd be said?" (*De Divinatione*, II, 47.)

But in fact, there have been a number of astrologers ready to draw up schemes for domestic animals like dogs, cats, horses, pigs, and purebred cattle, and even to this day the custom has not disappeared. For that matter, some astrologers have gone so far as to draw horoscopes for insititutions, nations and corporations. Very recently, an astrologer based the majority of his predictions concerning the world's future on a study of the sky at the time of the American Declaration of Independence, and at the time of the proclamation of the Soviet Republic. Inanimate objects have also attracted their attention. We have read that the French steamship *Normandie* was launched under a malefic sky (the sun was in conjunction with the moon). Its destruction by fire at the port of New York was, therefore, predictable.

Today, advances in astronomy enable us to raise new

objections to astrology in addition to the old ones. For instance, when Copernicus removed earth from its seat at the center of the universe and when Newton discovered the law of gravity, these discoveries provided a glimpse of new horizons and badly shook old anthropomorphic doctrines. Our sky is no longer the sky of the Ancients, nor is our conception of the world any longer the same as theirs.

But it is the discovery of the precession of the equinoxes that threatens astrology at its very foundations, namely, the signs of the zodiac. This was first noticed by Hipparchus, the greatest astonomer of ancient Greece (second century B.C.). A gradual shift in the lines of the poles is altering the position of the heavenly equator among the constellations. Since the time of Hipparchus, the gamma point (the first degree of Aries) has gone back the whole length of the constellation of Pisces, taking with it, by general agreement, the belt of zodiacal rectangles with their former names. Because of this precession, the belt of signs has slipped back by about one compartment since antiquity. Leo, for instance, now covers the constellation of Cancer. A child born under Leo is given the same characteristics as before, although the Sun is crossing another constellation at that time. The trouble is that the old lodgers have moved but their names are still on the doors.

Chapter Ten

THE VERDICT OF STATISTICS

As Montaigne said: "The question which is being asked is not whether Galen said anything of value, but whether he spoke these words or others!" The irony of this observation may well apply to criticisms of astrology, for although the arguments which are advanced against it seem powerful enough, they do not raise the essential question: do the claims of astrologers have any relevance to common experience?

It is useless to declare that astrology represents an infantile state of mind if well designed experiments prove that its pronouncements are correct. In that case it should once again assume an extraordinary importance. It matters little whether it is explained by symbolism or physics, or whether the stars are signs or causes. The essence of the matter is to find out if an astrologer's forecasts of the future actually happen. Are they right? That is the first question which astrologers should be asked today.

They might answer that their observations, and their day-to-day experience constantly prove to their satisfaction the accuracy of astrology. But somone who did not believe in astrology would declare the exact opposite, and say that all his observations had shown him the falsity of astrology.

We can take it, then, that the private feelings of the observer can entirely dictate his perceptions. Even if it only exists in his imagination, he will be no less firmly convinced of its reality. Whom then are we to believe, astrologer or anti-astrologer? Both have a "typical example" to cite in support of their cases. But one example is not everything. How can we find which one is right or wrong?

The difficulty of assessing the accuracy of an astrological forecast is a serious stumbling-block when one wishes to find out the truth or falsity of the subject. Here is an example which has the advantage of being both in the past and of recent date.

In November, 1963, fifteen days before the assassination of John F. Kennedy, a book written by a well-known astrologer came out, containing astrological forecasts of the world scene. Opening the book at the page where the author deals with the destiny of Kennedy, we read: "[For the U.S.A.] the major crisis is likely to break out on or around the 30th of May ... Convincing proof of this may be found in the constellation of the President himself, John F. Kennedy, who has a very good chance of being re-elected to the Presidency by the American people in the elections of November, 1964. .. His Sun – that of the 29th of May – is at 7 degrees of Gemini, in the exact place where the solar eclipse of the 30th of May, 1965, will occur. At this anniversary, how can we fail to conclude that he will be affected deeply in his power, authority and prestige? We do not think he will be involved as a private person, but as the representative of the U.S., of which he is the solar symbol."

It is obvious here that the astrologer has struck out: he has completely failed to see, or even get a glimpse of, the approaching death of Kennedy, since, fifteen days before his assassination, he has published a book in which he talks about the U.S. President's life up to May, 1965.

But the forecasts about Kennedy have not been concluded. The author starts a new paragraph and adds: "Having said that, it is certain that the signs in Kennedy's sky, with a dubious Saturn nearing its culmination, carry disturbing portents for his own course, if not that of his country, at the time of his presidential mandate."

Those who pay no attention to the dates referred to earlier by the astrologer might say that here the man had hinted at the truth.

Let us pass by the question of whether this assemblage of forecasts is a success or a failure, and merely note the fact that some people will claim that the astrologer did predict the President's death, and others will maintain that he did nothing of the kind but cleverly mixed good and bad omens so as to be sure of never being totally wrong.

This example illustrates the difficulty of reaching an objective judgment about an astrological prediction. Common sense is not enough; it is almost always swamped by personal prejudices unless a more rigorous method of approach is employed.

The statistical method evolved from theoretical considerations of the calculation of probabilities, a branch of learning distinguished by the names of Pascal, Laplace and Gauss. It enables us to reach logical conclusions in areas where, formerly, there were only tortuous arguments and misleading impressions. In astrology, this method may be profitably applied by accumulating a large number of specific cases which are noted down in quantified form instead of being judged only according to the vague impressions they have given us.

If, for instance, an astrologer claims that sailors are generally born with the sun in the sign of Pisces, how can we be sure of it? By getting together a thousand sailors' dates of birth, according to a random biographical selection, and noting down which sign each sailor is born under. Then one or two results will without any doubt come to light:

either the astrologers are right, and it will be seen that far more sailors are born under the sign of Pisces than under any of the other signs;

or the astrologers are wrong, and it will be found that no more sailors are born under the sign of Pisces than under any of the other signs.

Certain formulae in the calculation of probabilities enable us to assess, according to the number of sailors born under the sign of Pisces, the degree of certainty for or against this hypothesis. Statistical method therefore enables us to discard our personal feeling for or against an astrological claim, and replace it with a figure which we can no longer make a mistake over. This is a question of deciding whether the difference between the number of sailors actually born under Pisces and the number one would theoretically expect (in this case one-twelfth, since there are twelve signs of the zodiac) is too wide to be attributable to chance. Statisticians call a difference "significant" if the probability of its chance appearance is less than one in twenty, and "very significant" if this probability is less than one in a hundred.

It can be seen that the general idea is simple. However, its application is not always easy. "To come to a conclusion," wrote Lavoisier, 'one must evaluate the probabilities and estimate whether they are large enough to constitute a proof. This kind of calculation is more complicated than people imagine; it requires considerable shrewdness, and is beyond the average man. Mistakes in this type of calculation provide the foundation for the success of charlatans, tricksters, and all those, in general, who delude themselves, or seek to take advantage of the public's credulity."

Then what are astrological predictions about the world's future worth? Predictions, that is, of wars, economic crises, and various catastrophes? This type of forecast is, as we have seen, particularly inaccurate. However, an objective scrutiny of published forecasts and a comparison between what has been said and what has in fact happened shows that these forecasts are made at random.

Astrologers may broadly be grouped into two categories: those who make no claims except when common sense enables them to foresee an event as practically certain, and those who suffer from what might be called a "Cassandra complex," and wrack their brains to think up catastrophe after catastrophe. Unfortunately for the first, the practically certain event does not always happen: how often have astrologers not wrongly announced the death of President Eisenhower, while not one predicted the date of President Kennedy's assassination?

As for the "Cassandra complex," which the second group suffers from, here is a prime example: in his *Forecasts for the Year 1962*, an astrologer predicted the following events among others no less sensational: ". . . End of the 5th Republic; return of Soustelle; partial mobilization in Holland; proclamation of a republic in Iran; Kadar's dismissal in Hungary; severe epidemic in the Middle East; downfall of Nasser; very serious crisis in Israel; several monarchs will be dethroned; in China, a terrible epidemic, a famine worse than any known for millennia," etc., etc. Fortunately, none of these things happened!

There is no need to elaborate on a subject which science has discredited. It should suffice to quote from one of the leaders of the present generation of astrologers, who himself acknowledges the importance of statistical evaluation: "If an account had to be drawn up of accurate forecasts published over the last fifty years, it is certain that there would be a larger number of failures than of successes."

But let us leave these misty reefs where the modern disciples of Nostradamus have foundered. Neither science nor astrology will win new victories there. In order to make an objective assessment of probability precise categories must be established within the general area under investigation. Any serious analysis of astrology requires that the problems should be put in order and the fundamental rules abstracted from the jumble of everyday interpretations.

Curiously enough two astrologers have undertaken this task. They realized that statistics alone could provide a solid base for that doctrine of which they were convinced adherents. In spite of the comparatively modest aims they set themselves, they have remained, as a result of this attempt, famous figures in the circles of the star-gazers. As a consequence, their work deserves, before all else, impartial and thorough investigation.

These innovators no longer tried to read the whole destiny of a person from his horoscope. Instead, they tried to isolate a particular, specific, and limited aspect of the astrological field, in order to establish whether it corresponded to a fragment of the destiny of all those who had possessed it at their birth. By this method they examined the principal rules of astrology and published results which caused a sensation, for they appeared to verify those rules at every point. Thus, stone by stone, they hoped to build up once again, on solid and scientifically proven bases, the ancestral beliefs. It is therefore of the first importance to examine their work if one wishes to know what astrology is really worth.

Commandant Paul Choisnard (1867–1930), an alumnus of the Ecole Polytechnique, has for more than fifty years served as the bulwark from which astrologers have rebutted the attacks of men of science. The latter, it should be admitted, have shown little interest in verifying the different laws proposed by the astrologers' statisticians. A thorough examination of Choisnard's work is owed to his memory, for his basic principles were scientific. and can therefore be judged according to the methods used and the results obtained.

Choisnard put forward a certain number of fundamental laws of astrology which he tried, with courage and perseverance, from the beginning of the century till his death, to get accepted by the scientific world. But although Choisnard had the excellent idea of applying statistical methods to astrology, he unfortunately was ignorant of the most elementary principles of statistics. He was particularly ignorant of the laws of deviation. The significance of a deviation from the observed average must be estimated in terms of probabilities. It seems that Choisnard had never understood this, for he is satisfied, with evaluating the number of cases observed under a certain configuration in percentile terms. This procedure was to lead him, in his ignorance of the laws of large numbers, to formulate, as the expression of a new law, different chance results. In fact, when samples as small as his are used (samples of only one or two hundred), it is perfectly normal for the actual figure under consideration to be double the expected average sometimes (200% and even more). Such a result does not justify an appeal to the stars, but is a normal consequence of the theory.

One of the laws most often referred to by modern astrologers is that of the signs of "superior natures." Having chosen 123 "superior natures," Choisnard established the position of the Ascendant at their births in the signs of the zodiac. It will be recalled that the Ascendant, which is the point of the ecliptic which rises at the moment of birth, has traditionally held a position of fundamental importance in assessing the character of an individual. Choisnard published an outline which summarized his observations and showed, according to him, "the remarkable grouping of these Ascendants in the triple zone consisting of Libra, Aquarius and Gemini, with an extension from Libra onto the neighboring signs of Virgo and Scorpio." Libra, Aquarius, and Gemini are traditionally known as signs of the air. Their influence is supposed to make the subject more intelligent than, for instance, a native of a sign of the earth such as Taurus or Capricorn. Presumably air is more subtle and earth more dense and cumbersome. And he adds that "the signs of Sagittarius, Capricorn, Pisces, Aries and Taurus only possess very few Ascendants of superior natures. We can therefore conclude, with a probability bordering on certainty, that the Ascendant, and therefore the orientation of the whole zodiac at nativity forms, a kind of map of the human faculties. It therefore proves the influence of the stars."

But this statistic, even if it has been correctly interpreted, seems a little brief: 123 births is not many if the idea is to convince scientists that the signs of the zodiac can really induce an above average nature in certain people. But on closer examination from an astronomical point of view, one is struck by a serious error on the part of the author due to his ignorance of astronomical laws. He seems not to know that, in Europe where these "higher natures" were born, the signs of the zodiac do not all have the same length of passage at the Ascendant. After all, constellations of the zodiac vary considerably in size and the angle of their passing the ecliptic. Some pass though it in one hour, others in almost three hours. As a result, in some signs three times as many births must occur at the Ascendant than in others. Significantly, of the five signs well stocked with "higher natures," four are signs which pass the Ascendant slowly. Choisnard has therefore taken as a new and definitive astrological law something which is merely the natural effect of astronomical conditions in our part of the world.

Another important law, about which Choisnard has made many observations, concerns the ominous effect which the transit of certain planets could have on our vital energy at specific moments in our lives. These transits are defined by Choisnard as "the passage of the planets at certain points of nativity." This is an entirely traditional law of astrology invented by the Greeks.

Choisnard's study concerned "the roles played by the transits of Mars and Saturn relative to the sun at birth in the matter of death." Traditionally, Mars and Saturn are regarded as powerful malefics, and the sun is a sign of the life principle in a scheme. Choisnard therefore compared the position of Mars at the moment of death with that of the sun on the day of birth, and then the position of Saturn with that of the sun on the day of birth; he thus showed how often these traditionally inauspicious angles (conjunction, opposition, and quartile in an orb of 10 degrees) actually occurred. In the following table he sets out the results which he obtained:

Aspect of the transit of Mars or Saturn with the sun at birth	MARS (in a sample of 200 deaths)	SATURN (in a sample of 200 deaths)	Expected statistical rate of occurrence
CONJUNCTION	14.0%	10.0%	5.0%
OPPOSITION	7.5	10.5	5.5
QUARTILE	15.0	14.5	11.0

Commenting on these results, Choisnard wrote: "The most dangerous aspect is the passage of Mars over the sun at birth. This transit coincides with a death about three times as often as at any other moment whatever ... With Saturn, the conjunctions and oppositions seem about equal here, coinciding with a death almost twice as often as at any other moment ..." And he concluded: "This is clear proof that men do not die indiscriminately under any pattern of the sky."

These are precise and impressive facts, and they may be easily checked, if one wishes to take the trouble to do so. We therefore found it essential to repeat the experiment in order to be sure, but we used a much larger sample than that of Choisnard: 7,482 comparisons between horoscopes at birth and at death were collected, for each of the factors considered significant by Choisnard.

Now, all our results were random distributions, whether for Mars or Saturn or the three aspects under consideration. The percentages all approximated to the theoretical percentage so closely as to be virtually identical with it, as the law of large numbers would suggest (a law which could be operated in this experiment). The following table shows the matter clearly.

Aspect of the transit of Mars or Saturn with the sun at birth	MARS (in a sample of 7,482 deaths)	SATURN (in a sample of 7,482 deaths)	Expected statistical rate of occurrence
CONJUNCTION	5.7%	5.8%	5.5%
OPPOSITION	5.4	5.7	5.5
QUARTILE	10.5	11.1	11.0

In conclusion, it was established that the supposedly inauspicious passage of Mars or Saturn over the Sun at birth is totally nonexistent. But astrologers, in spite of everything, still continue and will continue for a long time to diagnose the combination of planets studied here as being a "malefic" influence.

Besides the disastrous events for which Mars and Saturn are held responsible, astrologers also claim that the presence of Jupiter in a scheme of birth augurs more cheerful predictions for the future. It will be remembered that, from the time of the Greeks, astrology has regarded Jupiter as the great dispenser of wealth and glory. If it is at its highest point in the sky, otherwise known as Mid-heaven, at the subject's birth, it is supposed to indicate a brilliant and successful future of money and fame. Choisnard applied this statement to a statistical test. He examined the position of Jupiter at the birth of almost one thousand people who had been very successful in their lives, and noted that the said planet was to be found at Mid-heaven (or within 10 degrees of it) twice as often in the case of these people than was normal (12% of cases instead of the average of 5.5%). The difference between these two percentages is all the more striking in view of the number of cases under review!

We took the opportunity to check whether this new law of Choisnard's was correct, using even larger samples. And we have established that, if the numbers of people who have been successful in their professional life (as actors, academics, painters, musicians, and so on) are collected into a single group, the position of Jupiter at Mid-heaven does not in any case indicate a happier or more brilliant future. Out of some ten thousand people examined, the percentage who had Jupiter at Mid-heaven was very near the theoretical figure, and is to be explained entirely in terms of the laws of chance. Jupiter is no more beneficent at birth than Mars and Saturn are malefic at death.

The astrological laws which Choisnard thought he had statistically established do not therefore stand up to thorough scientific examination. His attempt to secure traditional astrology on a serious and scientific base has merely upset it further, and tends to prove the exact opposite of what he wanted.

Karl Ernst Krafft (1900–1945), a Swiss astrologer, was a strange character who was involved with Hitler, as we have seen. It is said that he was in the service of the German government, his task being to discover the most propitious times for mounting the military offensives of the Wehrmacht. It is even said that the British War Office had also taken on an astrologer. Aware of the Nazi leader's weakness for astrology, the Allied Headquarters reckoned that such a man would know better than anyone the celestial configurations under which the German army would be tempted to intervene on different fronts. But perhaps all this is no more than the product of a British astrologer's speculation, for the level of the English command which these forecasts reached, and the effect they had, appear to be unknown.

It is certain, however, that on the German side Goebbels often sanctioned the cynical use of astrology as an instrument of propaganda. Many entries in his private journal testify to this in 1942. He writes there: "In the United States astrologers are at work and predict an untimely end for the Fuhrer. We are familiar enough with this type of propaganda for we have used it ourselves. Whenever we can, we will again exploit the possibilities which astrology has to offer. I anticipate important results from it, particularly in the U.S.A. and England. ... We will recruit on our side all the specialists in prophecy of every type. Nostradamus must once again authorize us to quote from him." [1]

In 1939 Krafft brought out a large volume filled with figures and graphs, called *A Treatise in Astrobiology* (Legrand, publisher). Like Choisnard, Krafft, who was an industrious worker, wished to prove the validity of astrology by means of statistics. Did he do any better than his predecessor in this undertaking? A single example will set the general tone of the "laws" proposed by Krafft, and the reader may judge what degree of confidence should be accorded them.

In the chapter entitled "Some Details of the Structure of Cosmic Influences," the author sets out to prove that certain configurations of the stars are "according to all evidence less favorable to the development of the artist." From a large number of musicians he chose to make his test on those born at the conjunction of the moon with Uranus; 115 musicians met this requirement, and he noted the positions in the ecliptic where the conjunction of the moon with Uranus occurred for them. A graph showing the distribution of these 115 conjunctions in the ecliptic is remarkable, for it reveals a con-

1. Lochner, *The Goebbels Diary*, *London*, 1948, pp. 142 and 145.

siderable concentration of births in some signs, and a complete void in others, stretching over 100 degrees of the ecliptic. It would seem, then, that some signs did have "musical" properties and, as Krafft wrote, "The virtually complete absence of the constellation (the conjunction, that is, of the moon and Uranus) in other signs must surely lead to the conclusion that, when it does occur in those signs, it has some kind of inhibitory effect on a musical career."

But it is astronomically impossible for a conjunction of the moon with Uranus to have occurred in the empty part of the zodiac, because Uranus had never been in that area in the period when the musicians were born, its revolution through the sky being very slow. This is indeed an example of how to invent laws from the void! Krafft is therefore completely unfounded in concluding that "The design of the ecliptic is not homogeneous, but some zones do have a particular influence. . . ."

It seems quite incredible that he could have made such a ridiculous error. However, such errors occur on almost every page of Krafft's book while the astrologers, dazzled by the apparent learning of the author, have been unable to see the enormity of his mistakes.

However, Krafft's study does contain a lesson. It shows the extent of scientific aberration to which a prejudiced and somewhat inflamed imagination can go. This book is a kind of statistical anti-methodology which is worth thinking about, and should be given to students of probability calculations to put them on their guard against the many pitfalls which lie along the road of discovery revealed by this difficult science.

Choisnard and Krafft, then, for all their praiseworthy efforts, only managed to erect a caricature of science, of which nothing remains. Of course these two theorists did not hold the whole of astrological science in their grasp, perhaps, but that does not make the outlook for astrology any better. Many other objective researchers have subjected its laws to statistical examination, and their experiments have always been to astrology's detriment.

This was the case with Farnsworth's work on the correlation between artistic predisposition and the sign of Libra. According to astrologers children born with Libra in the Ascendant will have better than average artistic qualities.

Farnsworth patiently examined the births of two thousand famous painters and musicians: Libra did not preside over the birth of these artists any more than any other sign. Nor were these artists more often born in the month when the sun is in Libra (between September 21 and October 21).

The same results emerge from the work of the astronomer Bart J. Bok, who demonstrated that there was no predisposition for the natives of any sign whatever to go into any particular profession. For his findings he consulted the whole list of *American Men of Science,* without finding the slightest unusual grouping.

We ourselves have established, using a sample of more than 25,000 celebrities' births, that the distribution in the signs of the zodiac was attributable to chance for the sun, the moon and for the Ascendant, whatever might be the hypothetical temperament or profession corresponding to the births examined. For instance, the sign of Aries does not produce any more soldiers than does Libra, despite the fact that an aggressive influence is attributed to the former, and a tranquil one to the latter.

ARE STATISTICS IRRELEVANT?

Astrologers remain unconvinced by the publication of these statistics totally destroying their doctrines. There was a time when they asserted, loudly and frequently, that statistics provided an ideal method of proving the truth of astrology, but this view was most popular during the period before the work of Choisnard and Krafft had been discredited. Today, astrologers have gone into reverse and claim, on the contrary, that statistics are irrelevant to astrology. For, they say, statistics isolate certain factors in a birth chart, but in such a chart everything is interdependent, and the same factor could, in different contexts, have a totally different interpretation. The validity of astrology ought, according to them, to be judged only on the basis of forecasts taken from whole charts, with all their components.

This argument is illogical, for astrology is a collection of apparently very precise laws. We are told that, as in the case of medicine, these laws have been discovered after millions of daily observations. In that case they would be nothing but empirical statistics, and therefore confirmable by mathematical statistics.

But let us nevertheless give astrologers the chance to justify their new claims, and see how well they can judge from total horoscopes, when they are really put to the test by the empiricists. On this theme, a remarkably penetrating study recently came out. Fourteen astrologers picked at random agreed to undergo the following test: they were given the co-ordinates of birth of three celebrities and, besides, the names of these people. The astrologers had to match each date with the name of whichever celebrity best suited that particular birth. These people consisted of a rather unlucky T.V. announcer who had had a number of troubles in the course of his travels, a four-time winner of the Tour de France cycle race, and a famous entertainer. All the astrologers failed. By a calculation of strict probabilities it can be asserted that if the fourteen astrologers had answered at random instead of consulting the stars, they could not have put up a worse showing than they did in this experiment.

But do astrologers know enough at least to distinguish between the horoscopes of people whose lives are completely opposed – between, for instance, a criminal who died on the scaffold and someone who spends his whole life quietly? Let us give an astrologer twenty dates of birth without the names, in which ten murderers are mixed up with ten dull lives, and ask him to separate one group from the other. Of course, he will not be expected to identify *all* the death-house names but at least to detect a number sufficient to make one reasonably believe that his choice has not been made at random.

We have asked many astrologers to give us this demonstration of their knowledge, but only a few have agreed. Some claimed they did not have the time, and others that this would teach them nothing, or else they proclaimed more ingeniously that inside every honest man there hides a killer and therefore their science could not hope to distinguish between real criminals and would-be criminals. But then what if anything can they find out from a birth chart, if everyone is potentially anything, by definition?

However, there were some astrologers brave enough to participate in the experiment. The results were conclusive: they chose law-abiding people as murderers in a manner which was quite indiscriminate and entirely in accordance with chance. Those prophets of the stars who were acting in good faith were completely taken by surprise, and there was even one astrologer who drew the inevitable conclusion that astrology is incapable of making a distinction, even when the final effect of a man's life is presented, between the birth chart of a criminal who will end up on the scaffold, and that of a decent, honorable family man.

It is high time to come to an end. Every attempt, whether of astrologers or scientists, to produce evidence of the validity of astrological laws has been in vain. It is now quite certain that the signs in the sky which presided over our births have no power whatever to decide our fates, to affect our hereditary characteristics, or to play any part however humble in the totality of effects, random and otherwise, which form the fabric of our lives and mold our impulses to action.

Confronted with science, modern and traditional astrology are seen to be imaginary doctrines. To predict the future by consulting the stars is to delude the world, or at least to delude oneself.

This is not to deny the possibility of predicting the future altogether. Astrology does not have a monopoly on forecasts. Besides astrological prediction there is the prediction of parapsychology. The great psychiatrist, Jung, has gone to some lengths to show the difference between the two. For a start, Jung denies astrology any scientific validity, because of its inconsistent and uncertain results. "If astrologers had concentrated more on statistics to justify scientifically the accuracy of their forecasts, they would have found out long ago that their pronouncements rest on unstable foundations."[1]

In the course of his life, however, Jung believed he had noticed that a few astrologers were sometimes able to make predictions which were so accurate that their effect became statistically disturbing. How were they to be explained? Jung then turned to the accumulated research into telepathy and clairvoyance, patiently and objectively worked out by Dr. Rhine of Duke University and others. If, says Jung, these writers are correct and we can sometimes predict certain future events, why should this effect not occasionally be apparent among astrologers? That would explain why some of their predic-

1. *Naturerklarung und Psyche*, Rascher Verlag, Zurich 1952.

tions have been remarkably accurate. Jung compares an astrologer to a medium or a seer able to have glimpses into the future. The stars, of course, have nothing to do with it; they are nothing but a pretext, a backing for these sudden premonitions.

Whether there are sometimes astrologers who are also mediums is a matter which still needs demonstration. The least that can be said is that statistical controls have shown them up as not very gifted in this respect. There might also be a danger in allowing this idea to gain credence among the general public. But in any case, it should be stressed that Jung and all the parapsychologists are agreed in asserting that the predictions of astrology as it now stands are in conflict with the documented cases of parapsychological clairvoyance.

Chapter Eleven

THE PUBLIC'S ATTITUDE

In these days the general public, even at its least sophisticated, has lost its old dread of the heavenly structure. The sky is no longer regarded as a threat or a promise. For most people it no longer represents a problem. Astrology, the belief in the influence of the stars on our destinies, should have vanished long ago. However, it lives on. Why? The answer is that although men no longer feel defenseless before the sky, they do feel this way when faced with themselves. The sky is no longer a painful problem, but man still is. So the sky has become a mirror for his self-searching, for no one manages to settle to his satisfaction the innumerable difficulties which assail his everyday life. Formerly, it was taught that the sky could settle them, and modern man wants to go on believing this. Many people whom life has not spoiled and who are confronted with an unforeseen obstacle seek to cling to something. The future still frightens them as it did in earlier times. It is a source of both fear and hope. How can they know whether they will have to rejoice or despair? The future is still hidden, as though by a veil, concealing the good and the bad which lie in store.

Perhaps I shall be more fortunate next year? Perhaps my lost son will come back from faraway lands? Will I win the state lottery? Will my cancer operation be successful? Will I sell my old motor-bike at a profit? ... a peculiar parade of questions, where the deepest and most honorable grief goes side by side with the most absurd preoccupation with financial gain.

Whom can they turn to in order to lose this fear of the future? Crystal balls, palmistry, Tarot cards? But none of these have the prestige of science, and this is where astrology wins out. It alone brilliantly combines mathematics and forecasts. Astrology thrives on credulous people, and people in distress; and the three big questions concern health, love, and money.

One thing is clear: people read their horoscopes in the

paper, or go and consult an astrologer in person, in the hope of hearing about a better future. If they are unhappy they hope to become happy; or if they are happy, they hope to be even happier. The astrologers promise that these people have only to come to them and they will know it all. This illusion is carefully maintained by charlatans who grow rich on the technique, and by newspapers which seek to increase their circulation. The popular press gives astrology prestige among the people, and reawakens the attraction the stars have always held for men. Even the latest discoveries of science have, para-doxicially, supported the notion of a magic of the stars in the popular mind: space extends without limit, and extraordinary things go on there; not a year passes without amazing discoveries being made. The list of mysterious rays emanating from outer space gets longer, to the enormous profit of astrologers and charlatans who turn these discoveries to their own advantage.

It is therefore not only emotional and unconscious factors which make astrology attractive; it is also nourished by naivete, lack of judgment, and suggestibility. Astrological prediction is like a Spanish tavern where the client finds what he has himself brought; for he can draw what he likes from the confused gibberish of horoscopes, whether it be his hidden aspirations or his most far-fetched hopes.

Scientists always emphasize the inordinate pride of men who believe that their insignificant persons could interest the stars. This is true, but the "appalling egocentricity" is more a temporary failure of intelligence than a serious defect of character. The client believes what the astrologer tells him because he lacks the capacity to distinguish, in the confusion of interpretations which are presented to him, the one which just happens to be right from the one which would be really unlikely without some kind of outside intervention. Our critical faculty may hold itself in abeyance when we ourselves are the subject under discussion. Astrologers both know it and play most skillfully on the sensitive organ of our self-esteem.

Some people we know are impressed by the forecast: "In your life there will be a motor accident!" Later, an accident actually does happen. It may have happened some ten years before or after the date specified in the forecast, but what does that matter! However, if they had the least idea of the calculation of probabilities, how could they be surprised at such a thing happening, one day or other, since it is so unfortunately likely in this day and age?

But the client is ready to believe, and he is impressed by an event which happened, so he goes back to the astrologer. The latter then has another weapon, for he now has what psychologists call a "halo effect" on his client. He was right once, so he will henceforth always be right. As a result of involuntary selection by his memory, the client will only remember, out of the hundred weird propositions proclaimed in his horoscope, the one which actually comes about, or the one which he very strongly wishes would come about. And so a kind of conspiracy grows up between the astrologer and his client, one which oscillates more or less violently between active and passive poles. And for both of them a single forecast which actually is realized wipes out all the innumerable ones which are not. In general, the astrologer is finally himself taken in by the admiration which his client displays, and he complacently admires himself in the mirror of his few successes, gladly forgetting the countless failures for which he is responsible.

The inability of these people to judge themselves and their close concerns dispassionately has been demonstrated by the experiment of Dr. Louis Couderc, a distinguished psychiatrist. Couderc wished to see how readers reacted to the astrologers' advertisements in the papers. He made one up himself, in a particularly crude style:

THE OCCULT SCIENCES. A new Messiah!
ANXIOUS people who are suffering now –
ANXIOUS people who will be in despair in the future –
UNBELIEVERS who mock –
A FREE trial is on offer to convince you.
DON'T WAIT: write to Professor L-H. Merric.
Put your questions to him, and ask his advice.
YOU WILL BE AMAZED.
Send name, date of birth, profession and stamp.

Having put this advertisement in the paper, he was swamped by letters from every class. To each correspondent he sent *the same unaltered letter*, and received a considerable number of replies. There were more than two hundred of them from which he could pick out dozens of sentences like this: "What you have told me of my past and my character is the absolute truth," or "You seem able to read my life like a book."

We too have designed an experiment of the same type. A horoscope was drawn up which was complete but false – that is, established by chance and without reference to the sky at the time of birth – and which was confined to fairly vague statements like "You have two personalities which are in conflict ... your character upsets those around you ... beware of road accidents ..." etc. We also received enthusiastic congratulations from our deceived victims. "I admire your knowledge of astrology and I envy you it!" one wrote, and another went even further: "My father has till now been dubious about astrology, but after reading your analysis of my character he is convinced that it is true." No one is easier to convince than someone who wants to be convinced at all cost!

Such experiments are useful, for they indicate how easy it is to trick people with a few clever words written in the learned style of a man confident of his art or science.

Astrologers have been accused of doing a lot of harm by taking advantage of the public's credulity. Some scientists of a moral turn of mind have even taken the matter to the courts, arguing that since the future cannot be predicted by the stars, as science has adequately proved, to take money for doing so is a swindle and a confidence game. However, punishments have seldom been imposed.

The scientists then protested that the courts had shown themselves to be culpably indulgent toward such people. Such shameless exploitation of human credulity dragged everyone down to a low level of intelligence. Mention was made of cases where astrologers had actually caused real catastrophes by their forecasts. The following is an example: A man goes to see an astrologer who tells him: "You cannot have a child." "But I've got three," answers the man. "In that case, they are not yours," hints the astrologer, to keep his reputation for infallibility. The client, impressionable as he could wish, begins to feel doubt and jealousy, which gradually poison both his and his family's existence.

In our opinion it is wrong to exaggerate these dangers. Astrologers are not all the cynical and paranoid charlatans described here. If they were, they would soon discourage their clientele. Some behave with decency, and though their conviction may be baseless it is nevertheless profound. These people, then, do not seek to exploit the public but to satisfy it. But to satisfy it in what way? The reason why so many people consult astrologers is that they offer something which scientists cannot provide. If psychology could cure all complexes, and medicine get rid of all disease, and politicians remove the specter of war and the atomic bomb from the future; if, in a word, science could make the future seem pleasant and without mystery, people would not go and confide their doubts and dreads to astrologers, and astrology, having become sterile and useless, would collapse by itself. But that is not the situation. Those who seek reassurance from the astrologers consider that they have found it. It is a false reassurance perhaps but probably worth more in many cases than nothing at all.

Any words of encouragement do some good when one is unhappy. Just as a sick man who has been written off by official doctors finds moral hope and comfort in trying miracle cures, so a man who is miserable about his future sometimes needs to be listened to, understood, and reassured. This is where the astrologer may function usefully as a placebo.

Naturally the knowledge of the placebo astrologer is nil, but his expertise may be considerable. If the client finds him to be a subtle psychologist, the astral consultation can be a kind of confession. He will find relief in knowing that there is someone to listen and to calm with soothing words ... at least until the next time.

But this group of astrologers, who tend to be fairly expensive to consult, should not distract us from the mass of charlatans who naturally make up the bulk of the business.

This brief survey shows the psychological reasons why popular astrology has survived, but it leaves one unanswered question: Why does it also gain support among highly sophisticated people? Why is it regarded as an important truth by many intellectuals, a fact which astrologers use to give themselves prestige in the eyes of the masses?

As in Roman times, astrology cannot be dissociated in our society from a kind of literary folly which is another form of credulity. As a result, it finds partisans who take up a philosophic or artistic position. If M. Gabriel Marcel, M. André

Breton, or William Butler Yeats believe in astrology, it is of course not for the same reasons as ordinary mortals. Besides, they believe in another sort of astrology. What fascinates these writers is the conception of the universe which is the base of astrology; it is the evergreen doctrine of microcosm and macrocosm. This way of explaining the world seems as good to them as any other, and above all it is very poetic. Visions can be embroidered onto this artistic theme.

Everyone is free to believe what he wishes, and sarcastic remarks will make no difference. But this "distinguished" belief in astrology should not allow us to forget the absurd "instant mysticism" which professional astrologers try to impose on us for a few cents.

If astrology's clientele is gathered from people who are credulous or in distress, the practitioners of the doctrine who spread it among us are generally not so much credulous as alienated. Beside the ordinary charlatans who use it as a "hustle" to make a lot of money, there are any number of deranged people who waste their time in vainly trying to revive this ancient conception of the world. The latter are serious cases, and there is no point in arguing with them over their principles. Fanatics, the deranged, and the mentally sick, they make a sad and discordant group.

For in the question of belief in the stars, the psychiatric angle should not be overlooked. Ravings about astrology are regularly symptomatic of certain mental illnesses, particularly those which include mystical ravings as well. For these people, the sky and the heavenly bodies are even more alive than they were in the ancient days of Babylon.

The psychiatric aspect also plays a part in the survival of astrology. Here, as elsewhere, is not the impotence of medical science to blame? Astrological delusions, like all other forms of raving, will be removed when a cure for mental illness has been achieved. The credulous, the distressed and the alienated ... but on reflection there is something else besides, something we underestimate because of its simplicity: that is, that man really is subjected to the influences of the cosmos which forms his environment!

Everyday observation shows the important part celestial phenomena play on terrestrial phenomena. Without the sun life would not exist on earth; without the moon there would be no tides; if the earth did not turn there would be no days or nights with their many effects on man. And so the idea has grown naturally among ordinary people, and also among scientists who are open to new concepts, that these influences which come from outside could well conceal others just as important, even though they are disguised today in forms of madness and humbug. The task of looking for such hidden but possible influences is one of clarification which well suits the scientist.

At all events, if such an enterprise could be set on foot, a lot of water would have to flow under the bridge before the primitive notion of astrology disappeared. One steadfast enemy has declared that it is only ignorance which makes people go on believing in astrology and that, if he had every such ignoramus visit a planetarium to understand how the motions of the stars and planets worked, soon there would be no one who believed in astrology. That is indeed a simplistic solution! The reasons for a belief in astrology are not all due to a lack of knowledge. They are chiefly to be found, as we have seen, in a dread of the future, in derangement, and in the impossibility which men experience in solving their inner difficulties.

It is time now to close the ancient record of astrological mistakes, and open one of fantastic truths.

Part Three

A NEW SCIENCE OF COSMIC INFLUENCES

Chapter Twelve

A NECESSARY CLARIFICATION

No one should regard it as impossible that, from the follies and blasphemies of astrologers, there should emerge a sound and useful body of knowledge, and that from mud and dirt there should come oysters, mussels, eels, good food; that from a heap of unclean worms there should emerge a silk-worm, that finally, in a stinking dung-heap, a hard-working hen may find a grain of corn, indeed a pearl or a nugget of gold, if it searches and scratches long enough.

KEPLER. *Tertius interveniens.*

You know that I believe in a disymmetric cosmic influence which naturally and constantly controls the molecular organization of those principles immediately necessary for life, and that, as a consequence, the types of controls of life are, in their structures, forms, and nuclear arrangements, in a relation with the motions of the universe.

PASTEUR. *Letter to Raulin, April 4, 1871*

It has been held that astrology had a monopoly in the study of the relations between men and the stars, and that any inquirer who makes a study of these relations must necessarily be branded as an astrologer. But this is a confusion which must now be clarified before a genuine science involving the relations between men and the cosmos can be established. It is important to put the matter on an objective footing in order to discover the pearl or the gold nugget in the stinking dung-heap of astrology.

These relations have always been felt intuitively, but for too long they have been hidden from the mind by the prejudices which held and continue to hold sway in scientific circles. A good example of these prejudices may be found in the writings of Dauvillier, Professor of Physics at the Collège de France. In a recent publication he makes the following unequivocal declaration: "Those who are a little further on in the study of natural philosophy will understand how many of the astronomical and physical reasons for our existence are fortuitous, and they will refuse to investigate a connection between the solar system and the human species."

However, great scientists of the last century like Pasteur and Claude Bernard were of a quite different opinion. The latter did not hesitate to write that "Living matter is no exception to the great universal harmony which requires adaptation in all things. It breaks no accord, it is not in conflict or contradiction with general cosmic forces. On the contrary, it is part of a universal concourse, and animal life is only a fragment of the total life of the universe."

Today an increasingly large number of scientists maintain that in its journey through space the earth is basically a huge cosmic vessel where each of us lives like an astronaut in his space capsule, continually subjected to the effects of the cosmos. They are not dismayed by the thousands of ancient legends against which they stumble in this shifting territory, preferring to agree with Chesterton that "A dreamer is not someone who plunges into mysteries, but one who refuses to emerge from them." Thanks to these men, a new science will replace the old fantasy.

Let us by all means plunge into the mystery, but we should take care not to be swept away by the current. The current of astrology is very strong, and at the start there is a risk that the diver may be drowned.

Naturally there is no question here of our being convinced by almost any story related to us concerning this or that marvelous event originating from the cosmos. In this matter we have taken special pains to separate the wheat from the chaff. Our criterion has not been the likelihood or unlikelihood of the observations put forward, but the burden of proof attached to them. But the science of the relations between men and the universe is still very young, and we do not yet have a sufficient perspective to be truly impartial. It is quite possible that we have been overindulgent to one writer and too hard on another.

We will begin with a collection of recent experiments which will not be without surprises. After an outline of our own work, we shall follow a more direct path leading from the simple to the complicated, from the general to the particular, and from inanimate objects to mankind.

We shall cover the many discoveries which illustrate how much the earth is shaken by effects originating from our environment of space. These influences on the planet Earth add up, in their totality, to something which is well worth considering: the period of its orbit may be shortened by them, and earthquakes and volcanic eruptions may occur as a result. We will also see the extent to which radio waves can be jammed by emissions coming from outside our planet, and the unexpected part which planets and the galactic field can play in wave transmission.

Then, going deeper into the matter, we will see how other investigators have studied the relationship between our weather and extraterrestrial influences. And if the weather depends on the motions of the stars, so too, presumably, will vegetation and the water levels. All this leaves its mark on earth, and the indelible marks of cosmic clocks may be rediscovered in this way, imprinted in nature.

But as the virgin forest grows thicker and the shadows deeper, we come to the influence of the satellite to which age-old traditions ascribe mysterious powers? Does it affect marine organisms? Does it regulate female menstruation, or disorder the mind? Investigators have given sensible answers to all these questions. As for the sun, what effect does it have on us besides that of its heat and light? Very recently, it has been shown to be the cause of an astonishing range of new and unsuspected effects. The sun can cause a proliferation of microbes; it can call forth certain epidemics; it has been shown to be responsible for sudden deficiencies in our bodies, and indeed in our minds.

But man is made in a way which does not allow him merely to establish something as fact; he also wishes to understand.

The last chapters of this book will be devoted to those who have wanted to demonstrate the mysterious structure of these cosmic effects on our lives. To attain this objective they had to have considerable courage, an unflagging zest for experimentation, and a complete absence of prejudice, which enabled them to break into territories still not understood. We will tell the story of those who have succeeded in this difficult enterprise: the Italian chemist, Piccardi, who brought to light the principal laws behind the cosmic forces which are all around us; the Japanese biologist, Takata, who worked to find out why human blood becomes violently agitated when the cosmos does; and many others who have taken up the challenge and persevered in its pursuit.

Finally, we shall see that their patient observations have led to overwhelming consequences for modern science, since they transform the very concept of what constitutes determining factors in science. Naturally, in the course of this march back from astrology the way may sometimes seem overgrown, and it is easy to get lost in the labyrinths of the new science. But only by following this difficult path will we be able to introduce scientific truth again into this province of charlatan astrology.

Laplace has said, "A philosophy which is really of use in advancing science must combine a deep imagination with great rigor of thought and experiment, and it must feel keenly both a desire to get at the causes of phenomena and a fear of assigning these wrongly." We may feel this fear but we should not hesitate to go forward.

Chapter Thirteen

UNPRECEDENTED
RESULTS CONCERNING BIRTHS

"What you look for is of little importance; it is what you find that is important," Pasteur said. Let me modestly put myself under the protection of the great biologist, for I have now reached a stage where I can no longer postpone a description of the strange results which I achieved almost in spite of myself. These results were obtained by the most orthodox scientific techniques, and they have been checked by many scientists who have failed to uncover any mistakes. They seem no more at home with reason than with superstition, for my findings are completely without explanation at the present time. One day, however, it is our hope that modern science will succeed in integrating the mysterious effects which these statistics laid bare.

Right at the end of the inquiry which I mounted to clear the humbug from astrology by means of statistical probability, I was one day confronted by a very strange anomaly: in one of the experimental groups (involving the birth dates of 576 medical academicians), the frequency of a certain position of the stars was suddenly far from normal. This result could not be put down to chance: indeed, any statistician would have considered it highly significant. Although the finding had no resemblance to any of the laws of traditional astrology, it was so striking that it could not be ignored.

What exactly had I observed? An odd preference among people who were later to become eminent doctors to be born at a moment when Mars or Saturn had just risen or was at the zenith.[1] Ordinary people, on the other hand, never showed this effect, and that made matters even more surprising. I had taken care to select ordinary groups of births taken at random from an electoral register. At the time of their births these

1. i.e. at its highest point. Throughout this chapter "zenith" could more accurately be rendered as "culmination". Ed.

151

ordinary people showed no preference for the rise or zenith of Mars or Saturn. The wheel of destiny which has apparently gone wild for senior doctors had behaved normally in the case of the man in the street.

This was both absurd and embarrassing. It was better not to ask too many questions but to repeat the experiment and see if the phenomenon recurred. Laboriously, I therefore again collected another group of 508 eminent doctors. I say laboriously, for it was not just a question of finding the names of the doctors. I then had to get their dates of birth, find the places where they were born, and write to the City Hall of each community to obtain the hour of birth. Without this there could be no statistical inference, because the motions of the planets under study quickly alter their positions in the sky, changing places from one hour to the next.

When all this had been done the evidence had to be accepted. As in the first group, these other famous doctors' births were inexplicably grouped around the rise and zenith of Mars and Saturn.

This happened in 1950; I was twenty at the time, an age when youthful enthusiasm forbids an admission that anything is impossible. Perhaps, I thought, I have put my finger on a new scientific fact. Why should unprecedented prospects not be born from the ashes of astrology, but this time according to the procedures of contemporary science?

Would I have agreed to embark on this dangerous road if I had been less young? I hardly imagined how long and how far from the beaten track this journey would be, for as the investigations increased the results became even more surprising.

To begin with, I got together data on the greatest possible number of French celebrities. This work produced such interesting results that I published them in 1955 to elicit comment and criticism from experts in the matter. The main reaction of those who examined the work was to advise me to try a repetition of the experiments abroad, to see if the same results would appear among births other than French.

I agreed. The scope of the experiments had to be extended if I wished to confirm the facts. Beginning in 1956, my wife and I visited a different country each year. During the holidays, and taking advantage of the thirty days of freedom at our disposal, we accumulated new records; during the rest of each year we worked on the statistical calculations. In this way German, Italian, Belgian, and Dutch celebrities were united. In all, 25,000 births were collected for analysis, all complete, indexed, and obtained from the registry office by means of an energetic correspondence with numerous City Halls.

Naturally, I was quite aware of what I was investigating: a man's profession indicated by his hour of birth! What an unnatural and alien notion! Only astrologers dared to maintain in this way that the influence of the planets could affect living beings.

However, when a new fact is suddenly glimpsed, one has to be very incurious to turn away without trying to find out whether it is true or false. My first results might not be repeated elsewhere, in which case they would have lost their significance, and I would have put them down to imagination or chance. But if they reappeared in five different countries, then indeed, chance could no longer be the cause. Instead, it would certainly be caused by something else.

From year to year it became clearer that this was no mere freak of chance; in every country investigated, the same results appeared. Although they were separated by frontiers and different customs and languages, the newborn who were later to follow a given profession chose to come into the world under the same planet, whether they were French, Italians or Germans. Absurd though it seemed, a closer and closer correlation was revealed between the time when certain great men were born and their professional careers. Doctors were not the only example, and Mars and Saturn were not the only planets to follow this rule. Jupiter and the moon appeared to have an equally large importance for other professions. But the most significant results regularly appeared for each planet just after its rise and its zenith.

Thus, when Mars appeared at the horizon or had just passed the highest point of its course across the sky, it was established that a greater number of people born at that time had a tendency to become great doctors, great athletes, or great soldiers. Future artists, painters or musicians, on the contrary, seemed to take care not to enter life at the times which suited doctors or athletes. Actors and politicians seemed to prefer to be born when Jupiter came to its rise and its zenith, whereas scientists chose an opposite timetable, only appearing at Jupiter's rise and zenith. For the four planets thus in play, the following table summarizes the data provided by the professional groups under examination.

Rise and zenith of:	High frequency of births	Average frequency of births	Low frequency of births
MARS	Scientists Doctors Athletes Soldiers Executives	Cabinet ministers Actors Journalists	Writers Painters Musicians
JUPITER	Team athletes Soldiers Ministers Actors Journalists Playwrights	Painters Musicians Writers	Solo athletes Scientists Doctors
SATURN	Scientists Doctors	Soldiers Ministers	Actors Painters Journalists Writers
MOON	Ministers Politicians Writers	Scientists Doctors Painters Musicians Journalists	Athletes Soldiers

It will be seen that each professional group has particular reactions to the four planets. A kind of cosmic vibration lasting 24 hours a day would seem to elicit more births of future doctors at some times, more births of future artists at others, and so on.

Let us keep the idea of birth as a train of life which is boarded at certain times, in order to grasp better the oddity of my observations. Each planet has a different schedule in the sky, so that Jupiter does not rise or reach its zenith at the same

154

time as Mars on a given day. The schedules of the four planets involved are like those of four different trains which, although they carry out a journey of about the same duration (24 hours) do not all leave at the same time. The train Mars, for instance, leaves the "rise" station at three in the morning and passes the "zenith" station at ten, carrying on its circular journey without pause. The train Jupiter would pass through the same stations some hours later. It would rise, for instance, at 5:00 p.m. and reach its zenith at 11:00 p.m. All the information about the planets' "schedule" is published each year by astronomers in the annuals and in guides to navigation.

Could such strange results have a meaning? What I established was that people of different professions were born at times which were not the result of chance. But what did it depend on? Could one talk about cosmic forces, since only the planets were involved? Could it be that they announced a propitious career, in which case the superstitions of the Chaldeans seemed vindicated?

It is obviously absurd to assert that Mars, for instance, is linked with this or that profession. But to escape from this absurdity I had to form new hypotheses and verify them with further experiments. If these strange results meant anything, then the explanation would necessarily have to emerge one day, or at least a minor fact would have to be discovered to make them admissible. So I went over a number of hypotheses with all their possibilities and raked up not a few figures and records before taking the next step in this maze.

Why should a child born at the rising of Mars have a better chance of becoming an eminent doctor? Why, if he were born under Jupiter, would he be more likely to take a career as an actor?

Let us first of all throw out all occult explanations whereby the rising planet would "cast a spell" of an invisible or symbolic kind on the newborn child, a spell which would be connected to his whole life and decide his fate. This kind of pronouncement is not pertinent, for scientifically, only concrete, limited, and precise hypotheses can be formulated.

From this angle, the first idea which occurred to me was that a ray (or any other modifying influence) might permanently affect the person whose birth coincided with it. When a child's birth coincides with the appearance of Mars above the horizon, the star's action could conceivably modify his fragile organism and leave a permanent mark on it. After this effect from Mars, the child would have something in addition to the determining characteristics inherited from his parents. This additional something might have sufficiently strong and lasting effects to predispose him in a definite direction.

But astronomers and biologists will rightly protest against this: "What nonsense! It is most improbable. If such rays existed, they would not be effective at the moment of birth, but right from the time of conception, when the random selection of heredity would decide the future qualities of the child. For birth is the outcome of nine months of gestation, during which the organism is completely formed. This ridiculous astral ray would then have turned up when the battle was over."

This logical and unanswerable objection would hold us up for a long time if we did not try another approach. But what would happen if we tackled this indefensible hypothesis from another angle?

A child's organism cannot be abruptly modified at birth by planetary influences; agreed. But why should it not happen the other way about: the child might have a predisposition to come into the world under certain cosmic conditions which corresponded to his biological constitution. In a way, the child would be waiting for the right time to be born, and this moment would merely be an indication of his biological make-up. The position of the planet might bring about the birth, but it would make no difference to the child's constitution. And it would be this constitution – the biological temperament inherited from its parents – which alone would give its life a specific direction, pushing it, for instance, into a particular profession. The star would therefore not play any part in predetermining the future.

Astronomers and biologists will object that this hypothesis is almost as improbable as the last. By what bizarre and mysterious process of physics would the star act as a releaser of births? However, this hypothesis has one big advantage: it lends itself to experimentation to establish whether it is soundly or unsoundly based. In this discussion, heredity will be the judge, for heredity is the single factor which determines our biological make-up. Everything we have at birth has been bequeathed us by our parents. A child with blue eyes necessarily has a blue-eyed ancestor. Let us assume, then, that the position of a star at the child's birth is the expression of one of his hereditary factors; in that case one of his ancestors must have had a similar position of this star at his birth. It is therefore possible to collect numbers of parents born when, for instance, Mars appeared over the horizon, and then see if their child is also predisposed to be born when Mars holds this position in the sky.

We shall establish the existence of planetary heredity if we can prove, through statistical means, a correlation between the position of the planets at the parents' birth with that at the birth of their child. If an indication of planetary heredity could be revealed, even though it were slight, then we would have taken another step in the solution of the problem, the interpretation of the absurd result obtained from the professional groups. The connection glimpsed between mankind and the planets would this time be attached to a recognized field of knowledge, namely, genetics, and would be more easily reconciled within the framework of modern science. The hour of birth could be explained as a kind of biological reaction to a spatial effect pertaining at that moment.

So once again I was on the hunt for dates of birth, but this time I was interested in the general population of men and women, and not members of an élite selected for a special purpose. In fact, planetary heredity had to be a general law of human nature, and no longer a perquisite of some people whose vocation was clearly marked.

For five years I worked on the birth registers at several city halls in the region of Paris. In the total figure more than 15,000 matchings of parents and their children were collected, which enabled me to calculate almost 300,000 positions of the planets. Then I applied the ten bodies of the solar system one by one to my hypothesis. Naturally, I was particularly concerned to observe the behavior in regard to heredity of Mars, Jupiter, Saturn, and the moon, whose performance with the professional groups was at the root of all my efforts.

The total picture drawn from the data examined *indicated a correlation between the birth sky of parents with that of their children*. This could consitute an important argument in favor of planetary heredity as I have defined it. In fact the degree of correlation was such that the probability of such an effect being produced by chance was five hundred thousand to one against. In other words, it was 499,999 to one that planetary heredity was a fact.

Moreover, planetary heredity followed rules of a consistency to satisfy the strictest critic. Its chief characteristic was its constancy, since it appeared in each of the areas studied, as much with the father as the mother, with the sun as with the daughter; and it regularly followed certain familiar genetic laws.[1]

Heredity is clearly indicated for Mars, Jupiter, Saturn and Moon, and also for Venus; it is impossible to find enough evidence for Mercury, Uranus, Neptune and Pluto. Now, Mercury is very small. Uranus and Pluto are very far away. The stars which produce results are therefore either the nearest (like the Moon) or the largest (like Jupiter). I do not draw any conclusions from this, but merely record the fact. For instance, the effect of hereditary characteristics was more marked with a child whose birth sky corresponded to his parents'. Another point of consistency was that, while the effect was constant when the births were natural ones, it disappeared as soon as induced births were subjected to experiment as a control.

A very important cross-proof of planetary heredity appeared when I concentrated on the irritating problem of induced births. Confinements today, as we know, are more and more controlled by doctors. In these cases, births occur at a different time than if it had been left to nature. Now, planetary heredity is established by the moment of birth. If this moment is artificially fixed, the hereditary predisposition to be born at one moment rather than another may still certainly exist in the newborn child, but we can no longer distinguish it. I have asserted that the planetary effect disappears in the case of births which do not occur at the natural time: when,

1. For a detailed description of this hypothesis, together with its statistical application, see *Die Planetare Hereditat* (Zeitschrift fur Parapsychologie und Grenzgebiete der Psychologie), Band V, No. 2/3, 1962, pp. 168–193. This also contains precise references to the data of births which were used. In French, *Planète* 6, technical note, pp. 82–83, may be consulted, and my forthcoming book, *l'Hérédité planétaire*.

that is, surgical intervention (forceps or Caesarian operations) or the use of chemical inducement are involved.

At the present time, therefore, I think it is possible to assume that planetary heredity is a fact. But, naturally, the experiments must continue, and my own conviction, like that of other investigators, will not be definitive until other people, using new material, bring out statistically verified evidence of the same kind as ours.

Although I obtained positive facts from material of apparent astrological origin, it is quite clear that these results, surprising though they are, must be explained in scientific, not astrological, terms. Indeed, they constitute a new and powerful criticism of astrology.

If the hereditary effect appears well founded, it does not indicate any return to obsolete traditions; it does not influence birth as a fundamental cause of our future life, precisely because the birth sky of a child adds nothing which it does not already have in it.

The planetary effect would therefore make no alteration in its constitution, would not imprint any influence on it at birth, and would provide no lucky or unlucky predestination in addition to the natural predispositions of the newborn child. In short, the birth would only be a reaction of our organism more easily indicated according to certain terrestrial conditions, and this reaction would probably not be the only one. It would still be nothing but a statistical datum, whose value would be relative. It would not have permanent meaning, unlike the pronouncements of astrology concerning each aspect of the sky.

Let us provisionally close this account of my research at the point where it began: with the professions. We can now understand a little better the potential meaning behind the improbable fact that people destined for brilliant success in a given profession tend to be born at a particular time. The reason would appear to be, simply, that such people have inherent constitutional (and therefore hereditary) elements which lead them by a natural tendency to a certain way of life which suits them particularly well. The time of these celebrities' birth would then be no more than an indication of their hereditary constitution. Any rational person who feels discon-

certed by this finding may rest assured that it is entirely heredity which, seen in the perspective of my research, determines
the general orientation of our lives. There is not, and there
never will be, any "planet of the professions," nor even a
"planet of character," but only cosmic clocks or "time-
keepers" which operate in a way which is still unknown but
seems to be connected to the earth's rotation.

Will science soon discover why a newborn child should be
able to respond to the still mysterious promptings of the cosmic clocks? Let us hope so. Meanwhile, it cannot be denied
that the correlation thus brought to light looks improbable.
The sum of the observations I have just proposed are, when
confronted with modern science, like so many monstrosities
and apparent impossibilities. The objections which experts can
and must raise against us are innumerable.

First of all, the objections from the medical angle. In order
to justify my interpretation of the results, it is necessary to
prove that the child plays an active and not a passive role during the process of confinement. Now, until recently at any
rate, it seemed clear that the effectuating role was played by
the mother. However, second thoughts are now being voiced
about this.

The objections raised in contemporary astronomical circles appear equally serious. How are we to appease the wrath
of the astronomers, or justify with any validity the fact that
planets may act as a "releaser" of birth, as our research would
seem to indicate? And what would be the organs receptive to
these strange influences?

We are surrounded by mystery and can only advance grop-
ingly. Our position is a little like that of a prisoner who, having made a hole in the wall of his cell, is still uncertain whether
this opening will lead to the way of freedom or whether it will
lead to the warden's office. But, putting this dilemma on one
side, we must continue on the way, holding firm to the conviction that although our observations were fortuitous in origin, they will lose their odd and occultist look when they are
successfully connected to the work of other investigators.

For example, the determinative factor which sets off the
beginning of labor is still one of the major unknown quantities in medicine. Professor Merger, one of the most eminent

of French obstetricians, admits it frankly: "The determinative factor in confinement is still not known."

On the other hand, if the old Hippocratic idea that the child could play a part in his entry into the world has been abandoned until the last few years, a great deal of recent research indicates that doctors are going to have to revise this position. For it now seems established that the child *can* play a part in the confinement, through the intermediary of hormones carried through the blood stream which influence the uterine contractions of the mother as long as the child is connected to her by the umbilical cord.

Now, modern science has a great deal still to learn about the relations between man and the cosmos. Let us continue on the road which leads away from astrology and on which we have now embarked, but this time in the company of accredited scientists. Perhaps at the end of it all some reasons will emerge to pay off the mortgages which at present weigh so heavily on the probability of our observations. For, and we are the first to admit it, we are very far from understanding all the mysterious and invisible threads which hold man a prisoner in the vast coweb of the universe.

With planets, just as with obstetrics, the old concepts are today being revised. Hardly ten years ago, for instance, it was discovered that the planets could emit electromagnetic waves toward us. Those which originate from Jupiter can even sometimes jam our radio stations. These long waves are of only weak penetrative power, but nevertheless it is beginning to be realized that they can affect living matter.

Naturally, we do not claim that this ties in with our observations. Besides, in this case planets would not necessarily affect us by a direct route. They could also bring about slight disturbances in the solar or even the galactic fields.

Chapter Fourteen

THE CELESTIAL BOMBARDMENT

Things are not only what our senses perceive them to be. If, for instance, our eyes did not make use of the visible light of the sun, but of its longer electromagnetic waves, the sun would not look like a sphere to us, but like a kind of firework display, or a burning bush whose multicolored parts were in incessant movement, like flames. And if our ears were capable of receiving the message of these waves, we would literally hear "the music of the spheres."

The sun emits a very great quantity of rays, sending us not only light rays but also radiations of every wave length in its infinite range, from the longest to the shortest. Moreover, its activity is variable, changing from one day to the next, one year to the next, and one century to the next. We have come a long way from the ancient doctrine of the immutability of the heavens. The star of day is constantly changing, and earth feels the repercussions a little as the humble employee feels the wrath of his boss. On its surface *sunspots,* huge dark flowers which whip up immense magnetic whirlwinds, spring up, develop, and then disappear. Fantastic incandescent clouds of gas suddenly occur in the sun's atmosphere, due to eruptions. The sun, which turns on its axis in 27-day cycles, periodically points its spots and eruptions like a lighthouse in the direction of earth. It then projects in this direction a suddenly increased quantity of waves and particles.

But a determinative factor has finally been found to underlie these sudden changes of mood, an order behind the apparent disorder: sunspots follow approximately an eleven-year cycle. The cause is still a mystery, but the fact remains that every eleven years the sun seems to suffer a sudden attack of fever, and the number of its spots and eruptions begins to increase. Soon this fever subsides, and the number of spots decreases. The sun's activity slackens, more or less, before beginning again and coming to a climax eleven years later.

Finally, it was realized as instruments of measurement became more advanced that the sun's atmosphere stretched considerably further than mere visual observation would have led one to believe. It is now known that the sun, in its actual substance and not only its radiation, stretches its atmosphere so far that we terrestrians can regard ourselves as living in the interior of the sun.

These vagaries of the sun are not without consequences for our planet. The duration of a day on earth can sometimes be altered as a result. Danjon, the astronomer and director of the observatory at Paris, announced that, during the three months of January, February, and March, 1963, the days had been shorter.

If there is a connection between the duration of a day and the sun's vagaries, might this not partly explain earthquakes? The slowing down or acceleration of the earth's movement by a fraction of a second might appear a derisory amount, but that would correspond to a considerable difference in kinetic energy. The earth being a solid body, and its deviations from the norm being imposed on it all at once, the effect on the terrestrial crust should be a considerable increase in tension. But the tensions in the terrestrial crust have always ended to free themselves seismically. Would solar eruptions be responsible for some earthquakes? Will they one day enable us to foresee these catastrophes? Whatever the position, it is worth pointing out that Danjon announced an important deviation in the earth's rotation before the disaster at Agadir.

If these months were shorter it meant the earth had begun to turn on its axis more quickly. Naturally, only a minimal difference, a fraction of a second, was involved. But the phenomenon is no less bewildering when one thinks of the enormous energy required to bring about this acceleration. It is actually rather an ordinary occurrence, regularly noted ever since our measuring instruments have been sufficiently sensitive to calculate the exact length of a day. Danjon, like many others, attributes these deviations to the influence of solar activity. When this is particularly strong it disturbs the rotation of the earth on its axis, a motion which had been thought so unalterable that it was chosen as the standard measurement of time.

Even gravity, for so long sacrosanct, appears to work in a

different way than had been thought till now. At the time of the total solar eclipse of June 30, 1954, the physicist Maurice Allais, who had long been examining certain apparently abnormal activities concerning the earth's attraction with the aid of a pendulum, made a particularly strange declaration: at the exact moment of the eclipse, the pendulum's level of oscillation changed suddenly. The variation in this level continued to increase until the twentieth minute after maximum eclipse, and then subsided until the phenomenon was over. It seemed that the moon, by putting a screen between the sun and us, had cut off a tiny fraction of solar attraction. Only one explanation was possible. There must be a cosmic force which was still unknown. But what kind of force could the moon screen us from? A question mark still hangs over the matter to this day.

Here is a phenomenon which has been observed on the planet Mars, and which has occasioned the greatest surprise in all those who have seen it. American experts have named it "the blue clearing." When Mars is in opposition (that is, when earth holds the same position in relation to Mars as the moon does in relation to earth during a solar eclipse), the blue screen which hides all the planet's details in some filters suddenly begins to disappear. The "blue clearing," like Maurice Allais' pendulum, remains a complete mystery. But one thing is certain: the sun's influence on earth, and the planets' reciprocal influences, are a great deal more complicated and mysterious than had been suspected before.

Yet another puzzle is this: could the planets themselves be at least partly responsible for the sun's vagaries which affect us? For some years astronomers have thought that the positions of some of them might well alter the sun's activity. It has been noticed, for instance, that the cycle of sunspots occurs every 11.2 years, on average, and that Jupiter takes 11.86 years to make its orbit. The astronomer Paul Couderc has himself raised this question: "These numbers are close to each other. Is this just a coincidence? People have for a long time wanted to ascribe the spots to disturbances caused on the sun by Jupiter. But further investigation has been brought up short by the gap of a year between the two. However, if Jupiter is the agent, the combined action of the other stars might alter the period, and I do not see this as a serious objection."

The same idea was more recently expressed by the astronomer, Link: "Earth does have an effect on the activity of sunspots, particularly when it is reinforced by a planetary conjunction. This is the case when a lower conjunction with Venus takes place: then earth and Venus are on the same side as the sun, and their effect on it is a combined one." If the earth's position in the sky modified the activity of sunspots, it would itself be the cause of the sun's atmospheric interferences which disturb it so much. In short, as the proverb says, as ye sow thus shall ye reap!

In 1942 astronomers discovered that the sun was an important source of emissions of radio waves. From that day, radio astronomy took on a new impetus and increased its range considerably. Radio telescopes were pointed toward the four corners of the universe, and it was discovered that the whole sky gave out sounds. This was a far cry from the "eternal silence of those infinite spaces" which had alarmed Pascal. Not only the sun but all the stars transmitted or reflected radio waves.

Beyond the solar system, the stars proved to be far more powerful transmitters. And beyond the stars the distant galaxies were even more powerful. But the planets in our own small solar system are also transmitters of radio waves, and "the sound of the planets" is now a recognized fact. In his historic lecture at the Palais de la Découverte in January 24, 1958, Professor Piccardi declared: "It may perhaps be of interest to say that sometimes the sounds heard on the radio are not caused by discharges from electric apparatus near our houses or by 'atmospherics,' but by electromagnetic waves created by great storms in the atmosphere of Jupiter or Venus."

Equally astonishing is the work of one of the technical directors of R.C.A. Communications, John H. Nelson, whose job was to study the quality of the reception of radio broadcasts. It had been established that this quality depended, among other factors, on the activity of sunspots and particularly the movement of the large spots at the zenith. However, an examination of the correlation between solar activity and radio broadcasts appeared to show an unexplained quantity left over. Nelson thought this might be explained by the heliocentric positions of the planets, that is, their relation to the sun. After various studies, he concluded his work as follows:

"Research carried out in this observatory since 1946 has shown clearly that sunspots are not the only answer to the problems raised (about the quality of radio reception). It is very clear that other forces are involved in addition to the sunspots. It is therefore necessary to find a new approach. Study of the planets has revealed encouraging results, and a more detailed examination is indicated. A highly developed technique of forecasting radio interference based on the motions of the planets would have the advantage of making possible long-range calculations, since the motions of the planets are well known."

By adding the observation of the heliocentric positions of the planets to that of sunspots, John H. Nelson brought about a significant improvement in the forecast of electromagnetic storms and days of poor reception. The latter could be predicted with 93% chance of success, a percentage which has never been achieved by observation confined to the sunspots alone.

But what arrangement of the planets causes radio interference? According to Nelson, the days when interference is worst are those when the planets are in the following relation to the sun: either at right angles to one another (90 degrees), or in conjunction (0 degrees) or in opposition (180 degrees). If Nelson's observations are confirmed, it will be of the greatest interest to learn how, through the intermediary of the sun, such planetary arrangements cause radio interference in this way.

In any case, the possibility that planets play a part in the solar field can hardly be denied. Directly or indirectly, they do cause effects; their image, as far as astronomers and radio astronomers are concerned, has changed. From now on they are no longer humble bit-players in the celestial dance. It is clear that they have an influence both on the earth and on us.

But besides being in the solar field, the earth, and therefore we ourselves, are also in the galactic field. In 1926 strange particles were discovered, almost by chance, which possessed an often considerable energy and pierced the atmosphere at a terrific speed. These were called cosmic rays.

Their origin is still obscure. It is not even known for certain whether they come from the stars of our galaxy, or more distant galaxies, or even from the great interstellar spaces which were long wrongly believed to be empty, and which are now thought to contain a fourth type of matter, plasma. To explain the stunning speed of these particles, the great physicist Enrico Fermi has advanced the hypothesis that our galaxy acts as a kind of giant cyclotron which would give them enormous acceleration.

Whatever the fact of the matter, a perpetual shower of these rays falls on every part of the earth in bundles and cascades, causing many different effects in their trajectory according to what they meet on penetrating our atmosphere.

The sun, then, is not an unchangeable sphere but is incessantly disturbed by inner vibrations. It is not confined in space, but its atmosphere extends to earth and beyond. The moon and other planets apparently cause strange upheavals in the solar field. The earth, carried along at a terrific speed by the sun in the galaxy, is ceaselessly pierced and struck by various forces and rays which may indeed be contradictory, and come from outer space.

All physical phenomena on earth necessarily feel the repercusions of these cosmic forces. The sun's vagaries, for instance, may alter the duration of the day, and perhaps even induce earthquakes. Connected with cosmic rays, they disturb the earth's magnetic fields and all the phenomena of the upper atmosphere. In relation with the planets they cause radio interference and no doubt many other things which we still do not know about.

Is it not natural to ask whether these vagaries might not also have other more subtle effects? The weather, the air we breathe, our physical and mental state, even the way we think – are not all these things dependent to some extent on disturbances in our cosmic environment?

Chapter Fifteen

THE STARS AND NATURAL PHENOMENA

In our examination of the effect of the stars on the earth and its inhabitants, we have just passed briskly through the first part concerned with these influences on the planet Earth taken as a whole. We must now enter the second and more obscure area, and ask the following question: does the cosmos influence the weather, nature, vegetation, and the quality of the air we breathe? This is dangerous ground, for it includes old tales which have survived tenaciously from an unscientific age.

When people are heard talking about weather forecasts, generally they agree to a series of fairly confused principles, but start from a fixed idea, namely, that the weather can be predicted if the prediction is based on the weather as it is at a given time. For instance, if it rains on St. Medard's day it will rain for the next 40 days "unless St. Barnabas cuts the ground from under his feet."

Sayings about the weather, often of a contradictory nature, have for a long time been sprinkled through calendars foretelling the future. These naive predictions and sayings are still repeated today, to console us for the troubles arising from constantly changeable weather conditions.

A leading daily paper headed the page on weather forecasts for the month of September in this way:

U.S. weather bureau: Heavy rain for the whole of September.
French weather prophets: Sunshine.
O. N. M. weather bureau: Cool on Sunday.

This is a significant point. Side by side with traditions which may be called rustic, there is the entirely modern point of view, as expressed by the meteorological bulletin for the morning. For many people it has become a daily ritual to hear or read this bulletin. But the Weather Bureau's performance in forecasts, particularly as regards a specific place on Earth, tend to be rather discouraging. Their statements, compared

168

with how the weather really turns out, indicate so large a proportion of failures that it might sometimes be said that the bulletin was worked out at random. And so as usual the public takes refuge, here as elsewhere, in the astrologers and clairvoyants whenever science is at fault.

However, many people do believe in the worth of the weather bureau's daily bulletins. But does this reflect much glory on the organization, since these are often the same people who are happy to believe in the influence of St. Barnabas or the effectiveness of the weather astrologers? Basically, these are not problems to the man in the street. The meteorological bulletin provides a scientific element to the weather forecast which he would like to believe, in which the stars often hold a place – especially the moon. Almost all the vagaries of the weather are put down to this star of the night, but the question whether all this has any basis in fact is not asked. Let us put this question firmly and muster all the arguments for and against.

Marshall Bugeaud (1784–1849) was a convinced believer in the influence of the moon on the weather. In addition to his conquest of Algeria and a satirical song about his hat, he has handed down to posterity a highly learned law called the *rule of Marshall Bugeaud:* "The weather for the whole lunar period," he said, "is the same as that of the fifth day, provided that the weather does not change on the sixth." The precision and the scientific caution of his pronouncement are both remarkable.

General Du Barail has confirmed that the marshall kept this rule in mind during his Algerian campaign. One day it was raining in the Ouarsenis; the troops were tired and the ground was sodden. Bugeaud was advised not to go on. "But I have looked at the moon," he said, "the weather will be fine. March on!" The weather was splendid, adds General Du Barail, and the operation was a complete success.

So Marshall Bugeaud's rule had a free run in the army – until the day when someone had the idea of balancing the forecasts against their factual confirmation. It was then noticed that the rule behaved exactly as in a game of chance, a game of heads and tails which couldn't be faked: it came out right ... five times out of ten! This story shows the extent to which a belief in the moon's responsibility for the weather is rooted in the human mind. The most widespread superstition has it that the weather changes at the full (or the new) moon, and remains thus until the next moon change (unless the first or last quarter reverses it all). Since a lunar period lasts only 27 days, it will be seen that all these alternatives enable the moon to be always vulnerable to accusations of changing the weather.

Some attribute to the full moon what others claim for the new moon, etc. It is necessary to clarify the matter with a simple statistical balancing. A careful scrutiny of the Weather Bureau's archives is all that is required, together with a comparison of the weather changes described there and the phases of the moon. This task will show that the moon has nothing to do with it. It is not to blame for the weather, whether it is full, or new, or going through one of its quarters.

Very well, someone will say, but I am not going to be persuaded that the appearance of the moon plays no part in the kind of weather we get: it will not be the same if its rim is clear as when it is surrounded by a halo. Is there not a popular saying to the effect that "if the moon has a halo, it is a sign of rain"? (The Chaldeans said much the same.) However, when the matter is looked at objectively, it is obvious that a moon with a halo is no indication of the forthcoming weather, but only shows a certain humidity in the atmosphere.

At the same time, many people still say today: "A red moon nips the buds." And it is a fact, this certainly happens. But the reason ascribed to it is false. In 1827, during a visit made by members of the Bureau des Longitudes, Louis XVIII caused Laplace considerable embarrassment by asking him to explain "the way the red moon worked." The great astronomer retired in some confusion, and the story was much enjoyed by the court. In order to avoid the same fate at Laplace, Arago, some years later, explained the ill effects of the red moon scientifically: "The actual light of the moon does not have any effect here; it is merely a sign that the sky is very clear and free from the nocturnal radiation which would induce only a slight fall in temperature. Whether the moon is above or below the horizon, the event would still take place while the atmosphere was so calm."

. The forecasting of weather is connected to that of the harvest. Many farmers are ready to assert that the lunar cycle influences the growth of plants. This belief is particularly widespread for melons and for all vegetables of the cucurbitaceous family. Could this be due to a similarity of shape?

Until these last few years, very few examples were known of the moon having a real effect on plant life, except for the part played by moonlight in opening certain flowers, Even in 1956, two experts, Rheinberg and Ghata, wrote that "the only authentic lunar rhythm in the reproduction of a plant is that of the *Dictyota dichotoma*, a marine alga. In North Carolina new sex cells appear with each lunar month. The same species at Bangor, Plymouth and Naples has a reproductive rhythm corresponding to the major tides, that is, two cycles per lunar period. The height of the tides makes no difference to the observed rhythms." A single marine plant is not much to go on. . . .

But some very recent work suggests strongly that the part played by the moon on plant life should not be treated only as a myth. Frank A. Brown and his fellow workers have shown, using very sensitive apparatus, that the oxygen consumption of the potato, the carrot, and other vegetables, and therefore their growth, could vary according to the position of the moon by month and day.

On the other hand, many other publications which are often quoted in the literature on the subject are purely imaginary. Consider, for instance, the writings of a certain Mme. Kolisko (an adherent of the Goetheanum, Rudolf Steiner's temple of anthroposophy), who recommends that cabbages, peas, tomatoes, radishes, carrots, and corn should be planted before the full moon. According to her, magnificent crops would be guaranteed by this procedure. Unfortunately, she is the only one to have obtained increased production by this method.

It will be seen that the reality appears disappointing enough when contrasted with all the marvelous powers which the moon is supposed to have over plant life.

Since the conventional wisdom seems to hold so little truth, should we conclude that the stars are totally uninvolved in meteorological disturbances? This was certainly the opinion of most experts in this field, until a short time ago.

Is there then no culprit in the sky? As we have seen, there is at least one, the sun. But to find even this out, scientists had to admit that there was a possible and even necessary connection between the fields of meteorology and astronomy. Then evidence proving the sun's guilt obligingly appeared for all to see, and could have been realized a long time before. It was known that the sun was responsible for spectacular disturbances in the atmosphere such as the aurora borealis. This is an effect of light which appears in the atmosphere, usually in the region of the poles; its changing forms and colors make it one of the most beautiful natural phenomena. It is now known that the appearance of an aurora borealis at the pole is a sign of momentary but violent increase in the sun's activity.

During violent solar eruptions, or at the time when important groups of spots move to the sun's central zone, a certain number of disturbances occur in our atmosphere, particularly the *aurorae boreales*, as a result of the greater ionization of the upper atmosphere, and magnetic storms, revealed by violent agitation of compass needles. Once this was known, it was inevitable that one day an expert would ask the question: "If the sun disturbs the atmosphere, could it not also upset the weather, since the weather is dependent on the atmosphere? And if the weather is influenced by solar activity, will we not be able to forecast it more efficiently in the light of our ability to predict this solar activity?"

The kind of weather we have imprints itself on nature: if it has been a dry summer, the grass in the fields is yellow and there are few flowers; if it has been damp, the grass is thick and the flowers plentiful. So if the sun influences the weather, it must have left traces in our natural surroundings.

As a matter of fact, the eleven-year cycle of solar activity is stamped and engraved everywhere on our earth. Examples are numerous: the level of Lake Victoria-Nyanza changes in accordance with the rhythm of the sunspots, also the number of icebergs, and famines in India due to the lack of rain. The *Bulletin astronomique de France* brought out a very interesting article on the relation between the activity of sunspots and the quality of Burgundy wines: excellent vintages corresponded with periods of maximum solar activity, and bad vintages with periods of minimum solar activity. Douglas, an American, and Schvedov, a Russian, have observed that the concentric rings formed in the growth of trees have a period of recurrence of eleven years as well. Finally, there is Lury's well-known statistical observation that the number of rabbit skins taken by the Hudson Bay Company follows a curve parallel to that of solar activity. All these phenomena evidently depend on the same cause, namely, the weather with its yearly variations in rainfall which is responsible for the growth of plants, the breeding of rabbits, the level of lakes, or the number of icebergs. So the weather is connected to the sun's eleven-year cycle.

On this subject, perhaps the most interesting study is that carried out on varves. These, says Piccardi, are many-layered deposits of sand or clay which are formed in calm waters, lakes, ponds, swamps, etc., in glacial zones. A varve's thickness also depends on the rainfall in a given year. Examination of these fossilized deposits in sedimentary rock formed through the geological ages reveals the same inevitable eleven-year cycle in the most distant past! Piccardi gives the following figures for the cycles during different geological ages: Pre-Cambrian: 11.3 years; Higher Devonian: 11.4 years; Lower Carboniferous: 11.4 years; Eocene: 12 years; Oligocene: 11.5 years. Hundreds of millions of years ago the sun was controlling, as it does today, variations in water levels and the fertility cycle in nature through the influence it exerts on the weather.

If, then the activity of sunspots lends its rhythm to the weather, could it become possible to forecast the weather which will occur *in a given year*? That cannot be claimed, for it would require moving from the statistical law of the eleven-year cycle to a case of one particular year. Of course, it seems to be established that the temperature over the whole globe is lower when sunspot activity is at a maximum, a finding shown by the confirmatory observations of Abbot and, more recently, Sir Robert Walker. The rainfall level also seems to obey the same determinative cause, that is, it rains more at a time of maximum solar activity. But in this case the whole earth is involved, and no certain conclusions can be drawn for a limited area during a single year.

Mention should be made of the effects of the sun's abrupt vagaries (sudden eruptions, movement of the spots to the meridian). According to the work of people like Hanzlik of Austria and De Rudder of Germany, it seems that the passing moods of the sun could provide the meteorologists with extremely valuable information on at least one important point, that of weather changes. This is what the experts call the movement of a warm or cold atmospheric front. These movements depend on variations of barometric pressure which change the prevailing winds: if the pressure rises, it will probably be fine; if it falls, there is a good risk of rain. Interestingly enough, in the last analysis these rises and falls in barometric pressure seem to depend on the sun's sudden eruptions.

But it must be added in fairness that the sun's influence here may in practice remain a fairly abstract concept for actual weather forecasting. For in the lower atmosphere localized phenomena can alter, or indeed completely transform, the sun's general effects at short notice, chiefly because of the basic inertia of atmospheric mass. That is why all efforts to establish a constant and scientifically rigorous correlation between solar activity and disturbances in the lower atmosphere have failed until now. It has been written that these relations seem to be as complicated as the relations between the two main characters in a psychological novel. However H. C. Willet in the U.S.A., and Y. Arai in Japan seem to have got some interesting results by applying data on solar activity to short-range weather forecasting.

For the moment, let us keep to the essential point: solar activity is connected with high and low atmospheric pressure systems; it follows that this has an influence on the wind currents and can induce (at least theoretically) heat waves, periods of rain or rainlessness, and alternations in temperature and humidity. Meteorology cannot afford to ignore solar activity, if it wishes to improve its efficiency in forecasting the weather. Such examination will be more useful than watching the barometric indicator go up and down its little scale.

People are often heard to say: "The weather is going to change because I can feel my 'pains' coming on: all my joints are hurting!" Is there anything in these words besides a mistaken impression, an idea which has gained currency through general usage? In fact, these "pains" cannot be written off as a myth. People suffering from rheumatism or diseases of the bone, or those who have had a limb amputated, really do feel these pains more strongly when the weather is going to change.

Besides, it has been established that before a storm birds behave in a particular way at a time when nothing in the clear air augurs the coming storm. Weather and its changes affect living creatures, as almost all scientists agree. But the question of how this is effected is not yet well understood. One thing is sure, namely, that the weather alters the air we breathe. In that air there are a number of elements which alter the state of our body and our sensations. Humidity is one obvious element. If it is low, people are more at ease; if it is high, the humid atmosphere is oppressive. The role of electricity in the atmosphere is also very important. But perhaps most important for our biological systems are the positive and negative ions, electrified particles whose effect was only recently discovered.

On November 4, 1952, a health disaster occurred in London; several hundred sick people died that day at a time when nothing suggested that this would happen. People with lung complaints were chiefly the ones affected as Professor Walsh MacDermott of Cornell University has made clear in *Scientific American*. That day there had been a heavy fog in London. The fog was so thick, and the humidity so high, that the sun seemed unable to rise. But was that enough to explain all those deaths?

One day in 1926 Professor Tchijewsky of Moscow University was brought a performing chimpanzee. The poor creature was in the last stages of tuberculosis, refused all food, and did not even wish to move. After four and a half months of treatment the chimpanzee had quite cheered up and his coat shone. He could once more be brought before the public, and he lived on for many years. The time came for Tchijewsky to announce his miracle cure to the world. At first sight it seemed simple enough: breathe for an hour or two with the lungs at full stretch. But the air which Professor Tchijewsky required his patients to breathe was not ordinary air; it was "curative" air.

What, then, are these mysterious seeds in the air we breathe which can bring death or life? They are ions, particles in the air which are positively or negatively electrified. Their effect on living creatures is marked, and differs according to whether positive or negative ions are involved. As a general rule positive ions are harmful and negative lions favorable to the organism. In 1926 Professor Tchijewsky was a pioneer in this field, but since that time a large number of scientists have been able to attest to the part played by positive and negative ions in the health of living creatures. All the experimental indications are that subjects breathing air charged with positive ions are likely to feel discomfort, headaches, and giddiness; whereas the same subjects feel cheerful, relaxed and in top form in an atmosphere full of negative ions.

The concentration of positive and negative ions in the air we breathe depends on the weather situation and, in the last analysis, on solar activity. Particles which induce a very high ionization in the upper atmosphere are directed toward earth by the sun: the ionosphere is filled with positive and negative ions. But unfortunately negative ions have a tendency to attach themselves to clouds, whereas positive ions tend on the contrary to accumulate on the ground.

When the weather bulletin announces that the next day there will be low pressure and that the winds will not be strong enough to disperse rain and fog, this will indicate an atmosphere where the concentration of positive ions will be more of a health danger. That is the explanation for the event which happened in London on November 4, 1952.

So it can be said that the daily weather forecast is a kind of medical prescription. Particularly in the cities and according to the mood of the sun and the atmospheric conditions, we may one day be subjected to an atmosphere where there is a heavy concentration of positive ions, and will therefore not feel well: sick people will feel even worse. On other days, on the contrary, the air we breathe will be full of negative ions, and we shall feel particuly well. It is evident that the weather, and therefore solar activity, have an important effect on our health through atmospheric ionization.

Now that the function of these ions is known, a course of action remains to be worked out by the scientists. As two experts, Krueger and Smith, have concluded: "It seems reasonable to predict that in the future we shall see the development of a control of the ions in the air in those places where people live and work, just as we now have developed controls over temperature and humidity."

But the formation of positive or negative ions in the lower atmosphere is not entirely dependent on solar activity. Ions are also a product of the natural radioactivity of the earth. In towns there are many additional "ion generators"; and automobile exhaust, smoke, and dust accumulate positive ions in large molecules. These, discovered by Langevin, have been named *heavy ions,* for they tend to sink to the earth's surface, and are really the "killer ions," as has been repeatedly demonstrated.

Chapter Sixteen

LUNAR INFLUENCES

One day Plutarch was asked: "Why do foals which have been chased by a wolf become faster runners than the others?"

"Because," replied the philosopher, "perhaps that is not true."

Another tale, not as shrewd a look at casual assumption of cause and effect but more to the point of lunar influence, is also taken from antiquity:

The poet Annianus was celebrating the grape harvest with Aulus Gellius and some of his friends. They were served with undersized oysters, and Annianus said: "The moon must be on the wane; because the oyster, like many other things, is small and dried up." He was asked what were these other things. "What?" he answered. "Don't you remember the verses of Lucilius?"

> The moon feeds oysters, fills sea urchins, puts flesh on shellfish and on beasts.

The moon has a very obvious effect on the sea, as is shown in the tides, and for a long time this has been associated with the idea that it also influences sea life. The assertion is to be found in Aristotle, Pliny, Saint Augustine, and Francis Bacon. It still exists in very widespread form today in the fish markets of large Mediterranean ports. At Suez, sea urchins and crabs are called "full" at the full moon, and "empty" at the new moon. At Nice, Naples, and Alexandria it is claimed that the finest sea urchins are those of the full moon.

Scientists have tested whether this belief is verified by the facts. They have found it to be so in one case, that of *Centrechinus setosus*, a sea urchin of the Red Sea. This sea urchin, and only this one so far, has a rhythm linked to the lunar month. In due season, at the end of July-August-September, at the time of the full moon, genital matter is released into the sea, where fertilization takes place. After the spawning period, the size of the ovaries and testicles decreases. Then, with the waning of the moon, the gonad cells take up production again, and this is carried on through the new moon to reach a maximum at the full moon, when the eggs and spermatozoa are mature.

It has been confirmed that no other kind of sea urchin acts according to a lunar rhythm. But in spite of everything, an explanation must be found for the lunar behavior of the surprising *Centrechinus setosus.* The question still remains open. Perhaps its behavior is due to some lunar side effect. However, it has been shown that neither the temperature of the water, nor the nocturnal light of the moon, nor even the fullness of the tides seems to be a determinative cause. Could the moon have some effect which has not yet been discovered? For the moment, nothing more is known about the matter.

Although *Centrechinus* may be exceptional among sea urchins, it does have imitators in the world of mollusks and worms. The most noteworthy of the mollusks is *Convoluta paradoxa,* which digs down into the sand at the sea's edge and keeps its rhythm even when removed to a laboratory and kept in tideless water. Another shellfish (*kammuschel*) produces eggs from January to July once a month, and always when the moon is full. The Californian cuttlefish always spawns at the mouths of rivers three days after the full moon, as does *Chalpopleura,* another mollusk.

THE FEAST OF THE PALOLO

Everything is ready well in advance: the Samoan natives have mended their nets and filled the leaks in their boats, for these inhabitants of the Pacific know the moon well. They have followed its phases and know that at the last quarter of the moon in October and November, in their neighborhood, the sea which is usually a deep blue will suddenly seem to change color. The Samoans shout with joy because the fun is going to begin. They rush to their boats to go fishing for *palolo.* They will come back with nets so laden that they will be able to satiate themselves with this delicious food. Then they will wait for its return next year.

What is this delectable *palolo* which the natives are so partial to? It is a worm, or rather, the rear part of a worm. *Palolo* is only its stage name; scientists call it *Leodicus viridix*. Of all sea worms, this one has the best known and most apparent lunar rhythm. It lives in the coral reefs of the Pacific. What happens is this: in the moon's last quarter in the months of October and November, the rear part of the worm, crammed with genital matter, splits off from the forepart. The latter stays at the reef and dies, while the genital section, like the last stage of a rocket, reaches the surface of the sea and sheds its load of eggs and spermatozoa. This spawn comes up at low tide, early in the morning, and the episode is repeated for several days. The number of worms involved in this phenomenon is considerable; hence the sea's apparent change of color.

How does the lunar rhythm trigger off the *palolo* and other organisms like it? In finding an answer to this and related problems H. Casper, a biologist, made a detailed study of the life of *Chironomis clunio marinus*, a kind of mosquito which lives in its larval stage in seaweed accumulations on the islands of the North Sea. Casper knew that this larva always turned into a mosquito after the full and after the new moon, when the tide was low. To find out if it was the height of the tide or the moon's direct influence which caused the transformation, Casper took seaweed containing the larva to Varna, in Bulgaria, and put it in his aquarium. He tried to modify the time of the transformation by inducing artificial tides at times very distant from those of the real tides, but there was no change in the hatching times of the mosquitoes. Then he tried lighting the aquarium on days other than those of the full moon. Nothing happened: the transformation always took place according to the moon's phases, unconnected with secondary causes like height of tides or moonlight. In the aquaria of Bulgaria, just as on the North Sea coasts, the larvae always turned into mosquitoes at the new and the full moon. Finally, Casper had to conclude: "A particular influence from the moon is certainly the factor controlling the birth of *Clunio marinus*."

FRANK BROWN AND THE FIDDLER CRAB

The American biologist Frank A. Brown decided to tackle one of the most perplexing problems of lunar influence. With his team of colleagues he has already been working for more than ten years, in his laboratory at Northwestern University, on the effect of lunar rhythms on the biological clocks controlling the activity of living creatures. This scientist has really opened up the question, and the numerous results which he has very recently achieved provide fairly definitive answers.

Brown deserves the credit for discovering one of the animals which was to become one of this issue's most famous stars: the fiddler crab (*uca pugnax*), so called because it has a giant pincer somewhat resembling a violin. Brown demonstrated that this creature changed color in relation to his environment, and particularly in relation to the position of the moon. And it did so even if it were enclosed in a dark room, apparently sheltered from the moon's rays.

Turning his attention to oysters, Brown carried out an entirely conclusive experiment, which confirmed Casper's work on *Clunio marinus*. He had the oysters transported in hermetically sealed containers by Railway Express from Long Island Sound to his laboratory at Evanston, 1,000 miles from the sea. There he studied the rhythm of their activity, the frequency, that is, and the extent of the opening of their valves. At the beginning the oysters kept to their original rhythm and regularly opened at the time of the tide at Long Island Sound. But at the end of a fortnight, Brown established that the rhythm of activity shifted progressively ... and soon the oysters opened to a rhythm *which would have been induced by the tide at Evanston if that town had been by the seaside*: the time, that is, when the moon reached the meridian there. The oysters had given up the rhythm for which real tides had been responsible, and now responded to an entirely lunar rhythm. It was as though their clocks had been "reset" by an unknown influence, which was directly related to the passage of the moon to the meridian at Evanston. And yet these oysters were shut up in completely sealed containers.

Intrigued, Brown wondered how a creature which had never seen the day or the moon, nor felt the effects of the tide, would behave. He chose a special variety of crayfish, called *cavernicola,* which lived in Mammoth Cave in Kentucky and was highly adapted to its environment. In this dark and completely enclosed cave the creature, without eyes or pigmentation, lives in a completely constant temperature. However, in the case of this species as well, Brown produced evidence for a 24-hour rhythm of certain metabolic processes which was probably based on the earth's rotation and would have some relation to the position of the moon.

In all the preceding experiments, however, only creatures of the sea were involved. What would happen with mammals? In 1959 Brown and Terracini demonstrated, working with rats, that these animals too are sensitive to the moon. For instance, they kept rats inside a closed room for several months, in absolutely constant laboratory conditions of light, temperature, pressure, etc. The rats could not have had any way of knowing whether it was day or night, whether the moon was above or below the horizon. Brown and Terracini then measured their activity and movement, which showed peaks of activity very clearly related to the position of the moon: the rats' activity was greatest during the times when the moon was beneath the horizon, and least when it was above; it was six times greater during the first hours of the lunar day than at the eleventh hour. In addition to this apparent recurrence of lunar rhythm, there was a lesser recurrence which seemed to depend on the movements of the sun. The experiment was checked several times successfully, and recently a study of mice has allowed the problem to be examined at greater depth.

Most significantly, if rats have a rhythm which adapts to the movements of some stars or planets, even when they are kept under rigorously controlled laboratory conditions, it must be that what we have always thought were constant conditions are not so in reality, and the sun and moon continue to affect the organisms by means which are still unknown. Brown puts it clearly: "We must revise some of our scientific concepts on this matter." It will be shown later how Piccardi, having quite independently reached the same conclusions, was able to isolate and identify the scientific and philosophical importance of this strange breakdown in the constant conditions of the laboratory.

Animals are therefore in some ways under the moon's influence. Would this influence not also apply to men? One question leads to the other. But in this matter scientific investigation has long been anticipated by popular beliefs formed in the earlier times.

In earlier times it was stated as a fact, and it is still widely claimed today, that the moon influences our moods, our reproduction, and regulates the female cycle. Popular opinions about the moon are not always without foundation. But would it be valid to extrapolate these assertions about the moon's effect and apply them to humans? "Man is descended from fish," argued Darwin in his *Descent of Man* (1891); "why should not the 28-day feminine cycle be a vestige of the past when life depended on the tides, and therefore the moon?"

The coincidence between the length of the menstrual cycle and the revolution of the moon has captured many imaginations, and it has been seen as more than a coincidence, a relation of cause and effect. There is often a pungent whiff of astrology here, as for instance in this description given by Doctor H. Duprat: "A woman's first menstruation, if she is in normal health, should occur at the time when the moon is in the same degree of the zodiac as it was at her birth, and, unless sickness intervenes, the function should repeat itself every month under the same conditions."

We therefore used statistics to check whether there was a relation between the menstrual cycle and the lunar month. Right at the beginning, the figures seemed to confirm it: the great Swedish scientist Arrhenius, having gathered together the times of menstruation in 11,807 cases, thought he had discovered a rhythm connected to the moon's phases. But many writers have followed his example and put the matter to statistical test, and they have never rediscovered this supposed rhythm. For instance, Bransom, Bjoernsson, Baumann and Gunn all worked on tens of thousands of cases, and they all concluded that their results do not demonstrate any such recurrence.

Scientists may be agreed that the moon has nothing to do with women's periods, but is it at all involved in certain diseases, or birth and death? Here, too, there are many often conflicting beliefs. In the North Sea islands, for instance, it is firmly believed that the moon is a "great midwife," so that children come into the world more often when the tide is rising than when it is falling. Schulze, a doctor in the island of Nordeney in northern Germany, decided to see whether this opinion was well founded. Using the island's registers, he went through all the births occurring when the tide was coming in, and all those when it was going out, and found ... exactly the same number in both cases. Therefore, neither tides nor the moon are responsible for newborn babies. However, Schulze adds with an amused smile that, in his country, his findings will never stop the midwife, summoned for a confinement when the tide is going out, from calmly telling the distraught father: "Don't worry, we have plenty of time. He won't be born before the tide comes in again!"

Another belief, and a more sinister one, comes to us straight from England. It is the notion that people always die when the tide is going out. All who have read Dickens' account of the death of poor old Barkis in *David Copperfield* will remember it:

> "He will pass away with the tide," Mr. Peggotty whispered to me with his hand over his mouth.
>
> My eyes were dim, and so were those of Mr. Peggotty. Nevertheless I answered very quietly: "Which tide?"
>
> "Along the coast," Mr. Peggotty told me. "People always die at the ebb tide, and they're born at the flow. He will go when the tide goes."

It is clear that this belief is in a way the corollary of the other. However, it is no truer, as one can see by going through all the recorded times of death and comparing them with the position of the moon and the times of the tide.

Doctors can be found who acknowledge that correlations exist between sickness and the moon. For instance, in his book on constitutions, Doctor Allendy declares that the fever crises and spitting of blood among tubercular patients at the sanitarium occurred most often at the first quarter of the full moon and least often in the following phase. He had observed this rule, he said, "in a spectacular proportion of cases." However, verification carried out on this matter indicates that this, without any doubt, is a case of erroneous interpretation of data.

"It is above all our nervous system which is most strongly affected by the moon," says Doctor Vergnes in his turn. "Madmen, maniacs, the unbalanced and the epileptic are more restless and nervous than usual when the moon is full. I have known an extreme alcoholic whose character changed markedly at the new moon. I have treated neurotic patients who declared that their sleep was troubled and interrupted with nightmares when the moon changed its quarter."

It is hard not to smile when these naive declarations are read. For sometimes it is the full moon which is laden with bad properties, sometimes the new moon, and sometimes the changes of quarter or two or three days after. Dr. Vergnes and other writers who share his beliefs unfortunately know nothing about probability theory, a subject which would stop them adding so much encouragement to the popular traditions of the "murderer when the moon is full" type.

There are even odder things to be found in the same category. A Doctor Castollani has described a "lunar migraine" induced by the full moon, "even when the curtains are drawn"; Father Moreux has described "a kind of squint which varies more or less in accordance with the moon's phases"; Doctor Elori has described a "meteor-opathological alternating hemicranium," characterized by headaches occurring on one side of the cranium, then on the other, and following the phases of the moon!

It would appear that all these are false affinities spread about by overly credulous people. In fact, to our knowledge there has been no systematic work done on man in this matter, like that which Brown has undertaken on animals. This is a pity, because although our satellite may not live up to all the hopes placed in it by enthusiasts of mysterious emanations, some of its effects do seem well established. Certainly they are still few and limited: a mosquito's hatching, a crab's color change, a rat's activity.... This is not much to go on in practice, but theoretically it puts us well on the way to a time when the thing will be incontestably proven. For then the question of the manner of the moon's influence would be raised – it emits so little radiation! Could it cause certain disturbances in the solar and terrestrial fields which have till now passed unnoticed? Writers have shown that the moon's influence could work through electricity or magnetism on earth. Physicists have long known that the magnetic field fluctuates in accordance with the positions of the sun and moon relative to earth. Brown and Terracini proved, in 1959, that some animals are sensitive to it.

It would be wrong to write it off *a priori*. We should

remember the strange shift in the gravity effect in the case of Allais' pendulum, when the sun was totally eclipsed by the moon. Also noteworthy is Bortels' discovery that microbes in test tubes facing the moon had a poor pattern of reproduction. And speaking personally, it would be ungracious of me to refuse any part to the moon in the concert of cosmic influences, for my own researches, it will be remembered, have revealed an effect which is not one of the least strange, and which will one day have to be explained.

Chapter Seventeen

SOLAR INFLUENCES

From the moon, we must now turn to the supposed effects of the sun on living creatures. Perhaps this will be a more fruitful field of inquiry, for it includes fewer old myths and flights of fancy.

Advances in medicine are achieved only through the observation of diseases and abnormal functioning of the body. The same procedure must be used to improve our knowledge of cosmic influences on life. Hence this chapter may appear to be a recital of all kinds of disasters: sudden catastrophes, recurring accidents, and serious and unexpected symptoms of disease. For this question must be asked: where do unforeseeable calamities come from? Could they, like the seven plagues of Egypt, be sent from heaven?

Between the two wars, Doctor Maurice Faure one day made a strange assertion. He has told his story as follows: "It was at Nice, a town where there was an automatic telephone service ... on certain days the telephones stopped working, or worked abnormally, for several hours without there being anything in the state of the apparatus to explain the disturbance. Different connections from those which had been dialed were obtained, or they were not obtained at all, or there were crossed lines, interruptions, and the like. Then the machinery would suddenly start to work normally again, without any human intervention.

"I was not particularly surprised to learn that this passing disorganization of the telephone service coincided with outbreaks of disease, and heralded serious atmospheric disturbances, which occurred immediately afterward. One day, when this unexplained disturbance of the telephone system was particularly serious, I read the news that a violent magnetic upheaval had occurred in the United States and had interrupted telegraph and telephone communications for several hours.

"I immediately got in touch with M. Vallot (an astronomer),

who informed me that these disturbances were fairly frequent, and were also revealed by disorganization of compasses, appearance of *aurorae boreales,* seismic tremors, volcanic eruptions, etc. According to him, one of the most certain causes of these magnetic disturbances was the movement of an important sunspot on the meridian. We decided, together, to investigate whether the movement of sunspots coincided, also, with an increase in diseases afflicting people.

"Doctor Sardou was informed and lent us his assistance. This is how the first investigation was carried out. M. Vallot noted the movement of sunspots from his observatory at Mont Blanc. At the same time, Dr. Sardou recorded the incidence of ill health which he observed at Nice on the Mediterranean coast, while I recorded that which I observed at Lamalou, a place in the mountains of Cevannes, on the edge of France's central plateau. None of us revealed his observations to his colleagues; but when, after 267 consecutive days spent in taking observations, we compared results, it was a simple matter to establish that they were chronologically interconnected. Out of twenty-five movements of sunspots, twenty-one were accompanied by significant increases in the incidence of ill health. . . .

"Afterward I established, as well, a correlation between movement of the sunspot with successions of sudden deaths, which occur twice as frequently at such moments as at others. . . ."

In his enthusiasm, Dr. Faure expressed his opinion that sunspots were also responsible for a whole series of accidents normally attributed to failures in the nervous system or the individual's psychology: the exhaustion of an airplane pilot, a locomotive engineer, or a crossing attendant could cause serious accidents at such times; and nervous tension could drive some people to crime or suicide. He also explained accidents which had been given wide press coverage in the same way, suggesting that they were more easily interpreted as outbreaks of madness than mere unfortunate coincidences.

Is Dr. Faure right in all this, or has he let himself be slightly carried away by his general hypothesis that everything can be explained in terms of sunspots? At any rate, he deserves the credit for having put the problem clearly. Confusion in the cosmos, which makes the barometric indicator rise and fall, could have similar effects on us too, both physically and mentally. Dr. Faure's observations were only the more spectacular symptoms of this, and they needed to be supported by numerous careful experiments.

Doctor de Rudder, a professor at the University of Frankfurt-am-Main, has written a considerable work, as impressive for its size as for the wealth of ideas expressed in it, investigating the cause of certain seasonal diseases which otherwise seem inexplicable. He examines epidemic diseases coming from outside (like poliomyelitis) as carefully as the sicknesses which occur within the system quite suddenly (like myocardial infarctus, angina pectoris, and pulmonary embolism). After a closely reasoned discussion of the causes which could explain them, he too advances the hypothesis of a potential meteorological influence.

Some patients are particularly sensitive to weather changes, as we have seen. Amputees, sometimes feel inexplicable twinges in the tip of their removed limb, rheumatics and arthritics suffer an increase in pain at such moments, and this happens long before meteorological instruments have recorded the slightest change. The reason for this has never been explained.

De Rudder therefore put the question clearly: do "meteorotropic" diseases exist connected with atmospheric conditions? In what way are they connected? And if they do exist, does solar activity have anything to do with them?

His question was heard, and in all the laboratories and hospitals investigators of an original turn of mind put forward their solutions to the problem.

Heart attacks. In a letter to the Academy of Medicine dated March 3, 1959, Doctor Poumailloux and M. Viart, meteorological engineer, wrote: "Our first findings point to a really remarkable correlation between increased frequency of myocardial infarctus at certain moments of maximum solar activity, and peaks of geomagnetic disturbance. For the two years under study, 1957 and 1958, periods of slight solar disturbance are, on the contrary, almost free from heart attacks." But the writers cautiously add that "these first findings require a long-range study based on a wider sample." If their findings were confirmed, they thought that the effect of this solar and geomagnetic activity might be a sudden increase in the coagulation of the blood, thus inducing a coronary blockage through blood clots, a direct cause of infarctus.

Similar findings were reached at Sotchi, Crimea, by the Health Director of the region, Professor N. V. Romenski, as regards heart diseases. He established that there was a maximum of aneurisms and fatal attacks during large magnetic storms. Special precautions are now taken in the hospitals and clinics of the Crimea when these magnetic storms, which are usually preceded several days earlier by intense and violent radio static, draw near. These precautions have led to a considerable reduction in the number of deaths.

Diseases of the lungs. Hellmut Berg, a professor at the University of Cologne, and a merciless critic of false correlations, announced the almost certain validity of G. and B. Düll's work on the deaths of tubercular cases. At an international symposium on relations between solar and terrestrial phenomena, which took place in Brussels in 1960, Berg declared: "G. and B. Düll have plotted different curves showing the distribution of numbers of deaths through tuberculosis around the days marked by severe chromospheric eruptions. They may be taken as indicative of a relation between solar and terrestrial phenomena within the biological field. . . ." This work takes as its subject Hamburg in the year 1936, and it produces evidence to show that, for this time and place under consideration, serious tubercular cases were in danger of dying on days when there was a violent eruption on the sun. At about the same time another investigator, Puig, found entirely similar results. On the other hand, Lingemann found no relation between pulmonary hemorrhages in a West German hospital and geomagnetic disturbances. He was about to come to an entirely negative conclusion when he was suddenly struck by a surprising coincidence which he had not noticed until then. During the period he was studying (1948-1952), the meteorological papers had made *eighteen references* to aurorae boreales occuring in Germany. These phenomena are highly unusual in Germany, and during their appearance the incidence of hemorrhage among the patients was one hundred times higher than a statistical calculation would have predicted. Since aurorae boreales indicate that considerable solar activity is disturbing the upper atmosphere, here too the sun's disturbance brought a risk of death to tubercular patients.

Eclampsias: For a long time, midwives have been blaming the weather and its sudden changes for a large number of eclampsias: a serious and sometimes fatal condition which may occur in the course of a confinement, characterized by spasms and convulsions of an epileptic type on the part of the woman in labor.

Much has been written on this subject without receiving much serious attention, but in 1942 two investigators, Bach and Schluck, finally tackled the question with the requisite scientific rigor. They produced evidence for "eclampsia days." These days were precisely those which had the greatest magnetic disturbance while on magnetically calm days few eclampsias occurred. The writers concluded: "In the last analysis the sun is responsible for eclampsia crises, since it induces magnetic disturbance." The practical effect of this conclusion is that astronomers could be of precious help to doctors by warning them of the days when, because of the sun's ill humor, women in labor need to be very closely watched.

So Professor de Rudder got his answer: there certainly are meteorotropic diseases connected to the sun's activity, as these researches have proved. However, they were a long way from clarifying all the obscurities. Each had concentrated on a different disease at different times and under conditions which were not comparable. Hence there are some contradictory results. Some amazingly close connections between a disease and the sun did not seem to appear any longer, or as frequently, a few years later when another researcher repeated the experiment on new material.

To get rid of these discrepancies, more research, comparison and criticism are required, so that knowledge of the sun's effects may be based on firm evidence, and this work should go on without pause until all the discrepancies have been definitely ironed out.

H. Bortels, a passionate and unconventional scientist whose insights sometimes amounted to genius, was director of the Institute of Bacteriology at Berlin-Dahlem where he carried out a considerable number of experiments on the activity and virulence of microbes under particular conditions of the atmosphere and the sun. He discovered a constant factor in his test tubes and cultures of bacilli: the shift from a high to a low pressure and from a warm to a cold front in the atmosphere altered the behavior of microbes to a considerable extent. As the weather changes, the *azobacter* devours nitrogen more greedily, and therefore reproduces itself more rapidly; the *pseudomonas tumefaciens,* in its urge to reproduce, forms magnificent stars; the *Bacterium prodigiosum* of saliva shows heightened activity, etc. In short, all the experiments were in accordance on one point: certain atmospheric conditions make micro-organisms more active, and therefore much more dangerous. But Bortels wanted to know whether the atmospheric changes which transformed the microbes' virulence had their origin in the sun. The sun emitted some very penetrating radiation; would their elimination halt the microbes' reproduction?

So Bortels had a huge plated apparatus constructed, the sides of which were 70 cm. thick (25 cm. of lead and 45 cm. of iron), and put his test tubes of microbes in it. Once inside this formidable tank, the microbes ceased to respond to weather changes. However, those which had been put in an ordinary themostat, an apparatus, that is, which kept heat and pressure at a constant level, continued to be active at recurring intervals.

Thus *Pseudomonas* behaved itself in the tank, whereas the one in the laboratory continued its scandalous genetic activity; in the tank, the nitrogen eater ceased to be overcome by sudden hunger pangs, etc.

All the microbes, whether in the themostat or in the tank, were protected from atmospheric conditions; but the microbes in the themostat were not protected from the penetrative rays of the sun. The cause of their activity therefore came directly from the sun. Bortels was preparing to carry out new experiments to confirm this when, unfortunately, the events of 1942 interrupted his work.

"How does the sound of the sea come about?" the philosopher Leibnitz has asked. Each wave, taken separately, makes a sound which is imperceptible to our ears, but millions of waves working all together make a noise like thunder. Perhaps Professor Tchijewsky was thinking of the great German philosopher when he established a connection between microbes and epidemics. It is hardly a serious matter that a microbe should be active when the cosmos is active, or that such a minor organism as a minute, isolated cell, a kind of base unit for life, should be disturbed when a sunspot moves to the meridian. But when a whole lot of microbes begin to be active, this becomes a serious matter indeed. That is how epidemics make a beginning, and in this way an epidemic is something like the sound of the sea. Tchijewsky was concerned to discover the determining cause of epidemics, those physiological crises which, often without warning, cover whole districts simultaneously and cause irreparable loss to humans. He had to find out the reason for the sudden emergence of these scourges which, even today with all our advances in preventive medicine, may appear on the least occasion. Tchijewsky thought that epidemics could be connected with a cosmic determinant, a solar one, for instance, and he decided to confirm the hypothesis objectively. He went through a considerable number of old records and histories, but he also used recent statistical documents which provided him with the dates of history's great epidemics. Here he found a justification for his hypothesis and published his theory before the last war: "During the years when there are most sunspots, a greater number of epidemics always emerges in history."

For instance, if his collection of dates is to be trusted, the frequency of diphtheria cases in central Europe, recurrent typhus, the great plagues, cholera in Europe, and above all, the death rate of smallpox victims in Chicago, obediently follow the eleven-year cycle of the sunspots. In the case of this last disease, the peaks of mortality were so closely correlated with the peaks of the sunspots during the three or four consecutive cycles since reliable statistics had been kept that Tchijewsky had high hopes of putting his theory on a solid foundation. In this respect, he was very disappointed when the introduction of vaccination virtually eliminated smallpox in a very few years!

Then Tchijewsky was seized with a new idea and, in order to settle the matter, collected all the statistics relating to deaths in Russia from 1867 to 1917 which he could find. He believed that he would be able to deduce from this that mortality in general, even without the help of bacterial infections, also followed the solar rhythm of eleven years.

Other investigators have turned their attention to less painful subjects. A fairly large literature even covers a happy biological event: birth. The problem here was to find out whether the number of confinements could reveal any increase or diminution in accordance with seasonal, diurnal or cosmic conditions. Some of the results are interesting.

First of all, demographers studied the basic cosmic rhythms which split up our earthly lives: the yearly movement of the earth around the sun and its 24-hour rotation on its axis. They established that births do not occur with the same frequency throughout the year. On average, there are more births during the months of May and June than in November or December. These frequencies are obviously dependent on the frequencies of conceptions nine months earlier, which means that there are more conceptions in August and September than in February and March. The reasons they give hold little mystery, but are evidently related to the movement of the earth around the sun, which causes the seasons. Summer and the holidays are more favorable to sexual relations than the end of Winter, for reasons which are as much material as psychological. But doctors have recently added a biological motivation to these: the number of hormones helpful to procreative power may increase and diminish in the course of the year.

Professor de Rudder, a specialist in pediatrics, has produced an interesting statistic on this matter which would tend to support the theory of hormones and the yearly cycle of procreative power. At the time of their birth, the weight of babies born in May and June is on average higher than those born in the depths of winter. So the strongest children seem to be those who are conceived at the time when the procreative tendency is strongest. Therefore, one can say up to a point that the month when a child is born does provide some indication as to the robustness of his constitution. If you were born in, say, June, you have a better chance of having good balance and being tall and strong, and even having well developed mental faculties. Another statistic even goes so far as to show that human geniuses have most often been conceived in April, and most often died in May. Naturally, the correlation here is a weak one. Young couples who read this book and wish to bring a future genius into the world ought not to confine their procreative activities exclusively to April for a great proportion of these couples would risk being disappointed!

In explaining the seasonal variations in reproduction and quality of newborn children, Huntington, an American, has advanced the hypothesis that this may be related to an early biological imperative bequeathed to us by our ancestors. For early man, it is said, was more directly dependent on seasonal variations and, therefore, cosmic rhythms.

Earlier statistics, like those of Quetelet, and recent ones, like those of Françoise Gauquelin, both show that as a general rule babies are in a hurry to be born at the end of night or at the beginning of the morning. The reason for these differences between the hours of the day is quite simply that the alternation of day and night not only controls our everyday activities, which are conscious and organized, but also, and to an even greater extent, the whole of our biological system. We have seen how the succession of day and night is the main clock, the most powerful cosmic "time-keeper" of the neural and hormonal activity of our bodies. Now, it is a hormone factor which appears to set off the beginning of labor in a woman. It is closely linked with the universal "time-keeper" of 24 hours. Hormones determining the term of confinement are secreted in greater quantities during the night, and so birth generally begins toward the end of the night rather than in the middle of the day. In the last few decades, induced confinements have become fashionable, and doctors can put the normal time of the confinement forward or back by the use of drugs and injections. This has the advantage of allowing births to take place more conveniently during the day. But the hour when the baby is born may also indicate its future health. In fact, confinements which have naturally started at a time which is physiologically often the best, that is, around midnight, are quicker and easier. Hence the saying that the child of the morning is generally more welcome than the child of the afternoon.

There are thousands and tens of thousands of them. They move forward in compact rows, annihilating everything in their path to satisfy their voracious hunger. Nothing stops them, not even the vast expanse of the sea when they meet it on their way. Then hordes of them rush forward into it and soon drown. That is a migration.

The determining factors of migrations are still very obscure. If the seasonal migrations of birds are determined by temperature conditions, how are those of locusts to be explained, or of ants, or of rats and lemmings? A frenzied desire for movement suddenly takes hold of them, for no apparent reason, and without any warning.

We are told that a migration takes place when a species of animal suddenly begins to reproduce itself in incredible quantity. But where does this burst of reproductive activity come from? The theory most widely accepted these days relates to the hormones: autopsies carried out on lemmings captured during a migration have revealed abnormal, indeed pathological, development of certain endocrine glands. But why should these hormonal glands have developed in this way? This explanation only takes us one step forward in an investigation of the phenomenon's original cause.

Some scientists have thought to examine whether cosmic factors could have justified this unhealthy reproduction of the species, for it resembles the sudden proliferation of microbes in Bortels' test-tubes. Chibirnikov and Derjavin, two Russian scientists, have concentrated on this angle. The first demonstrated that locust hordes in Russia followed the eleven-year cycle of sunspots, while the second proved that sturgeon in the Caspian Sea reproduce and then die in masses following cycles of eleven and thirty-three years, both of which occur during periods of sunspots. Other studies of the same type are in progress.

But what can be said at the present time about the huge colony of microbes which is humanity? Here too we find mass reactions which are unexpected and dangerous, upheavals which are often inexplicable, revolutions, wars, or just migrations bearing a close resemblance to those of animals. Entire nations have, one day, decided to leave their country of origin to set up house elsewhere and live in a new country: warrior hordes who spread across every country like a powder trail and sowed desolation. Are demographic, economic or other explanations always sufficient explanation for these sudden phenomena?

This question as well caught the imagination of the tireless Professor Tchijewsky. He collected the dates of a large number of recurrent social phenomena, and, as with epidemics, compared them with the fluctuations in the numbers of sunspots. In a huge study, a real panorama of history, he drew up lists of wars, revolutions and population movements from 500 B.C. to 1900, against the curves of solar activity. By means of these historical data, Tchijewsky felt justified in concluding that of all the "psychic epidemics" 72% coincided with peaks of solar activity, and only 28% with its low points.

Tchijewsky illustrated this conclusion with a certain number of examples, of which we print one or two of the more picturesque. The Jewish immigration into North America followed, according to him, a cosmic determining force; the succession of Liberal and Conservative governments in England did as well; between 1830 and 1930 this succession took place according to the following law: Liberals gained power during the peak years of sunspots, and Conservatives when they were at their low point. The idea behind Tchijewsky's thesis is evident: activity on the sun would tend to cause unrest among men, and this unrest might be expressed by the desire to immigrate or, more mildly, by a prepensity among the English electorate to back the least traditionalist of the parties, the Liberals.

These ideas have very recently even been applied to the political economy in an effort to find a cause in the sky for major economic crises. The statement that the great crisis of 1929 coincided with a peak of solar activity was a sufficiently worrying fact to pass for proof among certain people. The work of Tchijewsky is at the back of a lot of myths; these perhaps contain a grain of truth, but it cannot be denied that there are serious lacks in the records involving mass activities. As long as there is any doubt as to their accuracy, we should be very skeptical about them.

Caution, then, is required in assuming a cosmic interpretation of social behavior patterns, but individual reactions to some effects of the cosmos are more readily examined.

A record of such occurrences has been prepared, and it includes serious and mutually supportive research. Reiter has discovered a connection between solar activity and the number of road accidents. Martini has observed a link between mining disasters and the appearance of groups of spots at the sun's central meridian. Berg is in agreement with Martini in concluding that accidents may often be put down to delayed or inaccurate human reactions, in conjunction with very violent solar activity.

Delayed reactions are not all; there are also effects inducing serious depression or morbid excitement in the nervous system. G. and B. Düll have found a correlation between the number of suicides and solar activity. To confirm it, they collected 24,739 cases of suicide at Copenhagen, Frankfurt, and Zurich from 1928 to 1932. All this material, patiently collated, enabled them to conclude that the number of suicides was not unconnected with disturbances in the cosmos. It will be remembered that Dr. Faure and Dr. Sardou had come to the same conclusion about suicide as well as criminal acts.

As for the pathological stimulation of the nervous system by the movement of large sunspots, Father Moreux wrote as long ago as 1930: "The electric flow emanating from the sun affects our nervous systems, and I have often observed that many people, and especially children, are more irritable during times of excessive solar activity. The number of punishments in schools is always higher during magnetic disturbances caused by turmoils on the solar surface. These unconscious influences are expressed, in certain cases, by attacks of nervousness causing complex effects on morbid natures, such as dejection, attacks of gout or rheumatism, headaches, neuralgia, and even temper tantrums."

No doubt a certain naïveté is apparent to us today through Father Moreux's somewhat old-fashioned style. Tchijewsky's opinion, also, is astonishing since at about the same time he too reckoned that "The time is near when, before pronouncing sentence on the accused, the judge will ask to be provided with astronomical and meteorological data relevant to the time when the crime was committed. The nearer the crime to a time when sunspots were reaching their maximum intensity, the more diminished the responsibility of the guilty man." But the courts are a long way from acting on Tchijewsky's views.

However, very recently Tchijewsky's ideas have received unexpected support in the work of Dr. Robert O. Becker. A surgeon at the Syracuse Veterans Administration Hospital and New York's Upstate Medical Center, Dr. Becker stated in *Newsweek* on May 13, 1963: "Subtle changes in the intensity of the geomagnetic field can affect the nervous system by altering the living body's own electromagnetic field." His statement recalls the research already described on the effect of positive and negative atmospheric ions on human physical and mental health. Dr. Becker has established a direct relation between the number of admissions to psychiatric hospitals and the earth's magnetic activity, which is generally associated with sunspots. On the other hand, when magnetic disturbances decreased, so also did the number of patients admitted.

How could the earth's magnetic activity disturb the brain of a patient, a schizophrenic, for instance? Becker showed that the human body has areas responsive to positive and negative electrical discharges, located separately. The presence of electric waves carrying a different discharge would upset these areas. In some cases the effect may cause the patient to lose consciousness.

It may be seen, therefore, that outer space makes its presence felt among living organisms in a very unpredictable way. Not only is it unpredictable, but also it is not very well understood. Not all the different studies mentioned here have equal validity. Some are impressive because of their weight of evidence, but the premature conclusions of others may raise a smile.

But the point is this: what part does the moon play on life? It would seem to be a small one, whereas the sun is responsible for a mass of strange effects which seem to influence all of life on this sphere through the weather, the atmosphere, and magnetic disturbances.

However, perhaps not all cosmic effects on earth come from the sun and the moon. There remains in the universe a huge field of influences which have yet to be explored: the influence of galactic forces, the disturbing influence of planets in the solar field, cosmic rays coming from distant space, and no doubt many other things which we know nothing about at the moment. When we do know more, we will understand better what goes on between the sky and ourselves.

And then, a fundamental question still waits to be asked: if cosmic influences affecting men do exist, how do they work?

How are they imprinted on the inside of our bodies? The writers mentioned so far have hardly touched on this, keeping to factual discoveries rather than explanations. Someone has to throw light on this tangled network of influences, and put forward a theory resolving the difficulties and shortcomings of the experimental work.

Chapter Eighteen

THE PICCARDI EXPERIMENTS

Professor Giorgio Piccardi, Director of the Institute of Inorganic Chemistry at the University of Florence, is a great scientist who combines integrity in his work with enthusiasm The story of his research proves this.

In 1935, when he was still a young chemist, the famous Professor Beccari told Piccardi about a problem which had been worrying him for a long time, although it seemed ordinary enough: the descaling of boilers.

What happened in boilers? It was known that water left behind calcareous deposits in the containers where it had been kept, and these were sometimes important. Household saucepans are an example of this phenomenon, and, in industry, boilers follow the same rule. These calcareous deposits would impair their function if a procedure had not long existed for descaling them. The procedure is simple: at regular intervals *physically treated* water is put into the boiler. This special water, called "activated water," removes the carbonate of limestone when it is heated; instead of forming a hard and thick crust, like ordinary water, it removes the crusts already formed in a kind of scum. The procedure is very simple, but at the present time the way it works is completely incomprehensible to scientists. There is no theoretical base and no reasonable explanation for this phenomenon. How does this miraculous "activated water" differ from normal water so as to have an opposite effect on these calcareous deposits? No one knew. How did the effect work? That was another puzzle, and another question mark. But the very fact of its obscurity could not fail to stimulate the curiosity of young Professor Piccardi.

How is ordinary water made "active"? Piccardi has described the process: a mercury buoy, a glass phial containing a drop of mercury and low-pressure neon, is gently moved about in the water. As the buoy is moved, the mercury slides on the glass; the double layer of electricity between the mercury and the glass splits and produces a reddish glow through the neon. The water which comes in contact with the buoy thereby becomes "activated." Mercury buoys, like other apparatus, have been used in industry for the descaling of boilers. The scene is almost like an alchemist's laboratory in the Middle Ages, with red sparks leaping out of retorts.

But what was there about the water obtained in this way which could be called miraculous? In what way was the descaling thus achieved a kind of magic? Quite simply because after the "activating" treatment, the water's chemical composition was *exactly the same* as before. When Piccardi began his research, no one could explain how one had an effect and not the other, just because a dim red glow had been produced and a few electrical discharges had passed through it. Some chemists of that time decided to ease the confusion caused by this mystery by flatly denying that it played any part in the descaling of boilers, that scandal of physics, even though every day the effect of activated water in the industries where it was used completely contradicted them.

But in addition to their uneasiness in face of the unknown, another reason made many experts doubt the real role of activated water: the experiment did not always succeed, or was only more or less successful according to the day. The effects of activated water were certain enough, but they were subject to variations and eclipses. Its physico-chemical action on the calcareous deposits was sometimes less quick or less total than usual. This reaction apparently depended on the hour, on the day, on the month, and indeed on the year. So some people wondered whether perhaps the whole thing was an illusion, a myth, of the kind one can find elsewhere in science.

Piccardi disagreed. He was not someone whom the occasional failure in an experiment could discourage. He knew the effect existed, patently, and he decided to find an explanation for both it and its sudden changes of mood.

"All right," he said to himself, "let us put the problems in order. For the present I shall leave aside the delicate question of the difference between ordinary and activated water, and go deeper into the other problem: why is the experiment not always successful in the boilers? Why do the effects of the activated water vary according to the weather? It is not easy to observe what is going on in a boiler; probably the best thing is to repeat the effect in test tubes in the laboratory. By making the activated water react on different chemical bodies related to carbon of limestone, I shall see with my own eyes whether the reaction takes place more or less quickly. By carrying on the experiment over a long period I shall know when the fluctuations appear and why."

Piccardi got the project under way at once, and tried out a variety of chemical bodies. He realized then that all the reactions of these chemical bodies also revealed variations in line with the days. As with carbon of limestone, their dissolution showed an inexplicable inconstancy, in spite of perfectly identical laboratory conditions. The effect of activated water in the test tubes was never the same. There was surely a reason for that, one which had to be found.

"In 1939," said Piccardi, "I realized that the ceaselessly fluctuating variations in the behavior of the activated water depended in some way on our environment of space." One day, in fact, he covered the test tubes with a metallic screen, and this thin cover, although not touching the chemical bodies, had been enough to alter their manner of reaction. Something coming from outside, which the metal had screened, seemed to be the cause of the regular alterations affecting the progress of the chemical dissolution.

From that time he publicly invited physicists and chemists to collaborate with him in investigating so important a phenomenon, and proposed a clear program of experiment to elucidate the problem. "This was the first time that a relation could be made between phenomena from outside with, on the one hand, changes in the delicate physico-chemical character of the water, and, on the other, the behavior of some inorganic colloidal processes," he asserted in an historic account of his research. But the war intervened, and Piccardi was forced to break off his experiments for some years.

At that time Piccardi was not alone in his interest in problems which were scandalous for every conscientious and well-organized chemist. In places all over Europe and elsewhere incomprehensible happenings were occurring in scientists' test tubes. For instance, if water behaved oddly enough in boilers, there was another example of behaviour at least as erratic: sometimes it failed to freeze at a temperature several degrees below its freezing point. Why? The phenomenon was dismissed as a chance or accidental effect, and called an unimportant aberration; and then the experiment was repeated in the hope that this time it would work.

This hardly satisfied a German scientist, Bortels, the tireless investigator whom we have already described when he put microbes in a tank. In 1954, Bortels tackled this odd behavior of water, which the experts called "surfusion." He showed that surfusion was not a chance effect, but was connected to a precise determining factor, although it was difficult to express. For instance, it followed variations in atmospheric pressure and magnetic activity on earth. Water sealed in glass phials does not turn into ice, particularly when atmospheric pressure is low or when magnetic activity is on the decrease. By what mysterious means did changes in the atmosphere or the weather work on the physical elements of water kept in a sealed phial?

Madame Findeisen, a chemist, one day found herself confronted with no less strange a problem. She was examining the reaction speed of some inorganic chemical solutions in a hermetically sealed jar. One would not have expected these solutions to respond to any influence from outside, in the normal course of events. But after carrying out thousands of measurements, Mme Findeisen established that her colloids aged at different speeds according to the day and this was in response to changes in the barometric pressure. On some days the reaction was very rapid, and on others it lagged. Mme Findeisen was brought to the conclusion that: "Although they are in principle protected from all alteration in the weather, colloids do vary with weather variations. Might both the weather and colloids, then, be dependent on a more remote effect?"

But where did this first cause come from? The question was worth asking, for inorganic colloids, like those used by Mme Findeisen, are only a step away from organic colloids, which form the structural base of life. What was happening in the test tubes of Mme Findeisen and Bortels, or in Piccardi's boilers, might also be happening in our own bodies.

So these test tubes raised the same question as the unexplained appearance of certain diseases: did all this depend on the good or bad humor of the sun and of our surroundings of space at a given time? But neither Bortels nor Mme Findeisen went far enough in explaining the phenomenon to prove that an extraterrestrial factor was to blame. That honor was to be Piccardi's alone.

Professor Piccardi's method can be summed up in a few words: simplicity, ingenuity, and steadfast patience. That is why a few test tubes, a single chemical compound (*oxychloral bismuth*), water and a few metal screens were all he needed to achieve his goal. And he designed only three chemical tests in all and for all. But each test was unflaggingly repeated for more than ten years. Begun in 1951, they are still in progress, and up to the present time more than ten thousand measurements have been made.

To acquire a full knowledge of what was going on, Piccardi decided to vary three factors simultaneously. On the one hand, he wanted to see whether outside conditions played a part; to do this, he had to try to intercept them by putting a screen over the test tubes. On the other hand, to find out if conditions inside the test tubes were determinant, he had to alter the contents of the test tubes; here, activated and normal water were used as the means of differentiation.

That done, Piccardi decided to carry out only three routine tests, but they were to be repeated every day for years and they were intended to sum up the conditions he wanted to study. Piccardi observed the speed at which an inorganic colloid, oxychloral bismuth, dissolved. This colloid, which does not naturally dissolve in water, is prepared by pouring trichloral bismuth into water. It then dissolves, but this happens *at varying speeds*. Piccardi was interested in the speed of the reaction, and that was what he was essentially observing in the three tests.

Test F: Normal water in one test tube, activated water in the other. No screen over the test tubes. The speed at which the oxychloral bismuth dissolved in normal water was compared with its speed in activated water. How would the phenomena of space affect the two reaction speeds?

Test D: Again, normal water in one test tube and activated in the other, but this time a screen covered the two, to see if this barrier, by altering the conditions of space, had a different effect on normal and activated water. The criterion was still a comparison between the reaction speeds of oxychloral bismuth.

Test P: Normal water was poured into both test tubes, but the first was exposed while the second was under the screen. Observations were made to see if the screen affected the reaction speed, which ought to have been the same if the two test tubes were exposed. A difference would be explained in terms of the effects of space due to the presence of the screen.

Piccardi succeeded in formulting laws where others had only managed random probes, for he knew how to make use of a basic observation: since conditions in space appear to alter chemical reactions in response to the passage of time, experimental results cannot be the same from one moment to the next. So it was necessary to hold the experiments over a very long period of time, so that the effect of chance could be discounted, and, out of the apparent disorder, the outline of certain laws might emerge.

Having brought together this vast quantity of measurements, and having collated them according to numerous statistical calculations, Piccardi proved to his satisfaction that the reaction speed of oxychloral bismuth did not vary at random, but according to certain tendencies which depended quite clearly on extraterrestrial factors. Among these tendencies he distinguished three primary types of variation.

Short-length variation. Piccardi's chemical reactions varied at the time of sudden solar eruptions, powerful magnetic disturbances, or the occurrence of large collections of cosmic rays. When the earth undergoes sudden and exceptional cosmic bombardments, the reactions in the exposed test tubes are violent, whereas those under the metal screen remain more or less calm.

Eleven-year variations. The reaction speed of oxychloral bismuth also varies in relation to the general activity of the sunspots, which move from maximum to minimum every eleven years. Piccardi calls this the "secular variation."

Annual variation. This was the strangest of all the laws to emerge from the test tubes. What happened in the course of a year? The reaction speed increased or decreased according to the month. The same thing happened every year: in March the reaction speeds suddenly leaped up, and in September, at the other end of the year, another abnormal reaction occurred to a lesser degree. But these reactions were entirely independent of temperature or weather conditions. Therefore neither the seasons nor the sun's heat were the cause. Another explanation had to be found for why, according to the chemical reaction, these months behaved differently.

Piccardi found an explanation for this strange phenomenon in the earth's movement in the galaxy. He explains it as follows: "The behavior of chemical tests has suggested a working hypothesis according to which the spiraloid motion of our planet in the galaxy might be considered as an important factor, capable of inducing considerable effects. On the occasion of the International Geophysical Year, chemical tests were set up in different parts of the northern and southern hemispheres. The results obtained confirmed the predictions of my hypothesis."

The earth's movement through the universe is the cause of the annual variations in Piccardi's test. It should be said that this movement is not simple: while our planet revolves around the sun at a speed of 18 miles a second, the sun is moving in space toward the constellation of Hercules at a speed of 12 miles a second. Our earth therefore describes a spiral trajectory. It moves, drawn on by the sun, toward the constellation of Hercules, not a straight line but following a corkscrew route. Our sphere's complicated trajectory in the galaxy can be calculated, and the calculation shows, as Piccardi has written, that:

1. During March – and March only – the earth's movement is on the plane of the equator.

2. During September, the earth moves more or less parallel to the line of its north-south axis.

3. The total speed of the earth's movement varies during the year, from a maximum in March (29 miles a second) to a minimum in September (14 miles a second).

4. The earth always moves with its northern hemisphere in front, except for a brief period in March.

In our galaxy there are fields of force which the earth intersects as it moves along. As we mentioned earlier, Enrico

Fermi, the Nobel prize winner in physics, showed in 1947 that the Milky Way was a sort of friendly giant which held a magnetic field. This magnetic field, like a vast cyclotron, can speed up particles floating in interstellar space (which even recently used to be called a "void"), giving them a speed comparable to that of light. This, says Fermi, might be the origin of cosmic rays.

In its corkscrew route, the earth is sometimes parallel and sometimes perpendicular to these fields of force. During March, it meets them at right angles, and that is the time when considerable cosmic forces have their most important effects on us. On the other hand, during September the earth straightens up, and receives galactic influences on a line almost parallel to its course.

The major anomaly demonstrated by Piccardi in his test tubes whenever March came around is therefore explained in this way. His colloids behaved in a particular way at that time because they felt the shock of the galactic forces more strongly as the earth struck them at right angles. The impressive fact of the earth's mad career through infinite space could be read in those humble test tubes and in a substance with a name as peculiar as oxychloral bismuth. Penetrated every day by an inconceivable number of forces, by particles and waves from the sun and from galactic space, the earth and everything on its surface must react to this downpour.

Piccardi has advanced the hypothesis that, among these forces, electromagnetic waves of a great wave-length (like radio waves) play an essential part. It is known that these waves, which are constantly reaching us from space, are not absorbed by the atmosphere of earth, and represent what the experts call "the second window" in the spectrum of electromagnetic waves (the "first window" being waves of visible light) from which we get all our information about the surrounding universe.

Laboratory experiments carried out by Piccardi and also many other investigators (such as the Munich school in Germany) have demonstrated the effect of these waves on chemical or biological reaction speeds. Now, these waves reach us from every corner of the universe. The sun no doubt continues to be our most important source of radio waves, as well as the most variable. However, transmissions of electromagnetic waves have been detected from the moon, Venus, Mars, Jupiter and Saturn.

When, as a young scientist, Piccardi concentrated on the annoying "little" problem of boilers, did he think that this problem would take him so far afield, further than the earth and the sun right to the depths of the universe? Now, thanks to Piccardi, it was known why the magical descaling of boilers occurred more or less according to periods. The conditions of space controlled the effects of activated water on calcareous deposits. But all the mysteries of the business had not been cleared up, for it was still not understood why the results of normal and activated water were different, although all the chemists insisted that the two sorts of water were absolutely identical.

Water is a strange liquid whose behavior is often unexpected. We have seen, for instance, in Bortels' experiment, that there are occasions when it does not freeze below 32°F. Water is a "misfit" which many physicists and chemists have fallen foul of. A scientist who has specialized in the substance, Clement Duval, has declared in frustration that "all its components are abnormal."

For a long time water had been considered, taking the evidence on trust, as a perfect liquid. But this liquid, says Duval, "is reminiscent of the crystal structure of the ice from which it comes." In other words, to the surprise of investigators, water appears to have a structure like that of a solid, contrary to all the assumptions concerning liquids which had till now been current. The composition of its molecules has a particular construction and organization. In 1951 Pople advanced the hypothesis, later verified, that this composition of molecules is continuous; in other words, a glass of water is in a way "made up of a single molecule"! Water is indeed an old friend we hardly know at all. "Each time we go deeper into the structure of water, an important discovery is made," says Duval. We do not know whether this expert is acquainted with Piccardi's research. If so, he must surely feel some satisfaction to see such a striking confirmation of his remarks.

Since water does have a structure, Piccardi gradually glimpsed how the phenomenon of activating water by physical means, which till then had been so incomprehensible, had a "very clear and very simple" explanation.

Although they were chemically identical, activated water did not have the same physical structure as normal water. Hence their different effects. Hence, too, a hypothesis of how cosmic forces worked in the test tubes: without altering the chemical components contained in the test tubes, the cosmic forces could work on the structure of water they composed, break it down, and subject it to more or less violent twists according to the particular time.

But how were extraterrestrial forces able to break down the molecular structure of water? This structure, unlike that of solids, is slack and easily subject to alteration under the pressure of outside factors. That is why, in some cases, activated water descales boilers, whereas in other cases it does not do so. As they alter its structure, cosmic influences endow it with physical properties which change from one moment to another. That is also why different activities took place in Piccardi's test tubes according to whether the earth crossed the fields of force in one position or another, whether the sun was emitting more or fewer particles, or whether the atmosphere was receiving more or fewer cosmic rays or electromagnetic waves.

So space and cosmic forces can affect us through the intermediary of water. That is a conclusion of formidable importance. In fact, water is all over the earth, it is the planet's major liquid. The whole of physics and the whole of chemistry must take into account the variations which the structure of water undergoes, as do the pyramids of molecules submitted to continous alteration, distortion and pressures, according to the earth's trajectory and the cosmic forces which reverberate against it.

Water is also the liquid of life. The human body is more than sixty percent water, and in combination with colloids this forms the basic structure of our organism. So are we too not subjected to the effects of space even more than Professor Piccardi's test tubes?

One important detail should not escape our notice. Experts have shown that the structure of water becomes particularly unstable and easily influenced at a temperature of between 81° and 108°F. Now, it is a fact that human body temperature is fixed at the limit where water is on the point of leaving the structure which connects it with solids to become a perfect liquid. In our organism, therefore, the structure of water must react with particular readiness to the promptings of the surrounding space, even more, perhaps, than the water in the laboratory test tubes.

If this is the case, it is not only a cosmic chemistry which needs to be worked out from Piccardi's basic research, but also a cosmic biology.

Chapter Nineteen

THE TAKATA EFFECT

Some time before the last war, a Japanese doctor called Maki Takata had perfected a method of studying the ovarian cycle in women. Perhaps he was looking for an answer to the problem which has been of such concern to Japan, birth control. At any rate, his method produced good results, so good that Maki Takata became known not only in his own country, but also abroad, and gynecologists all over the world made use of the "Takata reaction."

The Takata reaction is a chemical method of testing the albumen in blood serum. Albumen, as is known, is an organic colloid. The Takata reaction gives the "indices of flocculation" of this colloid. To use the method correctly requires a delicate touch, and Takata has taken care to explain it with all his characteristic attention to detail. A blood sample is taken and put through a number of treatments, and then a reactive agent is mixed with it to make it "flocculate" at a greater or lesser speed. When only a little of the reactive is needed to make it flocculate the index of flocculation is said to increase; and in the opposite case it is said to decrease.

For patients treated by Takata, the flocculation index went up or down in response to the condition of their ovarian and menstrual cycles, indicating the activity of the albumen in the serum. So the Takata reaction enabled him to know what stage his patients were at in their ovarian cycle. On the other hand, the index of flocculation maintained a very constant level among healthy men, as Takata had checked with repeated experiments. The Takata reaction was therefore of excellent use to gynecologists.

.But suddenly, in January, 1938, doctors in every hospital in the country were warned of a new event: the Takata reaction was varying randomly among all the patients, and no longer meant anything. It had undergone an inordinate and incomprehensible increase, which took it beyond the limits of all the calculation systems set up for it.

212

Takata was curious to try his test once again on male subjects, and discovered an even more scandalous fact: he established that the blood serum of a healthy man, which a short while before had always been constant, had also gone wild. So everything was going very badly, and the doctor was much disturbed by it. Disturbed, but not defeated. His first thought was to doubt the evidence, and he therefore wrote off to every part of the world where his reaction was used by the gynecologists. Unfortunately, the same answer came back from Basle, Berlin, Zurich, Formosa and Manchuria: the blood serum's senseless behavior had been observed with amazement everywhere.

So all over the earth something had happened which overthrew the established physiological order, and which made the Takata reaction null and void. The Japanese doctor decided to solve the mystery.

To begin with, he resolved not to experiment with women any longer. As their index of flocculation was very variable at ordinary times, there could be no hope that any useful information could be gained from them in times as troubled as these. He had to study these huge variations, like sawteeth, in the index of flocculation of men. Perhaps he would find some order which would explain this apparent disorder. Takata therefore turned his attention to the stronger sex, whose reaction had been constant until that time. In looking for a pattern in the index of flocculation of blood serum, perhaps he could get to the root of this disturbance.

The first and most pressing question was this: were the sudden increases in the indices of flocculation the same for everybody? Did they occur at the same time for everybody? To be clear about this, Takata decided to carry out experiments at Tokyo, while his colleague Murasugi did the same at Kobe, a town in the south of Japan. A Mr. Kabagashi and a Mr. Hiramatsu allowed themselves to be used as human guinea pigs. Every day for four months (from February 1st to May 31st, 1939) examinations were carried out, at either end of the Empire of the Rising Sun, to see how the serum behaved when put to the test of the Takata reaction.

As the experiment went on, Takata compared the daily indices of flocculation of Mr. K. and Mr. H., and noted with great satisfaction that the two curves marking each day's

213

variation were admirably in parallel. Each sawtooth on one graph corresponded with the same increase on the other, and this continued throughout the four months of the experiment. When Mr. K.'s serum was disturbed, so was Mr. H.'s, several hundred miles away; when Mr. K.'s serum calmed down, at the same time, as though motivated by some obscure biological imitative instinct, Mr. H.'s also behaved properly.

The conclusion was that this experiment confirmed what doctors had observed all over the world. The factor responsible for the biological alterations in human blood worked simultaneously on all the subjects under experiment, wherever on earth they lived. All the inhabitants of the world had been affected together and at the same time.

But Takata still was not satisfied. He had discovered an effect,[1] but he still had to find the cause which had brought it about. "Since the whole world is affected at the same time," he argued, "the cause must be extraterrestrial. Otherwise, how could it have a universal influence on the planet?"

This was still rather vague. The idea that the sun might be the guilty party appeared to him as the most likely hypothesis. To check this, Takata worked with unflagging energy and ingenuity. At the same time, and all unknowing, Takata the biologist was, at the other end of the world, linking up with the ideas of chemists Bortels and Piccardi. Like them, he was looking for the cause of the incomprehensible fluctuations and unexpected upsets of his experiments in our environment of space. But his hypothesis was aimed more specifically at the sun. "Unless I am mistaken," he argued, "I must manage to prove that the sun's activity corresponds with the fluctuations in my subjects' blood serum."

Finally, after seventeen years of work, Takata could at last announce, in 1951, as the conclusion of his research: "Man is a kind of living sundial." His research had uncovered some intriguing effects.

Solar activity. "If the sun causes the irregularities of the blood serum," argued Takata, "these must necessarily follow that star's changes of mood." In actual fact, the experiment

1. For example, at sunrise, the indices of flocculation of all the subjects showed a sudden increase, which oddly enough began some minutes before sunrise.

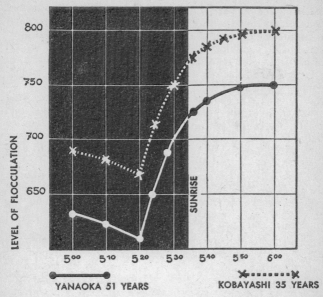

LEVEL OF FLOCCULATION

SUNRISE

●━━━● YANAOKA 51 YEARS   ✗┄┄┄┄✗ KOBAYASHI 35 YEARS

The rate of blood flocculation for everyone suddenly increases rather mysteriously a few minutes before sunrise. This diagram shows the flocculation activity of two individuals tested by Dr. Takata on September 4, 1940.

showed that the sudden increases in the indices of flocculation occurred in particular at a time when a group of sunspots moved to the sun's central meridian, that is, a time when the sun, in its 27-day rotation on its axis, directed a maximum of waves and particles, like a lighthouse, in the direction of the earth.

Sunrise. The Takata effect at sunrise is most peculiar: just at the moment when the sun is about to rise, the indices of flocculation, which are very calm at the end of the night, suddenly show an enormous increase. But the most surprising fact is that the increase in the index begins some minutes *before* the sun rises, as if this odd effect anticipated the emergence of the daystar. During the rest of the day, the index follows a typical rhythm similar to the variations in the upper atmosphere's intensity.

In an airplane. To confirm that this effect was definitely due to solar radiation, Takata decided to see what would happen above the protective screen which the atmosphere interposes between us and the sun. One of his close relations agreed to go up in an airplane to a height of twenty-four thousand feet. He took a small blood sample every fifteen minutes to check the effect at different altitudes. As he had thought, the flocculation index went up in a spectacular measure as the subject rose and the atmospheric layer became less thick. This experiment was repeated a second time.

At eclipses. When the moon comes between us and the sun, does it cancel out the Takata effect? To find an answer to this question, the doctor arranged to be in a front seat when a total eclipse of the sun was scheduled in his country. He had three opportunities to get apparatus and experimental subjects to a place where the eclipse was at its best, that is, in 1941, 1943, and 1948. His hypothesis was confirmed three times: as soon as the disc of the moon passed in front of the sun, the flocculation indices began to go down, reaching their minimum when the eclipse was at its maximum. The solar radiation responsible for the Takata effect therefore seemed to be intercepted by the moon. However, neither walls of houses, nor a thick layer of concrete prevented its action. Only an experiment carried out at the bottom of a mine 200 meters underground (at Mieken, Japan), brought the Takata effect to an end. So there was no doubt that an extremely penetrating ray was involved here.

Artificial radiation. To establish the nature of the radiation, the Japanese doctor experimented with various types of artificial radiation in his laboratory. For thirty minutes he exposed human guinea pigs to X-rays, gamma rays, or a bombardment of neutrons accelerated by a cyclotron. These powerful rays produced the same effects on the men in the laboratory as did the sun: their blood serum went wild. The greater the penetrative power of the rays, the greater the effect contained. But in spite of everything, none of the laboratory effects was as marked as the natural effect of the sun.

If the sun was the major cause of the disturbances in flocculation indices recorded in 1938, an explanation was still needed for why these disturbances had been recorded after that date and not before. It was not difficult for Takata to provide the reason: solar activity, as characterized by the number of spots which whorled and cracked its surface, had reached its maximum at precisely that time. In the course of its eleven-year cycle, the sun had caused confusion in the blood of human beings.

Takata thought he had covered the whole extent of the problem, but it was more complicated than he had thought. Unfortunately, Piccardi's research had not been published at that time, so the Japanese doctor did not have the chance to make use of his extraordinary galactic hypothesis. However, man is certainly not just a sounding board for the sun, but a sounding board for more universal cosmic influences as well. That is probably why scientists who have repeated Takata's experiments after him, have not always reached the same results. It was even considered from these that his conclusions were illusory.

But the world of science was not slow in informing itself on this point. In 1954, two German researchers, Caroli and Pichotka, took the view, after acquainting themselves with the work of Piccardi and Takata, that it was of great importance to check whether the behavior of inorganic colloids in Piccardi's boilers took place at the same time in blood serum, which was the organic colloid studied by Takata. Might these both be the same reaction to an effect from space? If so, it would be strong evidence that the Japanese doctor had been right.

So Caroli and Pichotka prepared to bridge these two experiments by simultaneously studying blood variations in their test tubes and also the variations in inorganic chemical bodies. Their results were such that they could conclude positively that variations in the length of time of blood coagulation and variations in inorganic colloids occurred at the same time. Like earlier writers, they considered that these variations were caused by something in space, for "they correspond to variations in electromagnetic wave radiation of a high frequency." So Takata was right.

This connection between our blood and extraterrestrial

phenomena is even better explained in the exceptionally important research of N. Schulz, published in the Report of the Academy of Sciences of the U.S.S.R. This scientist, showing a great attention to scientific rigor, has made more than 120,000 measurements since 1954 at Sotchi, in Crimea. These measurements have established an absolutely certain relation between the number of white cells in the blood of healthy subjects and the number of sunspots. The determining factor is even more remarkable when it is realized that, in 1957, a period of maximum solar activity, Schulz found an exact *monthly* correlation between the leukocyte content in the blood and the sun's activity. These data are as well established as Piccardi's, both as to accuracy of measurement and quantity of sample.

The Russian scientist concludes from the data: "Variations in the number of sunspots have an effect on all life on earth." And he adds, trying to find an explanation for this effect: "The problem becomes clearer when it is recalled that sunspots coincide with an intense emission of particles, and that solar activity implies magnetic conditions, cosmic radiation, and numerous phenomena released on earth through solar eruptions or through sunspots and electromagnetic waves coming from the sun. This influence is continually changing, and cannot be ignored."

The sun's vagaries are therefore able to increase or reduce the number of leukocytes in our blood. That is certainly an impressive fact ... so impressive that some people have even wanted to go further and link the sun with the word *leukemia*. However, that is to go too far too fast. Nevertheless, "thunderclaps in a cloudless sky," sudden failures of our bodies in response to extraterrestrial factors, and everything observed by investigators almost everywhere – are they not more convincing since the research of Takata, Caroli and Pichotka, and, even more, Shulz?

Giorgio Piccardi has given his answer as follows: "Since it is certain that exterior phenomena work on an inorganic colloid as much as on an organic colloid, the effects of these phenomena do not concern one particular organism, or one particular disease, or one particular biological function, but the complex state of living matter.

"Organisms must preserve, as far as possible, their conditions of life, and therefore must react to fluctuations in the

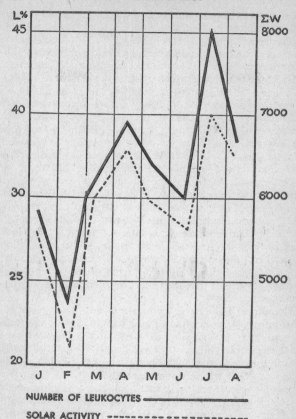

NUMBER OF LEUKOCYTES ——————

SOLAR ACTIVITY ---------------

From January to August 1957, the number of leukocytes in a group of healthy subjects increased at a rate similar to the rise in solar activity measured by sunspots. The coordinate to the left (L%) indicates the percentage of leukocyte increase. The parallel coordinate to the right (ΣW) indicates the number of sunspots.

properties of the space where they live and struggle to maintain their stability. In this matter a profound tension can be detected, a 'fatigue' throughout their colloidal systems and all their material substance. It may be assumed that the whole of living matter is disturbed in this way. Visible responses to outside disturbances, if they occur, are of very different types according to the case. That is why the research of Düll, de Reiter, and others has shown that *all* the biological and psychological phenomena which they have considered responds *to the same stimuli* from outside. On the other hand, widely different stimuli can produce the same biological effect. Individual 'reaction times,' pain felt by amputees, and the number of suicides all reveal a similar variation in response to sunspots, or atmospheric waves, or the earth's magnetism."

By means of the structures in our organism which can be broken down, the water which it contains, and the colloids which compose it, the cause of many of the changes in our bodies and even in our minds must be looked for far from the earth. Many of the diseases which de Rudder called "meteorotropic" do not depend only on the weather, as he assumed, but also on the passing moment and the continual fluctuations of infinite space. In the end, apparently, we are all "as old as our colloids." And the age of our colloids is decided by the cosmos!

Man is continually subjected to the effects of the cosmos, and that is indeed a fundamental discovery. But this statement implies even more; one of science's old assumptions is in the process of collapsing. All those enthusiastic and courageous pioneers, whose work shows flashes of iconoclasm and flashes of genius too, have, like industrious and intelligent termites, undermined the columns of the temple of established science.

Until this date it was believed that identical experiments, carried out under strict laboratory conditions, always had to produce identical results. But this remains true only of solids, systems which cannot be broken down. In the case of liquids, whose structure is eminently fragile, no precaution taken in the laboratory can stop it: water, blood, and all the colloids are broken down by cosmic effects. Because of these, the best designed experiments, if they are carried out at different times, will always yield variable results. This news should cause joy rather than concern, because we are beginning to know the reasons for this. Science is on the move, and soon enough we shall know even more about it.

But Piccardi has deplored our shameful rejection of so many results because they seemed meaningless to us, and unrepeatable, whereas what had been overlooked was simply the time of the experiment, which also was an important factor. Whatever might have been thought, laboratory conditions *were not* identical from one moment to the next. The cosmos, the space which is both an environment and a force of change, had taken care to "sign" the experiment with its elusive seal.

Time, then, is not an identical continuum without meaning for animals and things. It is a co-ordinate in the proper sense of the word, like length, breadth, temperature, and pressure. By forgetting to ask time to participate in their experiments scientists are in the position of the parents of the Sleeping Beauty: all the good fairies were invited to the baptism, but the fairy Carabosse had been overlooked; so Carabosse took her revenge. Apparently rigorous experiments produced absurd and unusable results. How many hours have been wasted by discarding this precious information!

Therefore, credit should be given to the patience, courage, and unflagging curiosity of those investigators who, instead of letting themselves be brought up short by the prejudices of the time, could say: "One hour is not identical to another, for conditions in space change. Our determinants are not confined to earth; our life is not bounded by the simple measurements which pertain on the surface of this little sphere. It expands to the dimensions of the universe. Man's measure has become the cosmos."

What justification, then, is there for the following communication, received quite recently, from a very highly placed scientist? "What vanity to believe that men are affected by these tremendous forces which are so far from us!" Not only does this humility today seem irrelevant, but, more seriously, it seems inconsistent with nature and the results of experiments.

Let us leave the last word to Professor Piccardi: "Although it is concerned with infinitely remote and powerful facts, our research does have human dimensions. It will be able to show how man is linked to his environment with bonds which escape his immediate apprehension, if not his awareness. Only by understanding the mechanism which connects him to the earth and the sky will man be able to understand better his physical and psychic position in the universe today. In the context of the universe as it is, man will find his natural role."

In Conclusion

Our age has purged the occult sciences, but it is not ungrateful, or should not be. Sometimes the old doctrines held a grain of truth in the folds of their multicolored veils. Modern physicists, replacing medieval alchemists with their retorts and alembics, create transmutations in giant cyclotrons; the statistical experiments of Rhine and his school in extrasensory perception stem from table-turning; Professor Rocard has demolished most of the claims of the adherents of radiesthesia, but he has demonstrated the reality of "the water-diviner's signal."

The controlled experiments of Piccardi, Bortels, Takata and many others are the successors of astrological dogmas. Their observations teach us that the time when a physical, chemical or biological event occurs carries a "signature" from space, which is its own and characterizes it. At its furthest point, science says that time is not an impartial witness but an actor in the drama of biological phenomena. And scientists may one day hope to explain results as inexplicable as those which I myself observed in relation to the date of birth. It no longer seems inconceivable that the planets and the moon could play a part in the totality of forces in our environment, a part comparable to the effects of solar activity on life. That is why the old notion of astrology cannot, without ingratitude, be treated only with frivolity or contempt. Astrology is man's first attempt to conceptualize the world, and to try to understand the meaning of his presence in the universe and the mystery of his life. Through the centuries it has fascinated peoples and influenced civilizations, and caught the imaginations of mankind's greatest geniuses: Plato, Aristotle, Kepler, Newton, Goethe, and many others.

But neither can one ignore the evidence which man's new knowledge is constantly accumulating, for to do so would be to fall into error and obscurantism. Aristotle's physics would make a schoolboy of twelve smile today, for physics has constantly evolved since Aristotle. This did not happen without difficulty, nor in a straight line, but it did happen. Astrology, on the other hand, has remained in the same condition ever since Ptolemy. This stagnation has been fatal to it, and has now turned it into a caricature of science. That is why it was necessary to put the claims of twentieth century astrologers in their right place. For them astrology is no more than an echo, a dead idea. The majestic river which was man's early thought about his universe has been swallowed up in a desert of foolishness. However, such as it is, and dead to our way of thinking, astrology should still be respected. Those who have passed away are owed respect. Let us honor the memory of this old and slightly crazy lady who was lively enough in her time.

Moreover, now a concept of astrology is about to be reborn, transfigured like a phoenix. Increasingly, a presentiment is growing as to the extent to which our bodies, and therefore our thoughts, are continually connected with the universe by invisible threads. In a time of interplanetary travel, the cosmic vision which gave rise to the first halting phrases of astrology is perhaps, after all, in its new form a necessary profession of belief, and the only way into the future. But today this vision is a scientific, not a magical, one. The superstition of personal forecasts no longer marks the limit of our understanding or conceals the truth from our eyes.

There is a deep gulf of ignorance as well as time separating the astronaut of today from the Chaldean priest who, on top of his tower and above the dust of the city, thought that he could almost touch the sky by stretching out his arms. This gulf exists, but there also exists the extraordinary continuity of the human intelligence and will. These may sometimes lapse into darkness, but they always rise again to go forward once more. The object, now and always, will be to slowly piece together a little of the great secret which the mysterious and everlasting circle of the universe contains.

Pioneers of the New Science

A. L. TCHIJEWSKY

Tchijewsky was Professor at the University of Moscow, and published his major work between the two world wars. His great virtue is to have been the first to seek methodically, in every direction, to establish a statistical correlation between the sun's eleven-year cycle and events on earth. He investigated the effects of recurrent solar activity on epidemics, general mortality, and even on large-scale social movements like wars, human migrations, and, indeed, changes of government.

It cannot be denied that his work is too systematized, and sometimes lacks the subtlety which a faultless experimental program would require. The science of tomorrow will certainly not be able to keep all the Russian scientist's conclusions. But his great basic premise, the effect of solar activity on life, has since been shown to be entirely correct.

It was also Tchijewsky who, as long ago as forty years, had the idea of emphasizing the sun's predominant role in the production of ions in the atmosphere, and in addition demonstrated "the effect of the ionization of the atmosphere on healthy and unhealthy organisms." Today, the effect of ions on life is being examined everywhere in the world, for it is a field rich in promise from a medical point of view. For this alone, Tchijewsky deserves our respect and gratitude.

H. BORTELS

Professor H. Bortels, director of the Bacteriological Institute of Berlin-Dahlem, is one of the first and most persistent of the investigators who gave an impulse to the new cosmobiology. From before the war, he carried out innumerable experiments which enabled him to establish that atmospheric conditions altered the reactions of micro-organisms. He was also involved in investigation of the phenomenon known as the "surfusion" of water: sometimes in response to certain meteorological conditions, water does not turn to ice at 32°F. Bortels made the vital observations that these deviant reactions took place even when the different entities under examination were enclosed in a thermostat, and thus sheltered from all variations in temperature, humidity and pressure. On the other hand, the reactions changed when the test tubes were covered by a metal screen. Bortels concluded that they were therefore caused by a new factor from outside, which was neither pressure, nor humidity, nor temperature.

It was then that he had a remarkable idea: he put forward the hypothesis that weather changes, like the chemical and microbiotic reactions, must all depend on the same extraterrestrial cause, and he thought of solar radiation. If he did not manage to demonstrate the truth of this hypothesis completely himself, it came to be completly demonstrated, a few years later, in the research of Giorgio Piccardi.

M. TAKATA

Maki Takata, doctor and Professor at Toho University in Tokyo, is one of the most engaging figures in this new science of the relation between man and the universe. Before the war he was known for having designed the test called "the Takata reaction." This test allowed the different stages of women's ovarian cycles to be estimated by means of a flocculation index in the blood serum. This index varied regularly according to the 27 days of the cycle, whereas it was constant in men.

In January, 1938, it was realized with astonishment that the flocculation index had begun to increase sharply among men as among women, and that this had happened everywhere on the globe where the Takata reaction was used. A phenomenon of a global scale was involved, the explanation for which could only be cosmic, Takata argued. And, by a great number of ingenious experiments, he succeeded in identifying the factor of disturbance: it was the sun. From this he deduced what is called "the Takata effect": the flocculation index in blood serum is responsive to the sun's eleven-year cycle, and to sudden eruptions occuring on the sun's surface; it alters at sunrise, and also at the time of eclipses. In short, as Takata himself concluded, "man is a living sundial."

The determining factor in the effect discovered by Takata is still obscure, and investigators who have wanted to find it again have not always succeeded. But his biological research has been remarkably developed through Piccardi's research in physico-chemistry. At the present time, Takata is one of the active organizers of an international committee for the study of chemical tests in connection with extraterrestrial phenomena. He is concerned with the Asian branch of this committee, in conjunction with Piccardi.

G. PICCARDI

Piccardi's story shows how someone who knows how to interpret a small fact correctly can, in science, make a great discovery. Giorgio Piccardi, born in Florence on October 13, 1895, was a brilliant scholar there, specializing in chemistry. One day, a famous Italian biologist, Professor Beccari, informed him of a strange and unexplained fact connected with the descaling of boilers.

Procedures for dissolving the calcareous deposits which blocked the boilers' pipes had long been familiar. One such made use of activated water. But how did activated water work? How did it differ from normal water? Why did the expected result not always take place? These remained unanswered questions. After years of work, Piccardi explained this scandal of physics. His conclusions were heavy with consequences, for they enabled a new science to be established on solid foundations.

Working on inorganic colloids, Piccardi discovered that these reacted with greater or lesser rapidity according to the conditions in outer space such as solar activity and the position of the earth in the galaxy. In addition, the results varied according to whether normal or activated water were used in the chemical tests. The scientists deduced from this that cosmic forces broke down the structure of water and colloids. The reason activated water had to be used in the descaling of boilers was that this water has a physical structure which makes it able, under certain conditions, to act on calcareous deposits, while normal water lacks this property. Descaling does not always occur in the boilers since our environment of space sometimes prevents it.

Although this may seem a minor discovery, the Piccardi

effect has important consequences; for the human body is essentially made up of water and colloids. Just as with boilers, our bodies and, as a consequence, our minds are continuously subordinated to effects from space, which affect us with varying degrees of force. Moreover, Piccardi's discovery amounts to a transformation of the concept of determining factors, for it is now known that many measurements relating to physics must indispensably record the exact time when they were made. For the cosmos which affects them alters from one moment to the next.

At age 77, Professor Piccardi is director of the Institute of Physics and Chemistry at the University of Florence, where he is actively engaged in research to identify the factors transmitting from the cosmos, and to clarify the problem, which is still obscure, of their method of biological operation.

M. GAUQUELIN

Michel Gauquelin was born in Paris on November 13, 1928. He was very young when he began his work on the stars' influence, and studied psychology and statistics at the Sorbonne with this in mind. To see if there were any truth in astrology, he applied methods of probability calculation to astrological laws and forecasts. In every case the results of this examination were to the detriment of astrology.

At the same time he observed, almost in spite of himself, a new statistical effect entirely independent of the doctrine he was examining. He discovered, in a study of the births of 25,000 well-known European professional men, that some planets appeared unusually often at that time in a position of rising or zenith. These results seemed incomprehensible to him. But the encouragement of several reputable scientists persuaded him to extend his research in an effort to find a rational explanation.

Gauquelin thought that the planetary effects which he had observed might be only simple reactions of the organism to the cosmos, dependent on the hereditary constitution of that organism. He was able to check the validity of this hypothesis by establishing, on a sample of 30,000 births, that there was in fact an hereditary predisposition among children to be born under the same cosmic conditions as had pertained at the birth of their parents. But answers still have to be found to the numerous objections raised by scientists against these curious experiments.

A. BROWN

Brown was born on August 30, 1908, and is Professor of Biology at Northwestern University, Evanston, Illinois. His problem was to find out whether internal clocks are "closed systems" which function independently of the environment, or whether they are "open systems" which can be put forward or back by factors coming from outside. In pursuit of this information, Brown experimented on a very wide variety of living organisms, from the potato to the rat, including the fiddler crab and the oyster. All these subjects, though enclosed for long periods in hermetically sealed rooms where the light, temperature, humidity and pressure were carefully kept constant, nevertheless behaved in a biologically inconsistent fashion.

Did their internal clocks work entirely on their own? Not at all: Brown observed that the rhythms of their behavior were based on the solar day, the lunar day, or even positions of these two in relation to each other. Thus, a rat shut in a dark room is twice as active when the moon is below the horizon as when it is above. However, the rat could not have seen the moon.

Brown therefore concluded that the rat had to be sensitive to very subtle geophysical alterations induced by certain cosmic rhythms. This led him to assert, like Piccardi, that an incredible hypothesis should be considered valid, namely, that influences from space penetrate to the heart of our laboratories and disturb organisms which have been put in conditions of apparently total constancy.

Bibliography

ASTROLOGY

Allendy, R., *Le problème de la destinée,* Paris, 1927
Bachelard, G., *L'air et les songes,* Paris
Barbault, A. *Défense et illustration de l'astrologie,* Paris, 1955
  Traité pratique d'astrologie, Paris, 1961
Berthelot, R., *La pensée de l'Asie et l'astrolobiologie,* Paris, 1949
Boll, M., *L'occultisme devant la science,* Paris, 1944
Bouché-Leclercq, *L'astrologie grecque,* Paris, 1899
Choisnard, P., *Preuves et bases de l'astrologie scientifique, Paris,* 1921
Contenau, G., *La divination chez les Assyriens et les Babyloniens,* Paris
Couderc, P., *L'astrologie,* Paris, 1951
Gauquelin, M., *L'influence des astres, étude critique et expérimentale,* Paris, 1955
Jung, C. G., *Interpretation of Nature and the Psyche,* Princeton, 1955
Krafft, K. E., *Traité d'astrobiologie,* Paris, 1939
Ptolemy, Claudius, *Tetrabiblos,* trans. W. G. Waddell, London, 1956
Rutten, M., *La science des Chaldéens,* Paris, 1960
Saintyves: *L'astrologie populaire,* 1937

THE SCIENCE OF COSMIC INFLUENCES

Basic Works

Berg, H., *Solar-terrestrische Beziehungen in Meteorologie und Biologie,* Leipzig, 1957
Piccardi, G., *The Chemical Basis of Medical Climatology,* Springfield, Ill., 1963
Rudder, B. de, *Grundriss einer Meteorobiologie des Menschen,* Berlin-Göttingen-Heidelberg, 1952
Schaefer, K. E., *Man's Dependance on the Earthly Atmosphere,* New York, 1958
Symposium international sur les relations entre phénomènes solaires et terrestres en chimie-physique et en biologie, Brussels, 1958

BIBLIOGRAPHY

Specialized Works

Aschoff, J., "Time-givers of 24 Hour Physiological Cycles" in *Man's Dependance on the Earthly Atmosphere*

Basche, E., and Schluck, L., "Untersuchung über des Einfluss von meteorologischen, ionosphärischen und solaren Faktoren, sowie de Mondphasen, auf die Auslösung von Eklampsie und Präeklampsie, *Zentralblatt für Gynäkologie*, No. 4. 1942

Bergier, J., "L'extraordinaire découverte de Piccardi," *Planète*, No. 5

Bortels, H., "Beziehungen zwischen Witterungsablauf, physikalisch-chemischen Reaktionen, biologischen Geschehen und Sonenaktivität," *Naturwissenchaften*, No. 8, 1951

Brown, Fr. A., "Living Clocks," *Science*, Vol. 130, 1959

Brown, Webb, Brett, "Magnetic Response of an Organism and Its Lunar Relationship," *Biol. Bull*, Vol. 118, No. 3, 1960

Caroli, G., and Pichotka, Jr., "Weitere Untersuchengen zur Beziehung zwischen Blutgerinnung und Wetter," *A.M.G.B.*, Series B, 1954

Casper, Cf article by H. Ullrich, "Ueber lunare Einflüsse auf Organismen," *Grenzgebiete der Medizin*, No. 10, 1949

Chauvin, R., "Quelques phénomènes étranges en rapport avec la météorologie et qui interessent les biologistes," *Année biologique*, Vol. 32, 1956

Couderc, P., *Dans le champ solaire*, Paris, 1932

Cyran, W., "Ueber die biologische Wirksamkeit solarer Vorgänge (nachgewiesen am Wehenbeginn)," *Geburtschilfe und Frauenheilkunde*, No. 10, 1950

Düll, T. and B., "Ueber die abhängigkeit des Gesundheitszustandes von plötzlichen Eruptionen auf der Sonne und die Existenz einer 27 tägigen Periode in den Sterbefällen," *Virschows* Archiv, No. 293, 1934

Duval, C., *L'eau*, Paris, 1962

Findeisen, E., "Experimentelle Untersuchungen über den Einfluss des Witterungsablaufes auf die Beständigkeiteines Kolloids," *Bioklimatische Beiblätter*, 1943

Florkin, M., "L'origine de la vie," Résumé du symposium tenu à Moscou en 1959, Paris, 1962

Friedman, H., Becker, R., and Bachman, C., "Geomagnetic Parameters and Psychiatric Hospital Admissions," *Nature*, No. 200, 1963

Gauquelin, Fr., "L'heure de la naissance," *Population*, No. 4, 1959

Gauquelin, M., *Les Hommes et les astres*, Paris, 1960
Méthodes pour étudier la répartition des astres dans le mouvement diurne, Paris, 1957

BIBLIOGRAPHY

"Existe-t-il une hérédité planétaire?" *Planète*, No. 6, 1962

"Die planetare Heredität," *Zeitschrift für Parapsychologie une Grenzgebiete der Psychologie*, Vol. V, No. 2/3, 1962

Halberg, F., *Physiologic 24 Hour Rhythms: A Determinant Response to Environmental Agents, Man's Dependance on the Earthly Atmosphere*

Heller, J. H., and Teixeira-Pinto, A. A., "A New Physical Method of Creating Chromosomal Aberrations," *Nature*, No. 4645, 1959

Hosemann, H., "Bestehen solare und lunare Einflüsse auf die Nativität und den Menstruations Zyklus?" *Zeischrift für Geburtschilfe und Gynäkologie*, 1950

Kirchhoff, Hr., "Unterliegt der Wehebeginn komischen Einflüssen," *Zentralblatt für Gynäkologie*, No. 3, 1933

Krueger, A. P., and Smith, R. F., *The Physiological Significance of Positive and Negative Ionization of the Atmosphere, Man's Dependance on the Earthly Atmosphere.*

Laborit, H., *Du soleil à l'homme*, Paris, 1963

Malek, Jr., Budinski, J., and Budinska, M., "Analyse du rythme journalier du début clinique de l'accouchement," *Revue Franc. Gyn. Obst.*, No. 5, 1950

Meyer, Jr., *Des variations saisonnières, mensuelle, quotidiennes et horaires du nombre des accouchements*, Lyons, 1956

Nelson, J. H., "Shortwave Radio Propagation Correlation with Planetary Positions," *R. C. A. Review*, Vol. 12, 1951

Piccardi, G., "Phenomenes astrophysiques et événements terrestres," conference at the Palais de la Découverte, January 24, 1959

Poumailloux, M. and Viart, R., "Corrélation possible entre l'incidence des infarctus du myocarde et l'augmentation des activités solaires et géomagnétiques," *Bulletin de l'Académie de Médecine*, March 3, 1959

Reiter, R., "Neuere Untersuchungen zum Problem der Wetterabhängigkeit des Menschen," *A.M.G.B.*, Series B, No. 4, 1953

Reinberg, A., and Ghata, J., *Rythmes et cycles biologiques*, Paris, 1957

Schultze, K. W., "Beeinflussen Flut und Ebbe den Geburtseintritt?" *Deutsche medizinische Wochenschrift*, 1949

Schulze, N., "Les globules blancs des sujets bien portants et les taches solaires." Report in *Toulouse Médical*, No. 10, 1960, pp. 741–757, of work done by Sotchi (U.R.S.S.) and published in *Laboratornoie Delo*, 1960, and in *Rapport au Conseil interministeriel de l'Académie des Sciences d'U.R.S.S.*, 1960

Täger, R., *Gehören erdmagnetische Störungen zu den Ursachen des Wehenbeginns?*, Göttingen, 1950

Takata, M., "Zur Ermittelung des Ovulationstages bei der Frau," *Archiv für Gynäkologie*, 1938

BIBLIOGRAPHY

"Zur Technik der Flockungszahlreaktion im menschlichen Serum, zugleich Intensitätsbestimmung der Vital-Ionisation bei der Bestrahlung des Menschen," *Helvetica Medica Acta,* 1950

"Ueber eine neue biologisch wirksame Komponente der Sonnenstrahlung (Heliobiologie)," *A.M.G.B.,* Series B, No. 5, 1951

Tchijewsky, A. L. de, "Action de l'ionisation de l'atmosphère et de l'ionisation artificielle de l'air sur les organismes sains et les organismes malades," *Traité de climatologie,* Vol. 1, 1934

"L'action de l'activité périodique solaire sur les épidémies," Vol. 2

"L'action de l'activité solaire sur la mortalité générale," Vol. 2

"Effet de l'activité périodique solaire sur les phénomènes sociaux," Vol. 1

Tocquet, R., *Cycles et rythmes,* Paris, 1951

INDEX